EMILE DURKHEIM

What are the connections between Durkheim's activities as a moralist and his conception of sociology? What were Durkheim's political hopes and how are they connected to his sociology?

International scholarship over the last twenty years has produced a new understanding of Emile Durkheim as a thinker. This book is the first to present the reader with an overview of the best of this scholarship, and provides a taste of research much of which is not available in English elsewhere. Although the essays included reflect a wide range of concerns and styles of thought, there is a startling coherence in the image they present. Durkheim was, from his first reviews to his last written work, a moralist, and this collection reconnects the two parts of the man that other writings have generally separated: the institutionalizer of sociology and the moralist. *Emile Durkheim: Sociologist and Moralist* provides us with a Durkheim, hitherto known only to specialists, who utilized the insights of sociology for the purpose of intervention into moral development.

'This collection by distinguished experts presents some of the best scholarship on the wide range of topics on which Durkheim wrote and had influence.'

Kenneth Thompson, *The Open University*

Stephen P. Turner is Distinguished Research Professor in Philosophy at the University of South Florida, Tampa, USA.

The book contains contributions from Stephen Turner, Robert Alun Jones, W. S. F. Pickering, W. Paul Vogt, Hans-Peter Müller, Howard F. Andrews, Paolo Ceri, Philippe Besnard, François-Andre Isambert, J.-C. Filloux and Hans Joas.

EMILE DURKHEIM

Sociologist and moralist

Edited by Stephen P. Turner

London and New York

First published 1993
by Routledge
11 New Fetter Lane, London EC4P 4EE

Simultaneously published in the USA and Canada
by Routledge
29 West 35th Street, New York, NY 10001

Phototypeset in Times by Intype, London
Printed and bound in Great Britain by
Biddles Ltd, Guildford and King's Lynn

British Library Cataloguing in Publication Data

A catalogue record for this book is available from the British Library

Library of Congress Cataloging in Publication Data
also available

ISBN 0–415–09437–2 ✓

In Memoriam
Howard F. Andrews

CONTENTS

CONTENTS

Part III The role of the sociological moralist and the moralist

CONTRIBUTORS

Howard F. Andrews was born in 1944 and died in 1988. He studied geography and economics at the London School of Economics and Political Science. After receiving his B.A. and M.Sc. degrees there, he completed a D.Phil. at the University of Sussex in 1970. He came to the University of Toronto in 1969 as a postdoctoral fellow, and became a member of the faculty of the Geography Department in 1970. From 1980 to 1983 he was director of the 'Child in the City (research) Programme' and subsequently served as Acting Director and then Director of the Centre for Urban and Community Studies. His teaching and research interests were exceptionally broad. His D.Phil. thesis was a quantitative-analytical study of changes in central place systems. He soon became concerned with the various processes that shape urban landscapes. A major research project on the design process of a cooperative housing project led to a lasting interest in perception studies and in urban political processes. His research on the mental maps of children led to his involvement in the 'Child in the City Programme'. As Director of the Centre for Urban and Community Studies he planned to extend his interests in children's living environments in big cities to Third World cities. His historical interests, reflected in his paper for this volume, were in the evolution of human geography in France in the late nineteenth and early twentieth centuries, and in the differentiation of geography from sociology. He spent many months in French archives, gaining an impressive understanding of French intellectual life in general and French academic life in particular.

Philippe Besnard was born in 1942. He is Director of Research at the Centre National de la Recherche Scientifique, Professor at the Institut d'Etudes Politiques de Paris, and a member of the Groupe d'Etude des Méthodes de l'Analyse Sociologique (C.N.R.S. and University Paris-Sorbonne). He is co-editor of the *Revue Française de Sociologie*. He has been, for many years, an active member of the Groupe d'études durkheimiennes, an international network he created, and has published extensively on the history of sociology, particularly on Durkheim and the Durkheimians. His current research interests include social rhythms and the empirical study, through the statistics of first names, of social taste and social transformation of taste. His major publications include *Protestantisme et capitalisme*, (ed.) (1970), *The Sociological Domain: The Durkheimians and the Founding of French Sociology* (1983), *Un prénom pour toujours, la côte des prénoms* (1986), *L'anomie* (1987), and *Moeurs et humeurs des Français au fil des saisons*, 1989. He has also edited five special issues of the *Review française de sociologie* devoted to the history of French sociology.

Paolo Ceri, born in Florence in 1944, is Professor of Sociology at the University of Turin (Italy). He previously taught at the Universities of Trento and Lecce. In 1978 and 1985 he was Directeur d'études associe at the Ecole des hautes études en sciences sociales in Paris and in 1991 he was Visiting Professor at the University of Bordeaux. He served as a member of the national board of the Italian Sociological Association from 1989 to 1992. Since 1978 he has been Editor-in-Chief of *Quaderni di Sociologia*. His numerous books and articles on sociological theory, industrial sociology and social movements, include *Industrializzazione e sviluppo urbano* (1978), *Potere e libertà* (1981), *I quattro volti dell'antisociologia* (1985), *Ecologia politica* (1987), *Impresa e lavoro in trasformazione: Italia e Europa* (1988) and *Social Exchange and Political Exchange* (1990).

Jean-Claude Filloux was born in 1921. He is currently Professor of Educational Science at the University of Paris X-Nanterre. His books include *La personnalité* (1957), *Durkheim et le socialisme* (1977), *Anthologie des Sciences de l'Homme*, with J. Maisonneuve (1991), and *Durkheim et l'éducation* (1993). He is also the author of a number of crucial articles on Durkheim, including 'Sur la pédagogie de Durkheim', *Revue française de pédagogie* (1978), 'Personne et sacré chez Durkheim', *Archives de Sciences sociales* (1990), and 'Notes sur Durkheim et la psychologie', *Bulletin de Psychologie* (1965).

François-Andre Isambert was born in 1924 in Koblenz, Germany, to French parents. He was a volunteer in the French Army during World War II. He was co-founder of the Groupe de Sociologie des Religions (CNRS) and the Archives de Sociologie des Religions in 1956. He was Professor at the University of Lille from 1965–69, and at the University of Paris X 1969–70, and Directeur d'Etudes at l'Ecole des Hautes Etudes en Sciences Sociales, 1970–1987, and founder and Director of the *Centre de Sociologie de l'Ethique* (EHESS), where he is currently. His major publications include *Christianisme et Classe ouvrière* (1961), *Buchez ou* *l'âge théologique de la sociologie* (1966), *Rite et efficacité symbolique* (1978), *Le Sens du Sacré* (1982), and *De la Religion à l'Ethique* (1992).

Hans Joas, born in 1948, is Professor of Sociology at the Free University of Berlin. He was formerly Professor of Sociology at the University of Erlangen-Nuremberg (1987–1990) and Heisenberg Fellow of the Deutsche Forschungsgemeinschaft (1984–1987), Visiting Professor at the University of Chicago (1985), University of Toronto (1986), University of Uppsala (1992) and Fellow at the Swedish Collegium for Advanced Study in the Social Sciences (SCASSS). His major works available in English include *George Herbert Mead. A Contemporary Re-examination of his Thought* (1985), *Social Action and Human Nature*, with Axel Honneth (1988), *Pragmatism and Social Theory* (1993), and *Communicative Action. Essays on Habermas' Theory of Communicative Action*, (ed.) with Axel Honneth (1991). Other works include *Die gegenwärtige Lage der soziologischen Rollentheorie* (1978), *Wissenschaft und Karriere*, with Michael Bochow (1987), and *Die Kreativität des Handelns* (1992), which will appear in English in 1993.

Robert Alun Jones is currently Professor of Sociology, History, and Religious Studies, and a member of the core faculty in the Program on Science Technology, and Society at the University of Illinois at Urbana-Champaign. As Director of the University's Hypermedia Laboratory, he has been a pioneer in the application of computer technology to the teaching of social theory. He is the leader of the Société d'études durkheimiennes (for which he is constructing an electronic bibliographic archive), the author of *Emile Durkheim* (1986), and the editor of *Durkheim Studies*. His articles, essays, and translations have appeared in the *American Journal of Sociology*, the *Journal of the History of the Behavioral Sciences*, the *Annual Review of Sociology*, *History of Sociology*, *History of Anthropology*, *Sociological Quarterly*, *Sociological Inquiry*, and the *Archives de sciences sociales des religions*. He has also published in *Academic Computing*, for which he is the Advisory Editor on hypermedia.

Hans-Peter Müller, born in 1951, is Professor of Sociology in the Faculty of Social Sciences at the Humboldt-University in Berlin. His major works are *Herrschaft und Legitimität in modernen Industriegesellschaften*, with Manfred Kopp (1980); *Wertkrise und Gesellschaftsreform, Emile Durkheims Schriften zur Politik*, ed. with Lucian Kern (1983); *Gerechtigkeit, Diskurs oder Markt. Die neuen Ansatze in der Vertragstheorie* (1986), *Sozialstruktur und Lebensstile. Der neuere theoretische Diskurs über soziale Ungleichheit* (1992). He is editor of Durkheim's works in German for the Suhrkamp-Verlag.

CONTRIBUTORS

William S. F. Pickering, born in 1922, studied in the University of London, taught for a time at the University of Manitoba, and was for twenty years Lecturer in Sociology at the University of Newcastle upon Tyne. He is now retired and is helping to establish the British Centre for Durkheimian Studies at Oxford University. Among his publications are: *Durkheim on Religion*, (ed.) (1975); *Durkheim: Essays on Morals and Education*, (ed.) (1979); *Durkheim's Sociology of Religion: Themes and Theories* (1984).

Stephen P. Turner, born in 1951, is Distinguished Research Professor of Philosophy at the University of South Florida. His books on the history and philosophy of social science include *Sociological Explanation as Translation* (1980), *Max Weber and the Dispute Over Reason and Value: A Study in Philosophy, Ethics, and Politics*, with Regis Factor (1984), *The Search for a Methodology of Social Science: Durkheim, Weber, and the Nineteenth Century Problem of Cause, Probability, and Action* (1986), *The Impossible Science: An Institutional Analysis of American Sociology*, with Jonathan Turner (1990), *Sociology Responds to Fascism*, ed. with Dirk Käsler (1992), and *The Theory of Social Practices: Tradition, Tacit Knowledge, and Presuppositions* (1993). He is currently chair of the Theory section of the American Sociological Association.

W. Paul Vogt, born in 1943, teaches sociology of education and research methodology in the Department of Educational Administration and Policy Studies at the State University of New York at Albany, where he is an Associate Professor. His recent works include: *A Dictionary of Statistics and Methodology* (1993); 'L'influence de *De la Division du Travail Social* sur la Sociologie dans les Etats Unis', in *De la Division du Travail Social d'Emile Durkheim, 1893–1993*, P. Besnard, M. Borlandi, and P. Vogt, eds. (1993); 'Political Connections, Professional Advancement, and Moral Education in Durkheimian Sociology', *Journal of the History of the Behavioral Sciences* (1991); and 'Equality and Literacy: Elements of a Social Theory of Functional Literacy,' *Review of Education* (1992).

ACKNOWLEDGEMENTS

The essays collected in this volume, except for Hans Joas's chapter and the Introduction, are to be published also in Italian, alongside others, in a volume under the editorship of Massimo Borlandi (*Emile Durkheim*, Roma: La Nuova Italia Scientifica). The Publishers and the Editor would like to thank Massimo Borlandi, who originally commissioned the essays, and La Nuova Italia Scientifica, via Sardegna 50, 00187 Roma, for making the English language publication of *Emile Durkheim: Sociologist and Moralist* possible. Joas's chapter is based on a section of his book *Die Kreativität des Handelns*. Making these texts available to an Anglophone audience has also required the effort of several translators, including H. Sutcliffe for the chapters by Filloux, Besnard, Müller, and Isambert, and for the Durkheim material in the Andrews chapter, and Jeremy Gaines and Doris Jones for the chapter by Joas. These chapters underwent additional changes after leaving the translators' hands. The final manuscript was typed by Karen Kier and Norma Walker.

INTRODUCTION
Reconnecting the sociologist to the moralist
Stephen P. Turner

The philosopher and moralist Alasdair MacIntyre closed his influential work, *After Virtue*, with a call for 'another . . . Saint Benedict' (1981: 238–45). The idea of calling for a moral exemplar and savior who could change both forms and practice struck him as the only kind of serious intervention the moral thinker can make under present circumstances. What is lacking in modern life, he reasoned, is a genuine tradition of moral reasoning – moral persuasion and reasoning presuppose such a tradition. So the only choice is to create one. But the creation of a tradition is not something that a professor can do in the study. It is an act, as MacIntyre conceived it, of community formation and the development of a common narrative – what St Benedict did when he created the religious communities of post-Roman Europe through the attractive example of his own way of living as a Christian.

MacIntyre was not sociologically naive in coming to this conclusion. MacIntyre constructed a sociological account of the history of ethics from the heroic societies of Homeric Greece to the present as a basis for a rethinking of the moral situation of the present day. Heroic societies, he reasoned, were societies in which not 'moral principles' but rather *virtues* were celebrated and formed the core of 'moral' experience. Virtues, he argued, were more or less directly connected to the good of the community, in a visible way. The Homeric heroes, for example, were persons whose excellence in fulfilling the roles set for them in their societies enabled their communities to achieve communal aims. The ancient virtues were closely connected to defined social roles, and when these roles were themselves transformed by the stabilization of Greek politics and the rise of urbanism, they no longer had much application to the actual problems of life, and this posed fundamental intellectual problems for moralists and ultimately for philosophers.

The flowering of Greek ethics at the time of Socrates, Plato, Aristotle and their students was a response to these changed social circumstances. Subsequent forms of moral reasoning were, similarly, fitted to the different social worlds of later societies, and came to be fitted in a specific

1

way – through intellectual effort. MacIntyre's own idea of the path out of the moral confusion of the present day is that virtue, and the associated sense of a purposeful life, need to be re-established in a central place in our morality. He considers that virtues can only be connected to our community existence through the creation of new narratives in which individuals and communities can tell their own story, in ways in which the individual has a place in a story of the community, and in which the acts of the individual and the virtues of an individual have a narrative connection to the larger story of the life of the community. Similar ideas are found in the writings of other 'communitarian' philosophers and sociologists today.

Like MacIntyre, Emile Durkheim was concerned with the problems of creating a morality appropriate to our times and also believed that the key to an understanding of the moral problems of the present was the understanding of moral change across long historical and evolutionary stretches. But the story told by Durkheim is quite different from MacIntyre's – it has a different center, and a different conclusion. In MacIntyre's historical narrative, the central figure is the individual moral agent, within a given social situation that is more or less fixed, who is faced with the task of conceiving and articulating solutions to immediate practical problems of action, but has access only to moral ideologies that no longer apply. The individual in MacIntyre is not merely a moral reflector, but an individual who is engaged in a particular human project or individual project – itself constituted out of the materials of a tradition of moral practice and reasoning, the received moral tradition with which one faces novel situations and in terms of which situations are pre-interpreted.

For Durkheim, the reasoning moral agent recedes, and is replaced by a person who is in the grip of social forces – particularly currents of feeling and desire – in ever-changing balance with one another, which are experienced phenomenologically in ways that do not reveal their true nature as causes – a true nature that Durkheim takes to be collective and immaterial. This argument, as it develops in Durkheim's own thought, shifts the center of Durkheim's narrative radically. It is this radical shift, and the novel conception of the proper role of the moralist it entails, that is the subject of this volume.

The manifest focus of Durkheim's writings, and the focus of the first two parts of the present volume, will be on Durkheim's central concerns as a sociologist – his deepening realization of the 'religious' character and roots of social institutions and his concept of the person. It might be supposed from this emphasis on the religious element that Durkheim was what has come to be called a 'normative functionalist.' A normative functionalist believes, on the one hand, that the normative element of action is essential to any understanding of action, but also that norms are themselves to be understood not, as for example MacIntyre does, as a product of individual action and reflection, much less as theories of ethics or narratives, but as a more or less automatic product of the needs of societal systems. Conflicts in normative orders, according to normative functionalism, may arise, especially where moral imperatives or norms and values come into conflict with one another for particular subgroups of society. In these cases there is the potential for 'deviance' or for lack of 'integration' into the prevailing, functional, normative scheme. But these difficulties are difficulties of individual adjustment to a prevailing normative order that is itself based on and explained by the functional demands of the social system as a whole.

The defenders of normative functionalism in sociology have found much to employ in Durkheim's writings, and in their eyes Durkheim was himself a normative functionalist. The points of commonality between Durkheim and normative functionalism are, indeed, many. The role of the individual moral innovator or the ethical thinker is radically diminished in both accounts of morality, in sharp contrast to writers like MacIntyre. But there is more to Durkheim than normative functionalism, and this 'more' is essential to an understanding of Durkheim's full project. Durkheim was as much a moralist as MacIntyre, and like MacIntyre he did not pretend to have discovered a new moral system but considered himself to be analyzing the conditions under which necessary changes in morality were to occur or could occur. Like MacIntyre and unlike the normative functionalists who appropriated Durkheim, Durkheim himself believed both that moral change of a constructive kind was inevitable and that a moral order appropriate to the present level of societal development would emerge, and moreover that the present moral situation was pathological and that some set of events or actions, preferably guided by the new discipline of sociology, was necessary to correct this pathology.

In the last part of this book, we will consider some of the ways in which Durkheim reasoned about the conditions for moral change and the necessary character of novel moral development in modern society. We will see, in this section, that Durkheim was centrally concerned with the problem of assuring commitment on the part of members of society to new moral ideas or their bindingness and less concerned with their content or with the specific problems they resolved (although, in general, he saw the moral problems of modern society as deriving from the central fact of the division of labor and the conflicts between the division of labor).

The results are as tantalizingly unspecific as MacIntyre's own. But they have the advantage of not resting directly on a problematic philosophical anthropology. Durkheim takes the problem of the diversity of morals seriously. He sees, as his competitors generally have not, that there are few if any human purposes that are not purposes within a societally specific sense of the world, a sense that is more deeply rooted than doctrine and ideology and impervious to mere intellectual change. MacIntyre himself is forced to adopt such an account – to substitute the claim that 'man is in his actions and practice, as well as in his fictions, essentially a story-telling animal' (1981: 201) for other versions of the human essence. Durkheim rejected the appeal to philosophical anthropology or 'human nature' as an account of social differences and social change. In the long view of intellectual history, this is a deeply radical step. It is also a deeply problematic one.

Durkheim's novelty in this respect was a matter of the radical character of his approach to the problem. Others had denied, in one manner or another, the idea of an underlying, ahistorical, human nature – notably Marx in his 'Theses on Feuerbach.' Herbert Spencer himself was revered, especially in American sociological circles, eager to declare their independence of economics, for showing that 'human nature' was not historically constant. But Durkheim went very far beyond either of them, to move large parts of the explanatory domain of traditional concepts of the moral agent to the realm of the social.[1]

Durkheim's slogan against the conventional uses of appeals to human nature was 'explain the social only by the social.' This proved a difficult commitment to keep, as Philippe Besnard shows in his chapter in the present volume, even in his own analyses of moral issues. More fundamentally, it seems to conflict with the whole notion of an applied science of morality or indeed with any sort of moralism. If the causes of moral change are in the collective consciousness, they are not open to manipulation through rational persuasion. Yet Durkheim's reasoning provides a strong basis for understanding why projects for novel moralities and moral regeneration typically have failed, and an approach to the most basic obstacle to any sort of applied moral science. The obstacle is one which is always lurking on the periphery of moral reflection. It is the problem of commitment. As Durkheim understood, ideas and commitments, thought and feeling, are or must be inseparable if the ideas are to have practical moral force. New ideas must not simply *promise* to bind, but must bind in emotional fact and in so binding transform the individuals who are bound. This problem was the core of his positive efforts as a moralist.

His recognition and tracing of the 'religious' character of social institutions and of such values as individualism, discussed in Part I of the present volume, represent a radical alternative both to utilitarianism, which faces the problem of commitment in the form of the free-rider problem, and to virtue moralities, in which excellence in the performance of social roles is visibly conducive to the common good. Durkheim made the connection between commitment or binding and social purposes at a far more basic level – at the level of the primal constitution of society itself (which he saw as fundamentally a religious phenomenon), in the echoes and reenactments of this primal constitutive moment, and in the moments of emotional communion in which society, and morality, are reconstituted. These moments are beyond the direct reach of the moral doctrinaire. But the moralist who seeks to apply the lessons of Durkheimian sociology nevertheless can constructively intervene. Part II examines Durkheim's revised conception of the moral agent. Part III examines his conception of the role of the scientific moralist.

PART I RELIGION AS *FONS ET ORIGO*

Part I of this volume begins with Robert Alun Jones's discussion of the origins of Durkheim's sociology of religion and the background to the idea that religion was ' "the most primitive of all social phenomena," the root from which all other institutional forms had derived' (Jones, infra: 40). Jones approaches Durkheim's arrival at this thesis through a consideration of Durkheim's response to Fustel de Coulages's work *La Cité Antique*, one of the most influential works of the century, which examined the religion of ancient Greece and Rome. Fustel challenged the notion that the Greeks and Romans provided useful institutional models for nineteenth-century France and challenged the idea that French society, and European society generally, could be seen as the heir of Greco-Roman political achievement. Fustel's means of arguing proceeded by substituting a mode of explanation in which religion is understood to be closely related to political institutions for the more familiar ideological approach, in which beliefs about institutions are understood as both their justifications and explanations. What separates us from the ancient world, Fustel argued, is the alienness of these religious beliefs and rites, such as their idea of the immortality of the soul and the connected fact of their focus on burial ritual. Fustel shows that these beliefs had formative effects on institutions such as the 'family, private property, law, morality and the ancient city itself' (Jones, infra: 31).

Durkheim, as Jones points out, took over Fustel's mode of comparative historical analysis. But whereas Fustel's interests in institutions were genealogical, Durkheim wished to extend the comparative method to the new findings of Australian and American ethnography. The results of these comparative analyses were striking. They confirmed Fustel's ideas about the 'priority and explanatory power of religious beliefs' (Jones, infra: 35) and, with the aid of the ideas and data collected by James Frazer and Robertson Smith, Durkheim extended these ideas to social development generally. They formed the basis of his lecture course on ethics taught at Bordeaux in 1898–1900. In this series of lectures Durkheim takes up another problem that Fustel had become famous for, the problem of the nature and origin of the general right of property. The puzzle Durkheim saw was that it is unclear how a 'universal' right could emerge from the familiar duties and obligations owed to co-members of small groups such as clans or families. Durkheim's conclusion was a generalization of the argument of Fustel, namely that the rationalistic ideologies or utilitarian justifications of these institutions were specious and irrelevant to their explanation. The roots of the idea of private property were in the sacralization of land implied in the rituals of the harvest. In this respect Durkheim followed Fustel in relativizing property rights to historical circumstances, and as Jones points out 'in this sense it belongs to Durkheim's lifelong attack on liberal individualism as much as to his sociology of religion' (infra: 40).

But for Durkheim, the deeper lessons were different. The idea of private property in its historical manifestations was relative. There was, however, a general lesson: that *collective* appropriation was a *pre-condition* for private appropriation. The sacralization of land was the collective appropriation of the utility of land, which was the source of the dignity of the right to property. The source of the right to property is thus in society rather than in the private needs and goods of the individual, and, most importantly, the original connection is made at the primal level of early religious practice, rather than as the result of quasi-utilitarian calculations or functional evolution.

The theme of primal religious origins is continued in Pickering's discussion of the origins of conceptual thinking in Durkheim. In Durkheim's *Elementary Forms of Religious Life* a particularly strong version of the argument that abstract categories (and the kind of thinking involved in abstraction) are religious in origin is advanced. This interpretation, however, creates a puzzle about the status of Durkheim and Mauss's 1903 monograph on classification. One interpretation is that the subject matter of the two books is the same and that the 1903 book is 'evidence for the general thesis of the later book' (Pickering, infra: 53). Durkheim himself advanced this interpretation. But the topics of the two books are quite different. The discussion on the elementary forms is concerned with such abstract concepts as space, time, cause and totality, deriving from Kant's critique of pure reason, which Kant calls 'categories'. The 1903 essay is concerned with *classifications*. The two are not the same. But what precisely is their relation in Durkheim's account?

Religion plays almost no role in the discussion in *Primitive Classification*. The sole reference to religion is to religious emotion. And this reference appears only in the conclusion. But this 'emotional' element in both classificatory and fundamental categories provides a link between the two texts. The argument of the monograph was that classifications of a cosmological kind derived in some fashion from social classifications. Pickering suggests that Durkheim in *The Elementary Forms of the Religious Life* and in his concern with the origins of abstract thinking as

6

such was forced to an even more distant historical origin, to the primal social situations of collective effervescence in which collective representations emerge. The centrality of the moment of fluidity in which collective representations can emerge and bind the participants is a theme that recurs in the final section of this volume. Although the notion of collective effervescence is a part of Durkheim's late work and is a small part of his discussion, it obviously plays an essential logical role in his analysis. The constitution of societies through collective representations and practices must be itself accounted for. Durkheim does so by the identification of a social situation within which collective representations and practices can themselves originate. Both the particular collective representations of a given moral order and the primal abstract categories of all thought must be accounted for, and there is an element of commonality in Durkheim's treatment of both.

Durkheim, of course, has other tools to explain the *transformation* of collective representations, for example in terms of the combination of pre-existing categories. But there is a limit to such explanations. They do not allow for the possibility of genuine moral and religious novelty. Collective effervescence fills the gap created by the limitations of these forms of explanation.

In modern societies, the law takes on the centrality of religious practice in primitive societies. But as Vogt shows in his essay on Durkheim's sociology of law, the thesis that 'Everything social is religious' (quoted in Vogt, infra: 79) is carried through here as well: 'All penal law is, more or less, religious,' (quoted in Vogt, infra: 78) Durkheim says in *The Division of Labor in Society*. But penal law is not the only law. The problem that Durkheim needs to explain, and to which his sociology of law is in large part devoted, is the transformation of the law in 'modern' regimes. The religious idea that informs modern society and modern law is the idea of the individual, and Durkheim is frankly enthusiastic about the social forms and political constitutional forms that are entailed by respect for the individual. He was, of course, concerned to establish – perhaps over-optimistically – that 'feelings of human fraternity' (quoted in Vogt, infra: 89) will derive from the enhanced social life and political life of modern orders, yet his vision of modern society is nevertheless, as Vogt points out, 'optimistic and liberal' (infra: 89).

Durkheim never constructed a systematic political sociology or political theory. Moreover, as the normative functionalist interpretation of Durkheim stressed, he was deeply distressed by the moral crises of modern society, crises that may readily be interpreted as a product of unrestrained individualism. Durkheim's political analysis of these problems and of the problem of solidarity is examined by Müller in his chapter on Durkheim's political sociology. Vogt made the point that in Durkheim's lectures, he was often much more frankly normative than his monographs. Müller shows Durkheim at the point of diagnosing the pathologies of development. Durkheim supposed that there was a normal process by which 'rules develop spontaneously in the course of social intercourse, as part of a gradual process of *habitualization* in which . . . exchange is first regulated provisionally, then as a habit and last of all legally' (Müller, infra: 98). The normal development of such rules, however, might be disrupted. Durkheim's diagnosis was that it had, indeed, been disrupted and that some sort of intervention was necessary to shorten the transition to the novel forms of social regulation that had pathologically failed to fully emerge. The first problem faced by anyone attempting to help such a transition along is in the correct identification of the new framework which is emerging. The political side of the problem, as Durkheim conceived it, was the lack of sufficiently large and sufficiently powerful institutions between the individual and the state, 'the result of the abolition of "intermediate bodies" during the French Revolution' (Müller, infra: 101) and the centralization of the French state. In contrast to Spencer, he regarded the problem of excessive state power as a problem of the lack of opposing intermediate forces rather than the excessive extinction of the state's activities and powers. Ordinarily, according to Durkheim, the 'stronger the state the more the individual is respected' (quoted in Müller, infra: 102). But this relationship holds only when there is a balance of power and communication between secondary or intermediate groups and the state which permits the development of individual autonomy.

Durkheim believed, as Müller shows, that the cult of the individual is the basic modern moral and political idea, and that regressions into archaic collectivism were abnormal and would, therefore, be transitory. But he did not take the fulfillment of the moral demands of the 'religious' idea of the dignity of the person to be automatic. He considered that moral individualism required political regulation and indeed required the political regulation of the economy. These considerations led to his most dramatic predictive errors, to the idea of corporate bodies as the building blocks of future society. In this prediction, and with respect to his concern for social solidarity and justice, Durkheim was a socialist. But, Müller concludes, Durkheim was basically right about the fundamental forces in European society. Individualism combined with the belief in the collective obligation to secure social justice *is* the basis of the modern European welfare state.

For Durkheim, the main competitor to his sociology, at least in the 1890s, was a large body of geographical and geo-political thinkers. The increasing emphasis on the religious origin and character of social institutions of forces of Durkheim's later career raises the question of what he thought in this later period of the causal conditions and forces that he had previously considered important. Social morphology is the broad heading under which Durkheim had originally addressed these problems, and the fate of these concerns is an interesting index of the changes in Durkheim's conception of his own task. The basic elements of 'social morphology' – population size, density and social integration – are given an important role in Durkheim's earliest writings. Indeed, we are told that the facts of social morphology play a 'preponderant role' in collective life and in sociological explanations (quoted in Andrews, infra: 118). His experience of 1895, in which he claims to have first recognized the importance of religion, marks a turning point in Durkheim's writings on morphological variables themselves.

In his later writings, the autonomy of collective representations and practices and their independence from their original morphological base comes to be more heavily stressed. But Durkheim, though he obviously became fascinated with the significance of crystallized facts of collective representation, never abandoned or repudiated his earlier claims about the concrete facts of social morphology. Indeed, in 1897 and 1898 Durkheim's yearbook, the *Année Sociologique*, provided for a new subfield of 'social morphology'. In his introduction to this section Durkheim restated many of his original claims about the importance of such facts as density of population. Andrews shows that much of Durkheim's discussion of these issues reflected the competition between Durkheimian sociology and geography. Durkheim came to the problem of social morphology in part as a critic of the explanatory ambitions of human geographers, and sought to annex much of this territory for sociology, understood as a broadly synthetic discipline. This effort was paralleled by Georg Simmel who, in Germany, was attempting to define a specific subject matter for sociology. Durkheim's vision was broader and more imperialistic. He believed that such specialized sciences as political economy, the comparative history of law and religions, demography and political geography had previously been wrongly pursued, and wrongly pursued because they had been conceived as independent wholes whereas they were in fact concerned with manifestations of 'one and the same collective activity' (quoted in Andrews, infra: 127). Durkheim thus did not so much abandon the explanatory variables that concerned him in his earlier writings as gradually reconceived them in terms of his more fully developed sociology.

The lesson of Part I may be summarized simply. Durkheim came to see the fundamental character of social institutions as 'religious.' The relevance to Durkheim's notion of morality and the possible tasks of a moralist is complex. First, by establishing the religious origins and character of the central phenomena that the moral reformer wishes to reform or treat as incorrect ideology, he shows that the moralist has made a fundamental error about the subject matter, and implicitly, an error about the possibility of intervening in the development of morality.

Second, by locating the connection between the fundamental institutional facts of society and 'religious' collective sentiment at this primal level – in the beginnings of history, coeval with conceptual reasoning itself – and by showing this 'religious' character to persist in the most fundamental, secular and 'individual' phenomena of modern life, such as the modern sense of personhood and individual dignity, he shows that any attempt to treat moral phenomena in a utilitarian fashion or to read the dictates of morality directly off of considerations of present social utility are doomed. The connection between social institutions, such as property, and collective feeling is at a level beyond that reached by utilitarian justifications of rights in philosophy and beyond the level reached by normative functionalism in sociology. Changes in deep collective sentiments, such as the individualism that arises in modern societies, are rooted in the longest and deepest processes of social development, and are not merely some sort of 'reflection' of the day-to-day functional steering demands of society.

PART II MORAL AGENTS, SOCIAL BEINGS

The individual as conceived by normative functionalism is, in Harold Garfinkel's famous phrase, a 'cultural dope'. The individual in Durkheim might also appear, superficially, to be merely the victim of larger forces originating in the collective consciousness. Nevertheless, Durkheim's conception of action is considerably more complex than that of normative functionalism. In his chapter, Paolo Ceri begins with the point that our conventional understanding of agents and human agency is itself informed by individualistic and subjectivistic premises. Durkheim, he points out, begins from collectivistic and objectivistic assumptions, so that in an important sense Durkheim's conception of social action falls outside the category of 'action theory' entirely. When Durkheim uses the term 'social action,' Ceri notes, he means the action of society on the individual (Ceri, infra: 140).

Society means durable associations between people living together. Duration as Durkheim sees it, can be explained only by reference to the existence of rules which are upheld as duties, and the fundamental relationship between the individual and the group is the reciprocal relationship between duty and interest. With this kind of reasoning, of course, we are in the conceptual world of the 'moral scientists' of Germany, such as Rudolph von Ihering, with the difference that where Ihering begins with interest and finds himself driven to accept the explanatory necessity of 'social' forces which morally constrain the individual, Durkheim's individual is first and foremost the product of moral rules.

Economic man, or interest-driven man, tears durable social orders

10

apart. Regulation and integration hold them together. These binding forces are 'made up of representations (especially values and norms) which are associated with more or less intense collective sentiments, reflecting the force of the associative relations within the group' (Ceri, infra: 144). These moral elements are bound in different degrees of crystallization. Some are established over time and become formal, others are momentary states of collective feeling. These 'crystals' are different not only with respect to stability over time, but with respect to concentration, the degree 'of nearness or farness from a state of collective fusion' (Ceri, infra: 144). One of these combinations, the state of fusion itself, a state of collective enthusiasm in which there is a high level of instability and closeness, is, as we have already noticed, of particular interest from the point of view of moralism. The moment of maximum cohesion, the moment in which collective life is strongest, is also the moment of creative social action. Creativity is possible because of the strength of group feeling. At this moment, the collective representations that arise can become greater than, and silence, individual representations and interests – in contrast to atomistic exchange situations, in which individual representations and sentiments dominate. But for Durkheim, as Ceri points out, the strength of moral forces is not so much a product of the specific content of moral representations as of the intensity and degree of diffusion of collective sentiments. Variations in clarity and intensity explain rates of specific individual actions.

The creative process, in which new moral orders are formed through the collective enthusiasm of groups in a high state of fusion, is countered by processes by which the force of these collective representations diminishes, such as is described in *Suicide*, which is a study of the decay of, or crisis in, social regulation. In *The Elementary Forms of the Religious Life*, Durkheim refers to political and moral crises which concern social integration. Crises of social integration are overcome in moments in which change and moral regeneration are possible, and these are the mainspring of the civilizing process. Durkheim's analysis implies that individual action is sometimes more, sometimes less, governed by collective forces. But he reasons that the explanation of variation in the strength of collective forces is, itself, collective. Individual freedom or autonomy, consequently, is not conceived in a utilitarian manner as something that the individual yields up to society, but as something which is granted within the framework of collective causality. The autonomy of individuals in modern societies is not a product of freedom *from* society, but results from the membership of the individual in 'multiple societies'.

Differentiation, meaning the creation of new but small crystals of determinate social order in such areas as occupations, produces an intensification of social life rather than a disappearance of collective forces.

Yet the result is a kind of individualization, since individuals no longer face a monolithic, localistic order and set of ties. The individual or person becomes sacralized, and the sacredness of the individual becomes the dominant element and the legitimization of the rules binding together groups at the highest and least 'local' level. This value is not in itself enough to insure social order, and it is for this reason that Durkheim seeks to promote intermediate groups such as corporativist bodies, and insists on the importance of educational institutions in assuring moral integration.

Durkheim, Ceri suggests, failed to explore adequately one of his own most important insights, the phenomena of differentiation understood as the creation of multiple societies and multiple membership. Of course he recognized that normative systems of different groups can conflict and that 'multi-membership' may lead to the weakening of moral control of the individual. But in such works as *Suicide*, where he might appropriately have pursued such thoughts, he did not. The idea of multiple membership and the general problems of the intensity of collective life implicit in the recognition of multiple societies are, Ceri suggests, a potentially fruitful path for the development of Durkheim's ideas.

The idea of integration, to which Ceri's chapter is largely devoted, is more developed in Durkheim's writing than the theory of regulation. As Philippe Besnard observes in his chapter on regulation, the lack of systematic development of Durkheim's ideas on this subject provides us with a series of interpretive puzzles at the core of Durkheim's most famous intervention into practical moral reform, his book *Suicide*. The lack of regulation, or anomie, is a major explanation given by Durkheim. But Durkheim confuses the issue by his presentation, and raises the question of whether his insistence on the need for greater regulation is special pleading. He minimized the importance of the phenomena of fatalistic suicide, the antithesis of anomic suicide. It is in connection with divorce that we find the clearest modern examples of this type, and Durkheim's handling of the problem of marital discipline is revealing with respect to his difficulties in applying his sociological ideas to actual problems of moral intervention and policy.

The legalization of divorce and the liberalization of divorce laws was one of the central issues for both moralists and social thinkers of the late nineteenth century. The legalization of divorce in France dates from 1884, three years before Durkheim's own marriage, and he himself was a participant in subsequent debates on the reform of divorce law. In his major contribution to this public debate, as Besnard shows, Durkheim claimed that the 'fragility of the matrimonial bond is just as harmful to married women as it is to married men' (Besnard, infra: 172). The possibility of divorce, he maintained, has scarcely any effect on female suicide. But he explained this by claiming that in general 'the state of marriage has only a weak effect on the moral constitution of women' (Durkheim, quoted in Besnard, infra: 172). In fact, as Besnard points out, this assertion is contradicted by the statistical material in *Suicide*. But the reasoning enabled him to say that divorce by mutual consent was harmful because it would destroy the matrimonial regulation necessary to moral health and happiness.

The thrust of his argument is to deny the distinctiveness of female suicide, and thus implicity to deny the existence of fatalistic suicide in its most obvious modern form. Besnard points out that Durkheim's original analysis concerned the discovery that 'the more frequent divorce is, the more the immunity of husbands decreases relative to bachelors and the more the immunity of wives increases relative to single women' (infra: 174). What Durkheim's own data indicate, however, is that the relationship holds differently for men and women in different regions. 'Since the marital tie is weaker in Paris than in the provinces, the fact that, in the provinces, the married woman is less protected than when compared to the single woman in the Seine', is a central finding of this data. What it suggests, however, is that fatalism is the cause of the suicide of married women in the provinces. Durkheim, however, forces a quite different conclusion, based on a theory of differences in sexual desire between the sexes. Regulation helps the married man who would otherwise suffer from the morbid desire for the infinite which always accompanies anomie. As women's desires are naturally limited, mono- gamous marriage is of no help to women. Since restraint on women serves no purpose, it is excessive. Women, in Durkheim's picture, are closer to children and animals in this respect.

This is, of course, a natural or biological rather than a social expla- nation, and as such is contrary to Durkheim's own principles of searching for explanations of social differences in other social differences. Besnard considers some ways of rethinking this explanation in Durkheimian terms. One remedy might be to reconsider the notion of fatalistic suicide. Durkheim elaborates the theory of anomie by distinguishing various modalities and forms such as chronic and acute, and progressive and regressive. As Besnard shows, some elements of this differentiated scheme are more properly assigned to fatalism. Besnard proposes a new scheme utilizing two distinct determining factors of anomie: acute anomie refers to the temporary absence of norms; chronic anomie refers to the presence of the ideology of progress at any cost. These absorb many of Durkheim's cases. The remaining cases of anomie may be reclassified within the categories of acute and chronic fatalism, with acute fatalism taking the cases of the individuals whose circumstances change in such a way that intolerable obstacles of a novel kind are placed before them, and chronic fatalism taking over the case of norms that are inflexible and impossible to interiorize.

13

Besnard's chapter illustrates several of the most important peculiarities of Durkheim's attempts to manage the relationship between himself as a sociologist and as a practical moralist and moral policy maker. On the one hand, Durkheim was not above stretching a point when his statistical data did not warrant it, nor was he above ignoring evidence that was contrary to his own basic conception, as in the case of suicides of wives in the provinces. The solutions to the problems he identified, on the other hand, were nevertheless consistent with his sociology. He did not simply rely on moral exhortation or direct legal repression of the activities he disapproved of, but rather considered policy, in this case divorce law, to serve the purpose of reinforcing a social institution that was itself a means or a framework in which a particular moral order, in this case a conjugal society, could be maintained. The means in this case are both indirect and supplementary. The main effects are effects of conjugal society itself. The law is merely a crutch, though a necessary one. By permitting what ought not to be permitted, the law may also have deleterious effects. For example, Durkheim considered that consensual divorce 'institutionalized' anomie in the marital relationship.

In this case, the policy implications of the data, as reinterpreted by Besnard, point to an ambiguous or at least ambivalent result, since it is clear that strengthening the marital bond through strengthening divorce laws does have a deleterious effect on provincial married women. It is this rather typical complexity of policy making that Durkheim's elaborate theoretical analysis of the case attempts to overcome, in favor of a simpler argument for stronger regulation of conjugal society. The causal ambivalence of policies is a feature that social policy makers have become considerably more cognizant of since Durkheim's time, and the very fact that Durkheim found himself wrestling with these difficulties indicates the significance of his rise to sociology from moralistic reformism. Durkheim appreciated, though he attempted to suppress, the difficulties in social policy making that the reformers of his own age tended to overlook. For them, sociology was a science of human welfare which unambiguously supported particular policies. Durkheim, though in an inchoate way, as Besnard emphasizes, moved beyond this to the beginnings of a sociological coming to terms with the problematic character of social intervention. The fact that he failed to fully abandon the moral convictions he brought to his analysis in the face of these difficulties indicates the extent to which Durkheim was still a moralist in the old sense.

Besnard also identifies a fundamental turning point in Durkheim's image of the moral agent. He began with an Aristotelian image of the individual who finds a happy medium between two extremes – a relic of philosophical anthropology. From *Suicide* on, this image changes to the image of an individual impinged upon by conflicting forces.

PART III THE ROLE OF THE SOCIOLOGICAL MORALIST
AND THE MORALIST

There is a fundamental conflict, at least from the point of view of the older idea of moral science, between Durkheim's reasoning about religion as the root of various modern social forms and forms of thought, and the idea of moral intervention. Phenomena that are fundamentally religious in character are not subject to policy manipulation in the usual ways, such as through the institution of new laws and regulations. Nor are they the product of rational moral exhortations or persuasion of the kind favored by some of Durkheim's German predecessors. Religious phenomena are *sui generis*. They arise spontaneously, though there are conditions that favor their development, and have unpredictable consequences. Thus, to envisage society or morals as phenomena closely akin to or derived from religion is to envision a society for which neither social policy nor self-conscious moral theorizing can have a significant constructive role. What role, then, can the moral thinker play in modern society?

Durkheim, it is clear, believed that sociology *could* play a constructive role in, so to speak, the creation of more satisfactory moral constitutions for the multiplicity of societies that modern individuals were members of. Yet his sociological principles limited the potential role of sociology, and did so in a way which his interpreters have found extremely puzzling. Part of the difficulty in determining whether Durkheim was a radical, a liberal or a conservative derives from this self-limitation.

In this final part, the conception of moral intervention that Durkheim accepted is examined in detail. Isambert's chapter stresses the continuity and volume of Durkheim's writings on morality and the role of the German moral science legacy in forming his description of the issues in the study of morality. One of these issues, central in particular to the work of Ihering, who is discussed in greater length in Joas's chapter, is the issue of the causal and emotional force of moral rules. This focus is equally central for Durkheim, as Isambert shows in his treatment of Durkheim's discussion of another German moral scientist, the psychologist Wilhelm Wundt. Durkheim's real innovation in this tradition, Isambert argues, was the notion of moral fact.

The problem of securing cooperation was central to post-utilitarian moral theorists. Durkheim applied the notion of moral fact to the problem of cooperative morality, the morality which obliges one to 'be useful'. Durkheim approaches the problem by looking for the moral facts that in the highly diverse situations and milieus of modern society actually do serve to ensure practically meaningful cooperation. Where Durkheim differs from such thinkers as Ihering is in his recognition of moral diversity, even diversity at the same stage of evolutionary development.

Thinkers like Ihering were evolutionists, but they did not, as Durkheim did, have a means by which they could identify what Durkheim considered to be pathological moral facts. This is highly relevant to the possibility of moral criticism based on 'science'. Durkheim could say that some moral facts found in modern societies are pathological and, consequently, not obligatory, and identifying these moral facts and arguing that they were not morally appropriate or binding could be a contribution of sociology to practical moral discussion.

Isambert examines a question that the preceding chapters raise implicitly: if the primary social forces and social institutions are religious in origin and partly religious in character, what is the role of morality? As Isambert points out, Durkheim identifies numerous connections of kinship between religion and morality, including common historical roots and the fact that social necessity and the phenomenological sense of externality are common to both. By social necessity, Isambert means the causal fact that moral and religious thinking is conditioned and, indeed, largely determined by the causal force of currents of the collective consciousness, on which we may as moral agents reflect. In the case of both the sacred and morality, there is a duality – between desire and duty in the case of morality, and fear and attraction in the case of the sacred. These two faces of morality and sacrality – sanction and collective desire for collective goods – are central to both Durkheim's analysis of morality and his analysis of the sacred. These commonalities might lead one to suppose that the one could be reduced to the other in some manner. But Durkheim refuses to reduce morality to religion or religion to morality, for fear, apparently, of falling into a utilitarian analysis of religion.

The duality between the disciplinary and the value aspects of morality, morality as a goal – or object-oriented science, such as utilitarianism would make it – and morality as disciplinary or a duty-oriented science, runs through Durkheim's writings on morality. The Kantian sound of Durkheim's discussions of duty raises questions about Durkheim's notions of moral freedom. As Isambert suggests, the kind of moral freedom Durkheim envisions is not Kantian autonomy or freedom of the will, but the reasoned acceptance of moral facts based on the reasoning of science. The science, of course, is sociology. The distinction is that the sociologist, unlike the Kantian moralist, must treat morality as an unknown quantity. But Durkheim supposes that this kind of study of moral facts can yield pure precepts or ideals rather than mere descriptions of moral practice, which is inevitably tainted by human weakness and other distortions. So the aim of this kind of study of morality is similar to the aim of traditional philosophical ethics of duty. Nevertheless, Durkheim's alternative image of moral fact creates a specific space for the sociological moralist and allows for a specific kind of appropriate intervention into moral debate.

The issue of the proper role of the sociologist in such discussions is examined in greater length in Filloux's chapter on inequality. Filloux begins with a crucial quotation from Durkheim's preface to the first edition of *The Division of Labor*: 'the fact that we propose above all to study reality does not mean that we should abandon the attempt to improve it; indeed, we would consider that our research was not worth a single hour's effort if it had no more than speculative interest' (quoted in Filloux, infra: 211). This overtly raises the question of what sort of attempt to improve reality Durkheim had in mind, and of the role he envisioned for his new science. As Filloux shows, the nature of the reforming mission Durkheim accepts is closely connected to his actual claims about the nature of modern society and the basic premises of his approach to it. Filloux identifies three crucial elements to this approach: structural functionalism, the hypothesis of the consolidation of the collective consciousness by stages, and the idea of the necessity of the 'cult of man'. Durkheim's conception of social development itself implies some form of socialism. The problem this creates for Durkheim is this: what form of socialism is consistent with individualism, or, as Durkheim thought of it, the cult of man? The notion of individualism as a moral force is itself conceived in a religious manner by Durkheim: individualism is a 'cult'.

By recognizing the necessity of these various collective forces for evolutionary developments, sociology reveals the necessity of a future society that is simultaneously individualistic, socialist and democratic. The means of reconciling the apparent conflicts between these forces or tendencies is the principal of merit, which Durkheim borrows from Comte and Saint-Simon. The principal is a means of reconciling the demand for justice and individualism. The sociologist can say what the 'normal solution' in modern society is to the problem of reconciling individualism and justice, meaning that the sociologist can explain what 'just' social stratification is. The solution to this question requires the solution of two other questions. The first is the problem of matching talents to roles in society. The second is the problem of paying people in conformity with the social value of the work they perform. Durkheim's solution to the latter problem is equal opportunity and competition, which is designed to avoid distortions and mismatches, particularly the lack of recognition of merit and social value. The problem with this general solution is in defining social value itself. Durkheim's solution to this problem is to argue that collective opinion itself contains an obscure feeling of the worth of various services, and that mismatches between these collective opinions and social reality were the primary source of the sense of injustice. Capitalists got more than they merited by public opinion, and workers got less. Yet public opinion is nevertheless an imperfect guide.

There are 'survivals', such as the respect for the upper classes and the respect for wealth.

The sociologist can usefully intervene here by helping to advance public opinion toward a better-defined meritocratic conception, an intervention made possible precisely because of the obscurity of collective feelings, and the sociologist can also persuade public opinion of the inevitability and necessity of meritocracy. This image of the role of the sociologist in moral discussion is in fact close to the moral science conception of Durkheim's German predecessors: the problem of moral science is to grasp historical development, to side with the achievably progressive elements in public opinion, and to focus and strengthen public opinion by more clearly defining principles. Filloux adds that the problem of change and the tendency for conceptions of moral worth to become stabilized, the same phenomena that produce survivals, mean that there is a *continuing* role for the sociologist in revising conceptions of merit. There is also a continuing tension between the need for more or less fixed ideals and opinions and the demand for precision in distribution of benefits that the cult of the individual ordains.

Durkheim was excessively optimistic about the solubility of the problems of justifying social stratification. He relied too heavily on the traditional utilitarian bugaboo of inheritance as an explanation of actual injustice in distribution. He did not recognize the extent to which meritocratic values themselves might be problematic and the source of conflict. Filloux argues that the spirit of Durkheim's approach to these problems remains valuable. But his chapter shows how difficult it is to apply this reasoning in practice. The familiar conflicts and paradoxes of policy science are evident in Durkheim's approach to these questions as well.

In the final chapter, Hans Joas reconsiders Durkheim's intellectual development in terms of another aspect of Durkheim as a moralist and as a sociologist of morals, namely his repeated return to the problem of the emergence of new moralities or moral creativity. Joas points out that the received image of Durkheim's intellectual development, in which Durkheim turns from his 'positivistic' early writings to 'idealist' later writings, depends on a neglect of Durkheim's earliest writings. These can best be understood, Joas argues, as the beginnings of a life-long attempt to answer the question of how a new morality can emerge. This approach his its roots in German Durkheim scholarship, in the work of René König, and also in the facts of the contextual relationship between Durkheim and the German moral scientists by whom Durkheim was influenced. His early essay on moral science in Germany is a major document for establishing this influence and shows that Durkheim intended to supersede, rather than take sides in, the conflict between Kantianism and utilitarianism. It is these moralists, as we have seen already, who provide the kernel of the idea of autonomous moral facts.

Durkheim's ultimate solution to the problem of creating new moralities is to be found in his final writings on religion. Joas suggests that his theory of religion is itself a solution of sorts to the problem, broached in *The Division of Labor in Society*, of the institutionalization of a morality of cooperation. His writings on education, Joas suggests, were always directed to this end. They are linked by the problem of finding an equivalent in education for the force of religion as a reinforcer of morality. The solution, Joas suggests, is in the idea that morality is formed in emotionalized collective states in which actors are attracted by ideals and lifted beyond themselves. The theory of religion is designed to show how the moments of collective effervescence transform or create social structures and interpersonal bonds. Yet these are also moments of moral creativity, moments in which new moral facts emerge. In his late lectures on pragmatism, this approach is extended, and defended against the competing claims of the pragmatists.

Durkheim's own account thus creates apparently insurmountable obstacles to a significant role for the sociologically inspired moralist. Sociology can aid in the clean-up work – clarify obscure moral facts or collective sentiments – and suggest institutional frameworks within which habitualized moralities can develop, as noted in Müller's chapter. But the creative work seems to be outside its scope. Moral facts cannot simply be invented by moralists, sociologically informed or otherwise. And moral progress cannot consist wholly in better defining moral terms and focussing moral reflection. So the relevance of science to the creation of new moralities is necessarily limited, and perhaps the contribution of sociology is necessarily trivial.

One way of overcoming these limitations would be to find a role for sociology in connection with moral creativity itself. Joas suggests that Durkheim did envision such a role for moral reasoning and the intervention of the scientifically inspired moralist in these contexts. In his final writings, he stressed that it was precisely the currents that permeate society that become the subject of debate and reflection, and that, with the help of the moralist, are the stuff from which new moral facts are created and crystallized in moments of collective effervescence. The scientifically inspired moralist has a specific role here in calling traditional morality into question and in emphasizing the conflicts within present morality. This form of moral reflection is a precondition for creative moral transformation, and this provides a role for the moralist in moral creation.

EMILE DURKHEIM

THE ROLE OF THE SCIENTIFIC MORALIST: DURKHEIM'S LEGACY

These essays have served to reconnect two elements of Durkheim that traditional sociological interpretations have generally sought to separate or to reinterpret by construing him reductively as an ideologist, particularly an ideologist for 'conservatism'. We can see instead a much more complex, but also coherent, picture – of Durkheim as a successor to the German moral scientists and a major moralist in his own right. Durkheim's analysis of the religious character of social institutions was a major advance on the moral commentary of his time. He pushed the problem of understanding the moral force back to a more basic, primal level, and in doing so gave a critique of, and solution to, the fundamental problems that were left by the moral scientists he recognized in his early essays as his predecessors.

Their central problem was that of the force of moral ideals. Durkheim's answer to this problem was that moral ideals of the sort they had considered under the headings of duty in the Kantian sense, or collective desirability in the utilitarian sense, were in fact more radically autonomous than they had appreciated. They were, Durkheim claimed, fundamentally religious or akin to religion. This kinship, given Durkheim's own analysis of the character of religion as the concealed worship of society, meant that the traditional model of scientific moralism was itself misguided. The role of the moralist was limited and defined by the facts that could be discovered by the sociologist.

Many of Durkheim's specific predictions proved wrong, but one proved right: that of the continuing and overwhelming importance of what he called the cult of man. The difficulties that modern societies continue to experience in the moral realm result, in large part, from the continued power of this cult and the conflict between, on the one hand, the principle of individual sovereignty, respect and dignity, and, on the other hand, other moral trends, notably those that arise from a desire for solidarity. In grasping this central moral fact Durkheim distinguished himself from his contemporaries in sociology, such as Weber, who considered the principle of individuality to be deeply threatened by tendencies in modern society. Weber, indeed, considered individuality to have already begun to be destroyed by the force of bureaucratic impersonalism and the domination of large organizations. One need scarcely add that the collapse of Communism, which Weberians, Marxists and communitarians alike would not, on their own premises, have foreseen, is fully consistent with Durkheim's basic intuition.

The Durkheim we see in this volume is closer to the whole man than the Durkheim of the specifically sociological writings. He is a quite different and in some ways more radically alien Durkheim than the

Durkheim of normative functionalism. But he also presents a more interesting and fundamental challenge to present-day thought. Durkheim believed that the sociologist – *and* the moralist – are obliged to respect the facts of the moral world just as the engineer is obliged to respect those of the physical world. This respect, which is crucial to Durkheim's achievement, means that major tendencies in modern society, such as individualism, cannot be simply denounced in favor of something more desirable, such as solidarity or community. This is a trap fallen into not only by moralists of Durkheim's time, but by sociologists of every generation since. The continuing relevance of Durkheim as a moralist and as a sociologist of morals is assured by the continued temptation, succumbed to routinely by sociological social critics, to foreshorten our picture of moral life – to see moral feelings that are deeply rooted as mere intellectual errors or deviations from human nature that could easily be corrected by a bit of propaganda and a government program encouraging the right organizational initiatives. Durkheim's point against these critics would be that the facts of collective morality that they decry are rooted deeply in circumstances, or, as Durkheim says, in conditions of existence, or in the religious constitution and roots of social institutions and collective opinions that cannot be eliminated without being replaced by new facts or a new morality of its own kind – not merely a morality of rationalized opinion, but a morality with the character of binding collective fact.

NOTE

1 The main element of the contextual background of Durkheim's innovation is perhaps to be found in a work, *Der Zweck im Recht* ([1877] 1913), by Durkheim's influential predecessor, the philosopher of law Rudolph von Ihering, whose thought Durkheim was exposed to in his formative German sojourn. Ihering, mentioned in several chapters in this volume, saw the law and political institutions generally (which both he and Durkheim saw as providing the essential forms within which economic life proceeded) as the product of successive collective solutions to conflicts of social interest. This step prefigured Durkheim, as did his emphasis on *fests* and the explanation of moral sentiment. For Ihering the law was fundamentally a product of social conflicts that arose under previous regimes of law. But the law itself had an evolutionary tendency toward the extension of rights to new groups and toward the greater achievement of utilitarian goals within societies. Ihering, an admirer of Bentham, made an important step away from utilitarianism by arguing that *society itself* in some sense provided goals or goods – 'interests' in his language – that had a kind of autonomous moral force that countervailed against the purely individual interests envisioned by utilitarianism.

Durkheim's sociology may be seen as a radicalization of this idea. Where Ihering had conceived of the conflicts of interest mediated by the law as central and the moral regulation of these interests as incidental but essential, Durkheim conceived of the moral character of public institutions as central. But although Ihering stressed the historical variability of 'interests,' he did so against the background of a general view of human nature that itself provided the motor for historical evolution in morals and the law, and explained, in conjunction with the facts of circumstances, historical variability in morals and the law. Durkheim rejected this well-established model of historical change and this solution to the problem of the diversity of morals.

REFERENCES

Ihering, R. von ([1877] 1913) *Law as a Means to an End*, Boston: Boston Book Co.

MacIntyre, A. (1981) *After Virtue*, Notre Dame, Indiana: University of Notre Dame Press.

Part I

RELIGION AS *FONS ET ORIGO*

1

DURKHEIM AND *LA CITÉ ANTIQUE*

An essay on the origins of Durkheim's sociology of religion

Robert Alun Jones

Durkheim's sociology of religion can hardly be considered a 'neglected area' in the study of his thought. It is a concern of sections or chapters in every major study of Durkheim's life and work (LaCapra 1972: 245–91; Lukes 1972: 237–44, 450–84), a favorite topic in the journalistic literature on the history of the social sciences (Isambert 1976; Jones 1977; 1981; 1986), and a central focus for edited volumes and monographs on Durkheimian sociology (Pickering 1975; 1984). Moreover, while these discussions frequently disagree on the precise nature, origin and/or significance of Durkheim's ideas on religion, there is virtual unanimity on one specific point – that is, that Durkheim was profoundly influenced by *La Cité Antique* (1864), the classic work on the religion of Greco-Roman antiquity written by Fustel de Coulanges, under whom Durkheim had studied at the Ecole Normale Supérieure in the early 1880s (Jones 1986: 621; LaCapra 1972: 30, 197; Lukes 1972: 60–3; Pickering 1984: 56–8). The ironic parallel to this unanimity is the relative absence, within the same literature, of any detailed discussion of their intellectual relationship.

This essay is part of an ongoing effort to redress this imbalance between assertion and evidence. As such, it begins with a brief account of Fustel's life and the social context of his work, and proceeds to a more detailed analysis of the ideas contained in *La Cité Antique*, noting agreements and disagreements with ideas later developed by Durkheim. The third section provides a still more detailed treatment of Fustel's profound but ambiguous influence on Durkheim's sociology of religion, particularly as this was revealed in Durkheim's posthumous *Leçons de Sociologie: Physique des Moeurs et du Droit* (1950). Finally, the brief conclusion attempts to place this influence within the context of Durkheim's other concerns, including the comparative method, the growing body of ethnographic evidence about primitive religions, the theories of

Robertson Smith and James Frazer about religion, and the social origin of our ideas of civic duty and obligation.

FUSTEL DE COULANGES: BIOGRAPHY AND SOCIAL CONTEXT

Numa Denys Fustel de Coulanges (1830–89) was born in Paris in the year of the July Revolution and the Barricades. Like his contemporary Ernest Renan, Fustel was of a Breton family. The early death of his father, a naval officer, left his education to his grandfather, and a family friend provided his support at the Lycée Charlemagne. At age 20, he entered the Ecole Normale Supérieure, where he studied with the historians Duruy, P. A. Chéruel and J.-D. Guigniaut.[1] Appointed sublibrarian, Fustel hid himself in the stacks, reading Montesquieu, Michelet, Tocqueville and Guizot.[2] But his chief early inspiration came from Descartes: 'Jules Simon explained Descartes' *Discours sur la méthode* to me thirty years ago,' Fustel observed late in life, 'and from that come all my works: for I have applied to history this Cartesian doubt which he introduced to my mind' (Thompson 1942: 363).

The early years of the Second Empire, however, were a period of political repression in the history of the Ecole Normale. The *coup d'état* of Louis Napoleon on December 2, 1851, was followed by the dismissal and even exile of some of the Ecole's most distinguished teachers, and the new director attempted to suppress most non-classical studies.[3] Like many of his contemporaries, Fustel turned to the study of Latin and Greek, then drifted into the history of classical antiquity. For all his Cartesian spirit, however, Fustel had already embraced the inductive method, writing an essay in praise of Bacon which shocked his fellow students (Thompson 1942: 363–4).[4] In 1853, he joined the newly established Ecole française d'Athènes, moving to the Lycée Amiens in 1855, then to the Lycée St Louis in Paris in 1857. In 1860, Fustel was called to the chair of medieval and modern history at the University of Strasbourg, where his 'vigorous and scholarly lectures' produced 'phenomenal success' throughout the next decade.[5]

During his sojourn in Greece, Fustel collected a number of manuscripts which provided the foundations for his earliest publications, including his *Mémoire sur l'île de Chios* (1856),[6] his highly praised French thesis, *Polybè ou la Grece Conquise* (1858),[7] and his Latin thesis, *Quid Vestae Cultus in Institutis Veterum Privatis Publicisque Valuerit* (1858). The Latin thesis in particular anticipates *La Cité Antique* for, according to Fustel, the goddess Vesta symbolized that domestic, familial religion which became the official cult of the ancient city, and thus the first phase of Aryan civilization.[8] But Fustel's masterpiece remains *La Cité Antique*, written over a six-month period at Strasbourg in 1864, comprising lectures

26

given the two previous years. Initially published at his own expense, the work quickly won Fustel a following at the court of Napoleon III and, by 1890, had seen its thirteenth edition. On the recommendation of Victor Duruy (the Emperor's Minister of Public Instruction), Fustel was thus called to Paris in February, 1870, to give history lectures at the Ecole Normale, and an invitation to provide a special course to the Empress Eugénie, and her suite followed quickly thereafter.[9]

Not surprisingly, therefore, the Franco-Prussian War significantly altered the course of Fustel's career, turning his interest from antiquity to what he perceived as his country's national interest. In an open letter, he protested against the 'religion of hate' preached by the German pastors, and in a pamphlet written in reply to Theodor Mommsen,[10] he defended the French character of Alsace on the principle of self-determination (Thompson 1942: 367). More generally, in 'La manière d'écrire l'histoire en France et en Allemagne' (1872), Fustel sharply contrasted the historiography of the two countries. In Germany, Fustel observed, science is 'a means to an end, and that end is the glorification of the fatherland,' but in France, royalists disparage the Revolution and its consequences while republicans despise the *ancien régime*. 'True patriotism,' Fustel insisted, 'is not love of one's native soil, it is love of the past, respect for the generations who have gone before us' (cited in Momigliano, [1970] 1982: 329; see also Gooch, 1913: 212–13). In short, Fustel called for a renewed respect for the pre-revolutionary *ancien régime* as the foundation for French unity after the humiliations of 1870–1.[11]

As a direct extension of these nationalist concerns, in 1872 Fustel launched what G. P. Gooch called a 'thunderbolt' in the pages of the *Revue des Deux Mondes* (1913: 209). For more than a century, the central question for European social history had been the institutional origins of feudalism. Arising in Germany, the debate soon spread to France and gradually resolved into two fiercely defended alternatives, the first insisting that the origins of feudalism lay in Roman civilization, the second equally insistent that its origins were Germanic (Thompson 1942: 360–2). By 1870, these two schools of interpretation, fuelled by the patriotic sentiments of their respective supporters, confronted one another in a precariously balanced opposition; and in 'L'invasion germanique au Ve siècle, son caractère et ses effets' (1872), Fustel 'set himself to the task of demolishing the whole fabric of early medieval history created by the German School' (Thompson 1942: 362). The much-discussed Germanic invasions of the fifth century had 'no direct influence on the history, religion, customs, government, or structure of [French] society. The barbarians brought with them nothing but confusion,' as Gooch summarizes Fustel's argument, 'and their arrival simply favoured the development of the feudalism already existing in germ' (Gooch 1913: 209).

The article created a sensation, and by 1874 had been expanded into a complete volume. Fustel hoped to follow this with a second volume on feudalism, a third on royalty and the States-General, and a fourth on absolute monarchy, bringing the narrative down to recent times. But the storm of criticism which greeted this first installment, and particularly the charge that it was more the product of Sedan than science,[12] led Fustel to abandon his original plan. Admittedly, like *La Cité Antique*, the first volume had presented Fustel's conclusions rather than the detailed historical research on which these were based. Returning to the 1874 volume, Thompson observes, Fustel now 'took the reader into his workshop', not sparing him

> page after page of criticism and exposition of individual texts; he lugged all his *apparatus criticus* out into the open. Each chapter grew to the dimensions of a volume, each page bristled with references and was sown with the marks of erudition . . . He convinced himself that his generation needed a lesson in historical method . . . By example and by precept he set himself up as the teacher and critic of the historiography of his time.
>
> (Thompson 1942: 368–9; see also Gooch 1913: 209–10)

The result, which occupied Fustel for the rest of his life and was completed only after his death, was the classic *Histoire des Institutions Politiques de l'Ancienne France* (6 vols, 1873–93).[13]

The *Histoire des Institutions Politiques* is important for two related reasons. First, it was the project which literally consumed Fustel during the period in which Durkheim was his student at the Ecole Normale.[14] Second, an essential element in the project was the detailed articulation of the method he had followed in writing *La Cité Antique* (1864), the same method employed by Montesquieu in *L'Esprit des Lois* (1734), and the method Durkheim would follow in *De la Division du Travail Social* (1893) as well. Essentially, as Fustel wrote to an admiring critic in 1865, this method relied less on the detailed accumulation of facts (something for which Fustel had no more patience than had Durkheim)   an on rigorous comparisons (of the Rig-Veda with Euripides, of the laws of Manu with the Twelve Tables or Isaeus and Lysias) until he had arrived at the conception of a community of beliefs and institutions among Indian, Greek and Italic peoples.[15] To these comparisons Fustel added a deeply Cartesian skepticism regarding secondary sources,[16] a commitment to the careful examination of primary texts,[17] an abhorrence of anachronistic analogies,[18] and an utter indifference to the role of the individual personality in the historical process.[19] The result was a work which deeply inspired the young Durkheim, and has an ineliminable place in any account of the development of his thought. (34)

THE IDEAS OF *LA CITÉ ANTIQUE* (1864)

Fustel's central purpose in *La Cité Antique* was 'to show upon what principles and by what rules Greek and Roman society was governed' (Fustel 1864: 11). The initial premise underlying this purpose was, as we have seen, that the ancient Greeks and Romans shared a common body of beliefs and institutions which they had inherited from Aryan peoples, indeed, Fustel argued, the Greeks and Romans represented two branches of the same race, spoke two variants of the same language, possessed similar governmental institutions, and passed through a series of similar revolutions. But at least a secondary premise was that these beliefs and institutions were decidedly *different* from those of nineteenth-century France. Fustel thus attempted 'to set in clear light the radical and essential differences which at all times distinguished these ancient peoples from modern societies' (Fustel 1864: 11).

This insistence on the radical discontinuity between Greco-Roman and French civilization was a direct extension of Fustel's effort to restore respect for the *ancien régime*. French school-children, he complained, learned about the Greeks and Romans from their earliest years, comparing ancient revolutions with their French counterparts, and ancient history with that of nineteenth-century France. Such comparisons not only perpetrated a complete misunderstanding of the past.[20] They also created a naive, idealized conception of ancient liberties which the French had then set before themselves as reasonable social and political aspirations, thus impeding the actual progress of modern society.[21] If, on the contrary, we study the Greeks and Romans 'without thinking of ourselves, as if they were entirely foreign to us,' Fustel suggested, then their institutions will be revealed as 'absolutely inimitable; nothing in modern times resembles them; nothing in the future can resemble them. We shall attempt to show by what rules these societies were regulated', he proposed, 'and it will be freely admitted that the same rules can never govern humanity again' (1864: 12).[22]

So dramatic a contrast between past and present presupposed an explanation for the transition from one to the other; and for Fustel, as Durkheim later complained (1893: 178–9), this explanation was provided by the progress of the human mind. In the present, Fustel argued, '[m]an has not . . . the way of thinking that he had twenty-five centuries ago; and this is why he is no longer governed as he was governed then'. For Fustel, therefore, institutions provided no explanation of their associated beliefs; for when we examine the institutions of the Greeks and Romans, they appear obscure, whimsical and inexplicable. But when we examine the religious ideas of the ancients, these institutional practices become quite transparent. 'If, on going back to the first ages of this race,' Fustel observed,

> we observe the idea which it had of human existence, of life, of death, of a second life, of the divine principle, we perceive a close relation between these opinions and the ancient rules of private law; between the rites which spring from these opinions and their political institutions.

(1864: 12–13)

La Cité Antique, as Fustel explained in his conclusion, describes the history of a *belief*. When that belief was established, 'human society was constituted. It was modified, and society underwent a series of revolutions. It disappeared, and society changed its character. Such was the law of ancient times' (1864: 396).[23]

These beliefs held in common by Greeks and Romans would have been inconceivable but for a common source – that is, those Indo-European tribes calling themselves 'Aryá' (hence 'Aryans') that invaded the Indian subcontinent during the middle of the second millennium before Christ, and whose language thus provided the basis for Sanskrit and Persian as well as Latin and Greek.[24] It was in this 'more ancient' epoch, Fustel suggested, 'in an antiquity without date', that the beliefs of the Greeks and Romans were formed, and their institutions 'either established or prepared' (1864: 13). So remote and undocumented a past, Fustel acknowledged, was inaccessible by traditional historiographical means; but it might at least be reconstructed hypothetically, by analyzing and comparing its 'survivals' – for example, the Indo-European roots still evident in the Greek and Latin languages, the legends still recounted by the peoples who spoke them, and especially the religious rituals practiced by Greeks and Romans down to the time of Christ: 'if we examine the rites which [Cicero] observed', Fustel suggested, 'or the formulas which he recited, we find the marks of what men believed fifteen or twenty centuries earlier' (1864: 14).

Above all, Fustel's reconstructive project revealed the belief in a life after death. No matter how far back we go, Fustel insisted, we find no point at which the Indo-European peoples thought that this life was the only life; on the contrary, 'the most ancient generations, long before there were philosophers, believed in a second existence after the present. They looked upon death not as a dissolution of our being, but simply as a change of life' (1864: 15). In particular, they believed that the soul remained associated with the body after death, was to be buried with the body, and that carefully established ritual precautions were to be observed upon such burials. In the absence of such precautions, the soul was condemned to wander as a 'phantom' or 'larva', without rest or sustenance, eventually becoming a malevolent spirit inflicting serious damage upon the living. Classical literature, Fustel thus observed, is replete with references to fear of privation of burial which, indeed, seems to have exceeded the fear of death itself. 'All antiquity was persuaded that without burial the soul was miserable, and that by burial it became forever happy' (1864: 18).

The souls of the dead were thus sacred beings, and the worship of these beings, initially through communal sacrifices[25] at the sacred hearth in every home, and later by sacrifices to the goddess Vesta (or Brahma, or Zeus, or Janus), was the oldest Indo-European religion (1864: 24–5). Like Durkheim, Fustel was little concerned with the particular symbol under which these beliefs were entertained; for whatever the symbol, the true object of worship was the moral nature of the human soul. '[I]t is certain,' he insisted,

> that the oldest generations of the race from which the Greeks and Romans sprang worshipped both the dead and the hearth-fire – an ancient religion that did not find its gods in physical nature, but in man himself, and that has for its object the adoration of the invisible being which is in us, the moral and thinking power which animates and governs our bodies.
>
> (1864: 33)

And having characterized these ancient beliefs, Fustel went on to trace their powerful impact on the family, private property, law, morality and the ancient city itself.

This ancient religion, Fustel began, differed from later religions in two respects. First, worship of the dead was necessarily worship of one's ancestors, and thus each family's rituals were private and domestic (1864: 34). Second, each family's religion was independent of every other, and its beliefs and practices were thus passed on, from father to son, as a kind of patrimony (1864: 38). But if the family was thus the instrument whereby religion was transmitted from generation to generation, religion was no less the constituent principle of the family. Indeed, Fustel insisted that the bond which held together the members of the ancient family was neither blood nor mutual affection, but the authority of the father, the *patria potestas*; and the source of this authority, he added, lay in the rites and beliefs of the ancient religion. 'The ancient family', Fustel concluded, 'was a religious rather than a natural association'.[26]

Consistent with this familial independence, the religion also required that the dwellings and grave sites of each family be separated from those of others. Both the hearth and the burial place, Fustel explained, had to be bound to a specific location, lest the families become confounded and the worship of one's own ancestors neglected or even abandoned. Each family thus took possession of a certain plot of land, which so became imbued with the religious sentiments of its members and eventually their moral responsibility. 'Without discussion, without labour, without a shadow of hestitation,' Fustel observed, the ancients thus 'arrived, at a single step, and merely by virtue of their belief, at the conception of the right of property; this right from which all civilization springs, since by it man improves the soil, and becomes improved himself.'[27]

Law and morality experienced a similar evolution. Upon its emergence, the ancient city found the law of the family already established and deeply rooted in custom and observance. Far from being instituted by some ancient legislator, therefore, the law rather had its birth in the religious authority of the father, and was thus imposed upon the legislator, who adapted it to the needs of the city by degrees.[28] Similarly, avoiding the suggestion that the ancient religion *created* moral sentiments, Fustel at least argued that these religious beliefs were *associated with* the 'natural sentiments' of morality, in order to 'fortify them, to give them greater authority, to assure their supremacy and their right of direction over the conduct of man' (1864: 95). Initially limited to the mutual duties of members of the same family, this ancient morality insensibly evolved to comprise the duties of citizens, and eventually those prescribed by natural law. Like Durkheim, Fustel thus accounted for the 'religious aura' of moral commands by referring his readers to their evolutionary origins in the institution of the family, whose own authority, as we have seen, was based upon the ancient religion.[29]

In *De la Division du Travail Social* (1893), Durkheim criticized Fustel for deriving these early forms of social organization from religious ideas; but in fact, Fustel's subsequent treatment of the evolution of legal, moral and religious ideas placed enormous emphasis on changing forms of social organization, in a manner strikingly similar to the conclusion of Book 2 in *Les Formes Élémentaries de la Vie Religieuse* (1912). A certain number of families, Fustel suggested, joined together to form a group (the Greek *phratry* or the Latin *curia*): 'Even at the moment when they united,' he added, 'these families conceived the idea of a divinity superior to that of the household, one who was common to all, and who watched over the entire group. They raised an altar to him, lighted a sacred fire, and founded a worship' (1864: 118).[30] When several *phratries* or *curias* joined together, forming a tribe, another religion was formed; and when several tribes gathered to found the confederation which constituted the ancient city, still another, more comprehensive worship was established. At each level, however, the function of religion was the same – 'among the ancients, what formed the bond of every society was a worship' (1864: 146).[31]

Fustel's account of worship in the ancient city also bears a strong resemblance to the later accounts of Frazer, Smith and Durkheim.[32] The city, for example, was a collective group of those who had the same deities and performed religious ceremonies at the same altar; and nothing in the city was more sacred than this altar, on which the sacred fire was maintained (Fustel 1864: 146; see Smith 1889: 114–19). The earliest religious act was a sacrifice upon this altar, followed by a communal meal in which the god shared (1864: 155).[33] Ritual far exceeded doctrine in importance, for rites were obligatory and unchanging, while doctrine was voluntary and shifted constantly.[34] Political authority was derived from religion, and thus the king was a sacred being, the hereditary priest of the sacred fire;[35] and the city's legal statutes derived, not from ancient ideas of justice, but from religion.[36] Citizenship was established entirely on religious grounds; and the stranger, by contrast, was 'one who has not access to the worship, one whom the gods of the city do not protect, and who has not even the right to invoke them.'[37]

The point toward which all these observations conspired, as we have already seen, was that the ancient city enjoyed nothing even remotely comparable to what we would call 'liberty'. Indeed, ancient peoples 'had not even the idea of it,' Fustel argued. 'They did not believe that there could exist any right as against the city and its gods' (1864: 223). Thus Fustel's account of ancient society, as Durkheim surely recognized and appreciated, unremittingly stressed the superficiality of merely *political* freedom: 'To have political rights, to vote, to name magistrates, to have the privilege of being archon – this was called liberty,' Fustel emphasized, 'but man was not the less enslaved to the state' (1864: 223). Only after the seventh century BC, when this ancient social organization was attacked by those classes deprived of its advantages, and still later when the triumph of Christianity introduced the separation of Church and State, did government become free of religious constraint. Henceforth, Fustel concluded, 'only a part of man belonged to society,' for, 'in what related to his soul, he was free, and was bound only to God' (1864: 394). Private virtues thus became distinguished from their public counterparts, and 'individual freedom' – that is, the possibility of elevating the former over the latter – became conceivable.

DURKHEIM, FUSTEL, AND THE SOCIOLOGY OF RELIGION

La Cité Antique enjoyed an almost instantaneous celebrity, and has remained a classic of French historiography. Its reputation survived the critical attacks of Charles Morel, Gabriel Monod and Henri d'Arbois de Jubainville,[38] inspiring new interest in the history of institutions among Fustel's followers.[39] Louis Gernet, a student of Paul Girard,[40] was a close friend of the Durkheimians Robert Hertz, Marcel Mauss and Marcel Granet, and served as general secretary of the *Année Sociologique* during the last years of his life; and Camille Jullian, who (as we have seen) edited six volumes of Fustel's manuscripts after his death in 1889, was

Durkheim's classmate at the Ecole Normale Supérieure and his colleague at Bordeaux. 'From his time at the Ecole Normale', Jullian later observed, Durkheim 'was profoundly affected by the influence of *The Ancient City*, and by the lectures and the example of its author. He himself has recognized this and proclaims it openly'.[41] There can be 'no doubt about Fustel's influence on Durkheim,' Momigliano agreed, but the precise nature of that influence, he added, has remained obscure in the absence of any detailed study of their relationship (Momigliano [1970] 1982: 339).[42]

The earliest indication of such an influence in Durkheim's works appears in his 'Introduction à la sociologie de la famille', the opening lecture of his course on the family given at Bordeaux in 1888–9. Pursuing the same strategy he would follow in *Les Formes Élémentaires*, Durkheim began his course with a discussion of the historical forms of the family, arguing (on the analogy with biological organisms) that '[t]he modern family contains within itself, in abbreviated form, the entire historical development of the family', and that, in any case, the constituent elements of the modern family are 'much easier to study' in their primitive forms (1888: 211). But if history thus contributes to the sociology of the family, Durkheim observed, sociology also has something to contribute to history; in particular, where most historical studies limit themselves to a single society, and are thus able to compare an institution only with its direct, linear antecedents, sociology promises to broaden the field of comparison to include analogous institutions in various societies of the same type.

To some extent, Durkheim granted, this promise had already been realized in Maine's *Ancient Law* (1861) and Fustel's *La Cité Antique* (1864): 'In order to account for the Roman family', he observed approvingly, 'we must compare it not only with the Greek family but with all families of the same type' (1888: 223). Durkheim thus viewed Fustel, together with Maine and Montesquieu,[43] as an early practitioner of the comparative method he would recommend in *Les Règles de la Méthode Sociologique*. But the significance of this introductory lecture on the family lies in its implication that Durkheim was already fully prepared to expand the scope of 'useful comparisons' well *beyond* Greek and Roman antiquity, to the growing body of Australian and American ethnography: '[E]ven different types of family,' he insisted, 'can help to clarify each other. From this point of view, the lowest species cannot be ignored. In this way, the domestic law of Australian or American tribes helps us better to understand that of the Romans' (1888: 224).

Steven Lukes is quite right, of course, to suggest that *De la Division du Travail Social* is relatively innocent of this growing body of ethnographic literature, particularly by comparison with Durkheim's writings after 1895 (1972: 159).[44] But Durkheim was at least as determined a comparativist as this relative innocence would permit. Referring again to *Ancient Law* (1861), Durkheim agreed with Maine's suggestion that the role of penal law was as great as societies were ancient, comparing Salic, Frankish, Burgundian and Visigothic law to that effect (1893: 144–6).[45] Admittedly, the famous passage criticizing *La Cité Antique* for deriving social arrangements from 'the religious idea' (rather than the reverse) follows almost immediately;[46] but Durkheim simultaneously praised Fustel for establishing, on the basis of the comparative analysis of classical texts alone, the principle that 'the early organization of [lower] societies was of a familial nature, and that, moreover, the primitive family was constituted on a religious base' (1893: 179).

Durkheim's full appreciation of the independent explanatory power of religious ideas came only in 1894–5, when he taught a lecture course on religion at Bordeaux, and confronted the mass of historical and ethnographic detail about primitive religious accumulated by Robertson Smith and his *protégé* James Frazer. It was only then, Durkheim later observed, 'that I achieved a clear view of the essential role played by religion in social life. It was in that year that, for the first time, I found the means of tackling the study of religion sociologically' (1907: 613; see Lukes 1972: 237). But for all the power of Smith's and Frazer's theories and data, there is a sense in which they simply returned Durkheim to Fustel, reinforcing and extending the observations of *La Cité Antique* concerning the priority and explanatory power of religious beliefs. Sociologists and historians, Durkheim thus wrote in his withering critique of Labriola's *Essais sur la Conception Matérialiste de l'Histoire* (1897), 'tend more and more to meet in the confirmation that religion is the most primitive of all social phenomena. From [religion], by successive transformations, have come all the other manifestations of collective activity: law, ethics, art, science, political forms, and so on. Everything', Durkheim concluded, 'is religious in principle' (1897: 129).[47]

The clearest sense of the relationship between *La Cité Antique* and Durkheim's *révélation* of 1894–5, however, is to be gained from *Leçons de Sociologie: Physique des Moeurs et du Droit*, the manuscript of Durkheim's lecture-course on ethics taught at Bordeaux in 1898–1900 (Durkheim 1898–1900).[48] The course began with discussion of the ethics of the family, the guild, and the State – that is, of those duties which people have toward one another because they belong to some specific social group. But Durkheim soon turned to duties independent of any particular social grouping, including the life, property and honor of human beings *per se*, regardless of their familial, occupational or national affiliations. Murder and theft, Durkheim observed, are the 'supremely immoral acts', and their immorality is in no way diminished if they are committed against the members of another society. This 'most general sphere' of ethics, Durkheim thus emphasized, is also 'the noblest in concept', for it concerns those duties 'considered by all civilized peoples as the primary and most compelling of all' (1898–1900: 110).

The distinctive element of the right of property, for example, is that the things to which the right refers are withdrawn from common use. The property owner alone may use such things, and this restrictive right is respected by all, regardless of the particular social group to which the property owner belongs. What are the causes, Durkheim asked, which have led to the rules governing this right? How are we to explain the respect that the property of others inspires? How are material things so attached to a person that they share that person's inviolability? Rejecting the solutions offered by J. S. Mill, Kant and Rousseau,[49] Durkheim followed his customary strategy of argument by analogy. This distinctive feature of private property (that is, that it is withdrawn from common use), he observed, is one shared by 'sacred' things: 'Whenever we have a religious ritual . . . the feature that distinguishes the sacred entities is that they are withdrawn from general circulation; they are separate and set apart' (1898–1900: 143).[50] And if private property and sacred things are thus analogous with respect to their distinctive character, Durkheim reasoned, perhaps they held a common origin.

Take the most ancient form of private property – namely, that in land. The clearly defined right to such property, Durkheim suggested, emerged only when small family groups began to establish relatively permanent settlements, and to set their 'mark' on particular parcels of land; and 'it is certain', he added, 'that this ancient family holding was permeated by a profound sacredness, and that the rights and privileges associated with it were of a sacred kind'. The proof of this, Durkheim insisted, lies in the fact that such parcels of land quickly became inalienable; and what, indeed, is inalienability, if not an insulation or setting apart more complete and more radical than that involved in the exclusive right of usage? An inalienable thing is one which must belong always to the same family – that is, not only at the present but in perpetuity – and which is withdrawn from common use. Moreover, Durkheim argued, such inalienability is precisely the 'most complete and best defined' example of appropriation, or private property; for here, 'the bond between the thing and the subject (or individual) who is the possessor reaches its maximum force, and here too that the exclusion of the rest of the society is most strictly imposed' (1898–1900: 150).

But this suggestion, supported by examples drawn from *La Cité Antique*, is still another measure of the extent to which Durkheim had been influenced by his reading 'of the works of Robertson Smith and his school' (Durkheim 1907: 613); for he immediately connected the origin of both sacredness and the institution of private property to Frazer's concept of *taboo*. The Polynesian institution of *taboo*, Durkheim observed, 'is the setting apart of an object as something consecrated, as something belonging to the sphere of the divine' (1898–1900: 143). The same effect is achieved in the observances of more advanced religions and in the respect accorded to private property, a similarity which strongly suggests that the origins of property were to be found, as Fustel had already found them, in the nature of certain religious beliefs. But in Frazer's work, Durkheim added, the link could be seen directly. In Tahiti, for example, rulers who are themselves sacred frequently preserve certain lands or properties for themselves by designating them sacred – that is, by ritually communicating a degree of their own sacredness to the land or property in question. 'Here', Durkheim insisted, 'we see the definite link between taboo and property' (1898–1900: 144).[51]

This observation, of course, was hardly new to either Frazer or Durkheim. On the contrary, it was part of a long-standing utilitarian tradition which interpreted such customs as expedients whereby the landed elite enforced respect for its property; indeed, this was Frazer's own interpretation, as Durkheim discovered to his enormous distress, once it had been extended to the mass of Australian ethnographic data made available in Spencer and Gillen's *Native Tribes of Central Australia* (1899).[52] Durkheim's argument, like Fustel's, was characteristically irrationalist and anti-utilitarian, insisting that such expediency was inconsistent with the notion of a 'living' religious belief, that these customs were 'far too primitive to have been expedients intended to safeguard worldly interests', and in any case, that the owners secured fewer advantages, and suffered more constraints, than any utilitarian interpretation could explain. 'Once consecrated,' Durkheim observed,

> even the master himself could do nothing to change the enclosure in any way. It was, then, an obligation he was under, rather than an expedient invented by himself in his own interest. If he adopted the procedure we describe, it is not because it was useful to him, but because he had to act in this way.
>
> (1898–1900: 153)

What, then, were the causes which lay behind this sense of obligation? Fustel's answer, Durkheim recognized, lay in the cult of the dead – that is, that the death of one's ancestors rendered them sacred and inalienable, and that this sacredness was extended, via the inherent contagiousness of the sacred, to the ground in which they were buried. But Durkheim also felt that Fustel's answer was open to several objections – for example, that it failed to account for property in the house as well as the burial field; that the widespread burial of dead ancestors in the field had a slim empirical basis; and that the focal point of sanctity in property lay not at the burial place as one might expect, but at the borders or periphery of the field in question (1898–1900: 153–4). Fustel's error, Durkheim explained, lay in his reduction of the ancient religion of the family to ancestor worship alone. On the contrary, ancient religion was a cult of 'all things that played a part in the life of the family,' including the harvest and the seasonal fruitfulness of the fields, as well as the fields themselves. 'We have to remember,' Durkheim insisted, following Frazer and Smith, that 'from a certain point in evolution, the whole of nature takes on a sacred character . . . gods crowd in everywhere. The life of the universe and of all things in it is related to an endless stream of divine principles' (1898–1900: 254).

Durkheim's conception of the sacred was thus far more capacious than Fustel's; and, as such, it required a different explanation, one which Durkheim fashioned out of the repeated analogies drawn by Frazer and Robertson Smith. The soil of the field, the harvest of the soil, the first fruits of the harvest – all were sacred in the same sense and to the same degree; for they all 'have a god within them and are this god made manifest'. Consequently, 'mortals may not touch them until certain ritual ceremonies have tempered the sacredness that resides in them, and in such a way that they can be made use of without peril' (1898–1900: 155). This was the function of the sacrifice of the first fruits of harvest – that is, the 'supreme and most formidable element' of sacredness was symbolically concentrated in the first fruits, which were offered to the god under severe ritual precautions. The remainder of the harvest, while retaining some of its sacred qualities, could then be used for utilitarian purposes, without fear of divine displeasure. 'The sacred element residing in the crops,' Durkheim summarized,

> has been prevented from passing over into the profane, for it has been separated from the profane, and by the sacrifice, it has been kept within the divine sphere. The line of demarcation of the two worlds has been respected, and this is the supreme sacred obligation.
>
> (1898–1900: 155)[53]

The details of Durkheim's argument here are important, for he insisted that these rites laid the foundations for one of the most important ideas in the subsequent history of the great world religions – that is, the idea of atonement. The sacrilege of having violated the sacredness of certain objects, Durkheim explained, was expiated through a ritual sacrifice, and the possibility of divine vengeance was thus averted and even transformed into a kind of benevolent, spiritual assurance (1898–1900: 156–7; see Robertson Smith 1889: 39, 121–4). But the argument is at least equally important for its explanation for the seemingly more mundane institution of private property. Only those who had performed the sacrifice, Durkheim insisted, had truly atoned for their sacrilege. This atonement forged a moral bond between the men practicing the rite and the god to whom it was addressed; and since a sacred bond already existed between the god and the land, the land in turn became attached to the men, and hence their property.[54] Durkheim thus attacked that long tradition of classical liberalism, initiated by Locke and later embraced by Hegel and Marx, which viewed the respect granted to the institution of private property as a quality originally inherent in men, only later extended to things. On the contrary, Durkheim argued,

> [i]t is in things that the quality originally resided, and it is from things that it has risen towards men. The things were inviolate in themselves by virtue of sacred concepts, and it is this derived inviolability that has passed into the hands of men, after a long process of being diminished, tempered and canalized.
>
> (1898–1900: 157–8)

In the primitive imagination, of course, this truth – that is, that the institution of private property has an origin exterior to the individual human being – is understood only under the symbolic forms of religion. But as always, Durkheim insisted that these symbols merely express the collective needs and interests of society.[55] The sacred character of the soil is thus 'a stamp the society has put on things, because [these things] are closely mingled with its life and form part of itself' (1898–1900: 161). In short, private appropriation presupposed collective appropriation: 'We have said that the believers took upon themselves the right of the gods,' Durkheim recalled,

> but we should now say that the individuals took upon themselves the right of the collectivity . . . Private property came into existence because the individual turned to his own benefit and use the respect inspired by the society, that is, the higher dignity with which it is clothed and which it had communicated to the things composing its material substitute.
>
> (1898–1900: 161–2)[56]

CONCLUSION

In the *Leçons de Sociologie*, therefore, we have the clearest evidence of Durkheim's profound but ambiguous debt to Fustel de Coulanges. Well before the *Leçons*, of course, Durkheim had seen Fustel as an 'early practitioner' of that comparative method whereby he hoped to abridge the hopeless mass of historical details and create a true science of society; but at the same time, he hoped to extend the field of 'useful comparisons' well beyond antiquity, to the growing body of Australian and American ethnography. The famous lecture-course on religion at Bordeaux in 1895 marked Durkheim's immersion in that literature, and the *Leçons* thus represented his attempt to synthesize the latest ethnographic evidence, the provocative theories of Smith and Frazer, and the idea he had first encountered at the Ecole Normale Supérieure – that is, that religion was 'the most primitive of all social phenomena', the root from which all other institutional forms had derived.

In the *Leçons*, of course, this idea was explored with special reference to the institution of private property; and in this sense, it belongs to Durkheim's lifelong attack on liberal individualism as much as to his sociology of religion.[57] But it should not be forgotten that, in the *Leçons*, the obligation to respect the right of property was treated as but one example of 'duties independent of any particular social grouping', that 'most general sphere' of ethics which Durkheim considered 'noblest in concept' because they bound not just one group to another, but all individuals to society as a whole. The central concern of the *Leçons de Sociologie* lies no more in the origin of private property than in the origin of familial obligation or of contracts or of duties to the State; rather, it lies in the social origin of duty *per se*.

But if the *Leçons de Sociologie* indicates the extent of Durkheim's debt to Fustel, it also reveals its limits. For while Durkheim approved of the unconscious, irrationalist and non-utilitarian aspect of Fustel's explanation for this sense of duty, he found the explanation itself, which relied on the equation of religion with ancestor worship, inadequate. Born and buried a Roman Catholic, Fustel had a conception of the sacred, intimately bound to the idea of individual immortality, while for Durkheim, the son and grandson of Alsatian rabbis, religion was synonymous with a community of shared moral beliefs and legal practices (Momigliano 1982: 340). Although inspired by Fustel's notion of the social significance of ancient religion, it was this community, not Fustel's idea of a personal immortality, that Durkheim rediscovered in Smith's *Religion of the Semites* and Frazer's *Golden Bough*. It was in this rediscovery that *Les Formes Élementaires* was born.

NOTES

1 Chéruel, Thompson observes, gave Fustel 'the habit of exactness and caution against preconceived ideas' (1942: 363).
2 Thompson argues that the influence of Montesquieu, Michelet and Tocqueville can all be seen in *La Cité Antique* (1864), adding that Camille Jullian, Durkheim's classmate at the Ecole Normal, emphasized the similarity between the beginning of *Democracy in America* (see Ch. 2 thereof) and the title of Fustel's introduction, that is, 'De la necessité d'étudier les plus vieilles croyances des anciens pour connaître leur institutions' (see the introduction to Jullian's *Extraits des Historiens Français du XIXs Siècle* (1897), cited in Thompson, 1942: 365). Thompson adds that it was Guizot's *Histoire de la Civilisation en France* (1829–32) that 'won [Fustel's] heart for history' (1942: 363).

3 A slightly more liberal attitude obtained after 1860, but significant educational reforms began only in 1868. See Thompson (1942: 363).
4 Thompson adds that it was under similar influences that Taine received his training at the Ecole Normale a few years later. The same effort to marry Cartesian rationalism to Baconian inductivism is a central theme of Durkheim's *Les Règles de la Méthode Sociologique* (1895).
5 'His success in the ten years he was there', Thompson reports, 'was phenomenal. He found a faculty "aux trois quarts morte," and his vigorous and scholarly lectures elicited, as he himself testified, "un enthousiasme naïf" ' (1942: 364).
6 This history of the island of Chios from its origins to the nineteenth century was subsequently republished by Durkheim's classmate, Camille Jullian, in his *Questions Historiques* (1893).
7 The French thesis was a study of the Greek historian Polybius' account of the Roman conquest of Greece, and thus dealt with the 'final phase' of the ancient city just as the Latin thesis and *La Cité Antique* dealt with its origins. Momigliano has suggested that the work had contemporary political overtones – that is, that Fustel's favorable treatment of Polybius, who viewed the rise of Rome to power and its conquest of the Greeks as the inevitable consequence of Fortune, was an implicit (and equally approving) reference to Napoleon III's 'Italian policy' of the late 1850s, wherein the Second Empire presented itself as the reincarnation of the Roman Imperial idea, representing the principles of peace, order, hegemony and the defense of private property (Momigliano [1970] 1982: 333).
8 Momigliano emphasizes, however, that the Latin thesis was not yet Fustel's masterwork of six years later; in particular, 'the notion that the principle of private property was derived from domestic religion – which is essential in the *Cité Antique* – is absent from the thesis on Vesta' (Momigliano [1970] 1982: 333).
9 Fustel was suspected of clerical and Bonapartist associations for years thereafter, and the chair in medieval history, repeatedly requested for him by the Faculté des lettres, received legislative approval only in 1878. In part, these suspicions derived from his defense of *l'ancien régime* (see below) and his open hostility to those German intellectuals revered by the historians Gabriel Monod and Ernest Lavisse. But they also derived from the prominent role granted to religion in *La Cité Antique*, the warm praise from Catholic readers this inspired, and the fact that Fustel chose to be buried a Catholic. In fact, this choice was out of respect for his ancestral faith, and he found the praise of the faithful an embarrassment. When a critic described *La Cité Antique* as 'reactionary and romantic', Fustel replied (as Durkheim would later) that he had always been a rationalist. Momigliano adds that he was probably an atheist as well (1982: 330; see also Edouard Champion, *Les Idées Politiques et Religieuses de Fustel de Coulanges d'après des Documents Inédits* [1903], which describes Fustel's correspondence with the paganist Louis Ménard, who conceived a violent distaste for *La Cité Antique*). Nonetheless, *La Cité Antique* remained a favorite of the French right well into the twentieth century. Léon Daudet (1868–1942) and Charles Maurras (1868–1952), the leaders of the *Action française*, admired it greatly. See Thompson (1942: 365–6) and Momigliano ([1970] 1982: 330).
10 Theodor Mommsen (1817–1903) was the author of *Römische Geschichte* (3 vols, 1854–6) and the most famous German historian of the nineteenth century.

11 Fustel did not desire a mere imitation of German patriotic scholarship, Momigliano insists, but rather a style 'si calme, si simple, si haute de nos Bénédictins, de notre Académie des Inscriptions, des Beaufort, Fréret' – in short, the historiographical style of the *ancien régime* (Thompson 1942: 367; Momigliano [1970] 1982: 329).

12 The temptation to cast Fustel as a patriotic historian reacting to the humiliations of the Franco-Prussian War is almost overwhelming; but even Monod, one of Fustel's strongest and most persistent critics, acknowledged that Fustel's anti-Germanist views were already on paper in his Strasbourg *cahiers* well before the war, and changed only on points of detail in later years. Jules Simon came to the same conclusion on the basis of transcripts of Fustel's lectures before the Empress Eugénie. On Monod, see the *Revue Historique* XLI (1889): 283; and on Simon, see the *Séances et Travaux de l'Académie des Sciences Morales et Politiques* XVIII (1894): 33–74 (both cited in Thompson 1942: 367; see also Gooch 1913: 213).

13 Of the six octavo volumes (of approximately 500 pages each) which constituted the *Histoire des Institutions Politiques de l'Ancienne France*, only the third and fourth of the series were completed by Fustel himself. These were *La Monarchie Franc* (1888) and *l'Alleu et le Domaine Rural Pendant l'Époque Mérovingienne* (1889). The other four were rapidly and piously edited from manuscripts and notes by Camille Jullian, Durkheim's classmate at the Ecole Normale. In the order of their appearance, these were *Les Origines du Régime Feodal: Le Bénéfice et le Patronat* (1890), *La Gaule Romaine* (1891), *L'Invasion Germainique et la Fin de l'Empire* (1891), and *Les Transformations de la Royauté pendant l'Époque Carolingienne* (1892). Jullian also edited two other volumes of Fustel's works: *Nouvelles Recherches sur Quelques Problèmes d'Histoire* (1891) and *Questions Historiques* (1893). See Thompson (1942: 370).

14 In general, Fustel prospered under the Third Republic, outlining a plan for the reform of the constitution in 1872 and declining an invitation from Thiers to write the official history of the defeat. He lectured at the Ecole Normale from 1870 to 1875, then moved to the Sorbonne, returning to assume the directorship of the Ecole Normale in 1880, shortly after Durkheim had arrived there. He found that administrative duties interfered with his research, and after four years he resigned, again for the Sorbonne, where he remained until his death in 1889.

15 In 1865, Fustal wrote to L. A. Warnkönig, who had written an extremely favorable review of *la Cité Antique*, that his type of mind was such that he 'could not be content with details,' and that his method had thus been 'the comparative one'. Ignoring Montesquieu, the introduction of the comparative method is frequently ascribed to Henry Sumner Maine's *Ancient Law* (1861); but Fustel was clearly unaware of Maine's work in 1864. Durkheim's dedication of his Latin thesis to Fustel, Momigliano emphasizes, was 'more than an act of homage. The link between Montesquieu and Fustel was in everyone's mind during those years' ([1970] 1982: 339; see also 337 and 326).

16 In the same letter to Warnkönig, Fustel also emphasized the value of ignoring modern interpreters, pointing out that he had not only not read what the moderns had written, but had also imposed upon himself the principle of not reading them (especially Mommsen) until he had almost finished the book. 'If the *Cité Antique* is haughtily devoid of refernces to modern authors while revealing an enviable familiarity with classical texts', Momigliano observes, 'one must deduce from this not simple ignorance, but intentional disregard'

([1970] 1982: 337). Fustel 'warned his students against the preliminary reading of secondary works', Thompson adds. 'They would obtrude a cloud of preconceptions before their eyes; perhaps confirm them in error; at any rate obscure the new truth that the source, objectively studied, might reveal' (1942: 370; see also Gooch 1913: 210–11).

17 'Analysis – as the chemist detects the elements in a strange mixture and notes their behavior and peculiarities – analysis of the sources was the historian's task. Every student of history,' Thompson observes, 'knows Fustel's saying: "It requires years of analysis for a day of synthesis." Fustel gave many instructions as to how this intensive analysis was to be carried out. Documents should be read in their entirety rather than second-hand in fragments and without the context. The historian must assimilate the spirit of the age he studies. . . . Yet every document must be studied separately and by itself. . . . A historian must not read into a text things which are not there. Each word must be examined and scrutinized minutely, not only for its etymology but for its contemporary usage. . . . Fustel's own word-studies have been universally acknowledged as models' (1942: 371).

18 Fustel 'abominated the philosophy of history,' Thompson observes

> He believed that drawing analogies in history was a dangerous method. That favorite device of many historians, of comparing or contrasting some other age or problem with the present for the sake of vividness, or clarity, he regarded as almost criminal practice. As a student of Greek and Roman history, Fustel had observed how some modern writers treated Roman consuls as modern kings or princes, if the writer was a monarchist, or as revolutionary leaders, if he was a republican. It was absurd to compare ancient Gaul under Roman rule with modern Ireland under English domination, or Poland subject to Russia!
>
> (1942: 372)

(See also Gooch 1913: 211.)

19 In particular, Fustel was critical of Tacitus' analyses of historical personalities: '[P]rofundity of psychological observation' Fustel insisted, is 'not precisely the most precious quality of an historian who, in the study of societies, should be less concerned with searching out the hidden depths of the human heart than with clearly perceiving social forms, usages, interests, and all the truths solely relative to changing humanity' (see Fustel, *Histoire des Institutions Politiques*, II, p. 240; cited in Thompson 1942: 37 n. 9; see also Gooch 1913: 213).

20 'Hence spring many errors', Fustal observed. 'We rarely fail to deceive ourselves regarding these ancient nations when we see them through the opinions and facts of our own time' (1864: 11).

21 'Having imperfectly observed the institutions of the ancient city', Fustel insisted

> men have dreamed of reviving them among us. They have deceived themselves about the liberty of the ancients, and on this very account liberty among the moderns has been put in peril. The last eighty years have clearly shown that one of the great difficulties which impede the march of modern society is the habit which it has of always keeping Greek and Roman antiquity before its eyes.
>
> (1864: 11)

22 Fearful of the revolutionary intoxication which had identified the ancient heroes with the protagonists of the Terror,' Momigliano observes, 'Fustel

deepened the gulf which separates our conflicts from the ancient ones and made it virtually unbridgeable' ([1970] 1982: 333). This contrast between ancient and modern freedom, Momigliano adds, had already been formulated in Benjamin Constant's *De l'Esprit de Conquête* (1814); but in Fustel it led, not to a defense of modern liberalism, but to the religious ideas of ancient peoples.

23 The contrast between these views and those of Robertson Smith (1889) and the later Durkheim (1912) could hardly be greater.

24 Only the Indians, Momigliano thus emphasizes, figure alongside the Greeks and Romans in *La Cité Antique*. The Bible and Jewish history are completely ignored, and the Celts and Slavs enter Fustel's intellectual horizon only after 1875, in connection with the problems of property. 'Whether or not this was simply a matter of prudence,' Momigliano observes, 'Fustel is addressing himself, as an Aryan, to Aryans' – something the Jewish philologist, archaeologist and art historian Salomon Reinach (1858–1932) realized immediately. Some notes taken by E. Graussard in Fustel's course on Greek history (1876–7) at the Ecole Normale suggest that, upon turning to the Semites, the instructor remarked: 'The whole is completely different: we find no relationship from any point of view; it is an absolutely different world from our own' (Momigliano [1970] 1982: 333–4, 341).

25 Fustel's discussion of the role of the communal, sacrificial meal strongly evokes the later treatments of the same theme by Robertson Smith (1889: Chs 6–11) and Durkheim himself (1912: 366–92). This rite, Fustel observed,

> consisted essentially of a repast, partaken of in common; the nourishment had been prepared upon the altar itself, and was consequently sacred; while eating it, the worshippers recited prayers; the divinity was present, and received his part of the food and drink. . . . The explanation of these practices is, that the ancients believed any nourishment prepared upon an altar, and shared between several persons, established among them an indissoluble bond and a sacred union that ceased only with life.
>
> (1864: 118–9)

26 Fustel was no less appreciative than Durkheim of the integrative functions of religious ritual, repeatedly asking his readers to consider the centrality of religion to the ancient family – for example, they met every morning to address their prayers to the sacred fire, and in the evening they prayed again; during the day, they assembled near the fire for the meal, which was accompanied by prayers and libations; during all these events, religious hymns, passed down from ancestors, were sung; and just outside the door was the tomb where the family periodically offered funeral meals, offerings and sacrifices: 'This caused the family to form a single body,' Fustel emphasized, 'both in this life and in the next. . . . Religion, it is true, did not create the family; but certainly it gave the family its rules; and hence it comes that the constitution of the ancient family was so different from what it would have been if it had owed its foundation to natural affection' (1864: 42).

27 Although less explicitly than Durkheim (see below), Fustel contrasted his own explanation with that of John Locke. Fustel emphasized the strength of the bond thus created: 'Found property on the right of labor,' he observed, 'and man may dispose of it. Found it on religion, and he can no longer do this; a tie stronger than the will of man binds the land to him. Besides, the field where the tomb is situated, where the divine ancestors live, where the family is forever to perform its worship, is not simply the property of a man,

but of a family. It is not the individual actually living who has established his right over the soil, it is the domestic god. The individual has it in trust only; it belongs to those who are dead, and to those who are yet to be born. It is a part of the body of this family, and cannot be separated from it. To detach one from the other is to alter worship, and to offend a religion' (1864: 67). Momigliano suggests that Fustel's goal was to refute any idea of primitive communism (1982: 333). Durkheim embraced this idea, but was no less opposed to the labor theory of value (see below).

28 Ancient law 'had its birth in the family,' Fustel observed.

> It sprang up spontaneously from the ancient principles which gave it root. It flowed from the religious belief which was universally admitted in the primitive age of these peoples, which exercised its empire over their intelligence and their wills.
>
> (1864: 86)

29 In the ancient family, Fustel argued, there is 'an imperious religion, which tells the husband and wife that they are united forever, and that from this union flow rigorous duties, the neglect of which brings with it the gravest consequences in this life and in the next. Hence come the serious and sacred character of the conjugal union among the ancients, and the purity which the family long preserved' (1864: 97-8).

30 This suggestion that Fustel was sensitive to the influence of social organization on the development of religious ideas must be qualified by a constant recognition of his more typical, eighteenth-century notion of the inexorable progress of the human mind. Ancient man, he observes only a page earlier

> could not have contented himself long with these gods so much below what his intelligence might attain. If many centuries were required for him to arrive at the idea of God as a being unique, incomparable, infinite, he must at any rate have insensibly approached this ideal, by enlarging his conception from age to age, and by extending little by little the horizon whose line separated for him the divine Being from the things of this world.
>
> (1864: 117)

This more Cartesian element in Fustel's thought is one with which Durkheim was extremely uncomfortable.

31 Speaking in particular of the confederation, Fustel emphasized that

> the social tie was not easy to establish between those human beings who were so diverse, so free, so inconstant. To bring them under the rules of a community, to institute commandments and ensure obedience, to cause passions to give way to reason, and individual right to public right, there certainly was something necessary, stronger than material force, more respectable than interest, surer than a philosophical theory, more unchangeable than a convention; something that should dwell equally in all hearts, and should be all powerful there.
>
> (1864: 132)

Fustel's argument here should not be confused with that of Montesquieu in *L'Ésprit des Lois* – that is, that the Romans adopted such a religion in order to restrain their people. Such a religion, Fustel insisted to the contrary, could not have had so artificial an origin and, in any case, 'every religion that has come to sustain itself only from motives of public utility, has not stood long' (1864: 166). If anything, Fustel added, 'the state was enslaved by its religion;

or, rather, the state and religion were so completely confounded that it was impossible even to distinguish the one from the other' (1864: 166–7).

32 It is reasonable to suggest that Frazer, who was a frequent visitor to France, and whose ideas closely resemble those of Fustel (see Thompson 1942: 364–5), incorporated many of the latter's ideas into *The Golden Bough* (1890), whence they were passed on to his protégé Robertson Smith and to Durkheim. Unfortunately, there is no direct evidence of Fustel's influence on Frazer's thought. See Ackerman (1987) and Jones (1986).

33 'These old customs,' Fustel observed,

> give us an idea of the close tie which united the members of a city. Human association was a religion; its symbol was a meal, of which they partook together. We must picture to ourselves one of these little primitive societies, all assembled, or the heads of families at least, at the same table, each clothed in white, with a crown upon his head; all make the libation together, recite the same prayer, sing the same hymns, and eat the same food, prepared upon the same altar; in their midst their ancestors are present, and the protecting gods share the meal. Neither interest, nor agreement, nor habit creates the social bond; it is this holy communion piously accomplished in the presence of the gods of the city.
>
> (1864: 158)

(See Smith 1889: 313; Durkheim 1912: 366–92.)

34 To the ancients, Fustel argued, religion meant

> rites, ceremonies, acts of exterior worship. The doctrine was of small account: the practices were the important part; these were obligatory, and bound man (*ligare, religio*). Religion was a material bond, a chain which held man a slave. Man had originated it, and he was governed by it. He stood in fear of it, and dared not reason upon it, or discuss it, or examine it.
>
> (1864: 167)

Again:

> All these formulas and practices had been handed down by ancestors who had proved their efficacy. There was not occasion for innovation. It was a duty to rest upon what the ancestors had done, and the highest piety consisted in imitating them. It mattered little that a belief changed; it might be freely modified from age to age, and take a thousand diverse forms, in accordance with the reflection of sages, or with the popular imagination. But it was of the greatest importance that the formulas should not fall into oblivion, and that the rites should not be modified.
>
> (1864: 169)

(See Frazer 1890: I, 62; II, 245–6; Smith 1889: 18–22; Durkheim 1912: 121.)

35 'It was not force . . . that created the chiefs and kings in those ancient cities', Fustel insisted. Rather,

> authority flowed from the worship of the sacred fire. Religion created the king in the city, as it had made the family chief in the house. A belief, an unquestionable and imperious belief, declared that the hereditary priest of the hearth was the depository of the holy duties and the guardian of the gods
>
> (1864: 178)

(See Frazer 1890: I, 167–71; II, 242–3.)

36 'In order that there should be a legal relation between two men,' Fustel observed,

> it was necessary that there should already exist a religious relation; that is to say, that they should worship at the same hearth and have the same sacrifices. When this religious community did not exist, it did not seem that there could be any legal relation.
>
> (1864: 193)

37 The ancient religion, Fustel observed,

> established between the citizen and the stranger a profound and ineffaceable distinction. This same religion, so long as it held its sway over the minds of men, forbade the right of citizenship to be granted to a stranger.
>
> (1864: 194–5)

(See Smith 1889: 39, 121–4.)

38 See his *Deux Manières d'Écrire l'Histoire* (1896) which insisted that, despite his avoidance of secondary sources and critique of thoretical preconceptions, Fustel's work simply elaborated his own *a priori* ideas.

39 See, for example, G. Glotz's *Solidarité de la Famille dans le Droit Criminel en Grèce* (1904), *Le Travail dans la Grèce Ancien* (1920), and *Cité Grecque* (1928); Paul Guirard's *La Propriéte Foncière en Grèce jusqu'à la Conquête Romaine* (1893) and *La Main-d'oeuvre Industrielle dans l'Ancienne Grèce* (1900); Paul Girard's *L'Education Athénienne*; and L. Gernet's *L'Approvisionnement d'Athènes en Bléau Ve et au IV Siècle* (1909), *Recherches sur le Developpement de la Pensée Juridique et Morale en Grèce* (1917), and (with A. Boulanger) *La Génie Grec dans la Religion* (1932).

40 Girard, a student of Fustel's, was the biographer of Paul Guirard, whose own biography of Fustel appeared in 1896.

41 Jullian, 'Le Cinquantenaire de *la Cité antique*,' *Revue de Paris*, 23e année, no. 4 (February 15, 1916): 857; cited in Lukes (1972, p. 60).

42 See, however, the suggestive discussion in Lukes (1972: 60–3).

43 Durkheim's Latin thesis on Montesquieu was dedicated to Fustel. 'The link between Montesquieu and Fustel,' Momigliano observes, 'was in everyone's mind during those years' ([1970] 1982: 339).

44 In particular, Lukes suggests that this led Durkheim to understate the degree of interdependence and reciprocity and overstate the role of repressive law in pre-industrial societies.

45 Durkheim disagreed with Maine's (admittedly 'incomplete') explanation for this correlation, which referred to the 'habitual violence' of those societies in which such laws were initially conceived. On the contrary, Durkheim argued, penal law is the natural consequence of a society in which the *conscience collective* is extensive and labor not yet divided.

46 'After setting up the religious idea, without bothering to establish its derivation,' Durkheim complained,

> [Fustel] has deduced from it social arrangements, when, on the contrary, it is the [social arrangements] that explain the power and nature of the religious idea. Because all social masses have been formed from homogeneous elements, that is to say, because the collective type was very developed there and the individual type in a rudimentary state, it was inevitable that the whole psychic life of society should take on a religious character.
>
> (1893: 179)

47 No one, Durkheim added, pursuing the specific materialist arguments of Labriola, has shown under what economic influences naturism arose out of totemism, or what technological modifications made naturism into the abstract monotheism of Jahweh and Greco-Latin polytheism. Moreover,

> it is indisputable that in the beginning the economic factor is rudimentary while religious life is, on the contrary, rich and overwhelming. How then could the latter result from the former, and is it not probable, on the contrary, that the economy depends on religion much more than the second on the first?
>
> (1897: 129–30)

48 This text is based on a course which appears on Steven Lukes' list of Durkheim's lecture-courses given at Bordeaux and Paris, which refers to a course entitled Cours de sociologie: *Physique Générale des Moeurs et du Droit*, taught each year from 1896–7 to 1899–1900 (Lukes 1972: 618). Momigliano has already emphasized the significance of *Professional Ethics and Civic Morals* in understanding Durkheim's relation to Fustel, albeit for different reasons. Specifically, Momigliano suggests that Durkheim's early interest in socialism and the division of labor was one wholly alien to Fustel, and that this led to the critical remarks of *De la Divison du Travail Social*. By the time of *Professional Ethics and Civic Morals*, however, Durkheim had become interested in Fustel's notion that private property had a religious origin, and this made Durkheim more receptive. But the type of corporate socialism in which Durkheim was interested in the 1890s was perfectly consistent with, and may even have inspired, the arguments of *Professional Ethics and Civic Morals*. The decisive factor in limiting Durkheim's early attraction to Fustel thus seems to have been that he had not yet encountered the theories of Robertson Smith and Frazer; and when he had, after 1895, the power of Fustel's comparative method became clear.

49 Here Durkheim was clearly referring to Mill's *Principles of Political Economy* (1848) and Rousseau's *Discours sur l'Origine et les Fondements de l'Inégalité Parmi les Hommes* (1753). The reference to Kant, though less certain, was probably to the first part of the *Metaphysische Anfangsgrunde der Rechtslehre* (1797), where the concept of private right is developed.

50 In addition, Durkheim noted, sacred things and private property share two other characteristics. First, the relationship between a sacred thing and a sacred person parallels that between a property owner and his or her property – in both cases, there is a kind of 'moral community' between the object and the person such that each participates in the social life and status of the other. Second, both sacred things and private property exhibit the phenomenon of *contagion*, whereby their special attributes are transferred to those objects with which they are in close contact (Durkheim 1898–1900: 147–8).

51 '[T]here is a sacred basis for property being property,' Durkheim insisted.

> It consists . . . in a kind of insulation of the thing, which withdraws it from the common area. This insulation has sacred origins. It is the ritual procedure that creates – on the confines of the field or around the house – an enclosure that in each case makes them sacred, that is, inviolable, except for those who conduct these ceremonies, which means the owners and all that belongs to them in the way of slaves and animals. What amounts to a magic circle is drawn about the field, which shields it from trespass or encroachment, because such intrusions, in these circumstances, become sacrilege.
>
> (1898–1900: 152)

52 Frazer's interpretation was developed in 'The origin of totemism' (1899: 647–65, 832–52) and the second edition of *The Golden Bough*. Durkheim's response, which drew heavily on Robertson Smith in its effort to construct a less utilitarian interpretation, appeared in 'Sur le totemisme' (1902: 82–121). For a more detailed account of this controversy over the important Australian data, see Jones (1986).

53 The ritual consecration of the boundary stones of the field performed an analogous function: 'The field is sacred', Durkheim explained,

> it belongs to the gods, therefore it may not be used. To enable it to serve profane ends, recourse is had to the same procedure as is used in the harvest or the vintage. It has to be relieved of the excess of sacredness in order to make it profane or at least profanable, without incurring peril. The sacredness, however, is indestructable: it can therefore only be shifted from one point to another. This dreaded force dispersed about the field will be drawn off, but it has to be transferred elsewhere, so it is accumulated at the periphery. This is the purpose of the sacrifices described.
>
> (1898–1900: 156)

54 'Before the ritual was carried out,' Durkheim reminded his readers,

> everyone had to keep at a distance from the things entirely withdrawn from profane use; afterwards, everyone was bound to the same stricture, these others alone excepted. The sacred virtue that until then protected the divine domain from any occupancy or trespass, was henceforth exercised for their benefit: it is that virtue which constitutes the right of property. It is because they have enlisted its service in this way that the land has become theirs. A moral bond has been forged between themselves and the gods of the field by the sacrifice, and since the link already existed between the gods and the field, the land has therefore become attached to men by a sacred bond.
>
> (1898–1900: 156–7)

55 'The gods', Durkheim observed in this particular restatement,

> are no other than collective forces, personified and hypostatized in material form. Ultimately, it is the society that is worshipped by the believers; the superiority of the gods over men is that of the group over its members. The early gods were the substantive objects which served as symbols to the collectivity and for this reason became the representations of it: as a result of this representation they shared in the sentiments of respect inspired by the society in the individuals composing it.
>
> (1898–1900: 161)

56 Durkheim considered this conclusion consistent with another hypothesis – namely that of a primitive communism – with which he also agreed: 'Indeed, we know that it is the clan that owned the land in common, land that it was settled on and which served for hunting or fishing' (1898–1900: 162).

57 In his extremely insightful essay on Fustel, Arnaldo Momigliano observes that, while Durkheim seems to have agreed with Fustel on the religious origins of private property in *De la Division du Travail Social* (1893), this theme disappears from Durkheim's later work, either because he had lost interest in the problem of the origin of property, or because the very nature of Australian societies rendered its treatment difficult (see Momigliano 1982: 340). But in fact, the origin of private property is not a central theme even in *De la Division*, which is rather concerned with the origin of the right of

contracts. Durkheim's concern was consistently with the concept of the sacred itself, and with its sociological explanation.

REFERENCES

Ackerman, R. (1987) *Sir James Frazer*, Cambridge: Cambridge University Press.
Arbois de Jubainville, H. (1896), *Deux Manieres d'Écrire l'Histoire: Critique de Bossuet, d'Augustin Thierry et de Fustel de Coulanges*, Paris: Emile Bouillon.
Durkheim, E. ([1888] 1978) 'Introduction to the sociology of the family,' in Mark Traugott (ed.), *Emile Durkheim on Institutional Analysis*, Chicago and London: University of Chicago Press.
—— ([1982] 1960) *Montesquieu and Rousseau: Forerunners of Sociology*, trans. R. Manheim, Ann Arbor, MI: University of Michigan Press.
—— ([1893] 1933) *The Division of Labor in Society*, New York: Free Press.
—— ([1897] 1978) 'Review of Antonio Labriola, *Essais sur la Conception Matérialiste de l'Histoire*,' in Mark Traugott (ed.), *Emile Durkheim on Institutional Analysis*, Chicago and London: University of Chicago Press.
—— ([1898–1900] 1957) *Professional Ethics and Civic Morals*, trans. Cornelia Brookfield, Glencoe, Il: Free Press.
—— (1902) 'Sue le totémisme', *L'Année sociologique* 5: 82–121.
—— (1907) 'Lettres au Directeur de *la Revue Néo-scolastique*', *Revue Néo-scolastique* 14: 606–7, 612–14.
—— ([1912] 1915) *The Elementary Forms of the Religious Life*, New York: Macmillan.
Frazer, J. G. (1890) *The Golden Bough: A Study in Comparative Religion*, 2 vols, London: Macmillan.
—— (1899), 'The origin of totemism', *The Fortnightly Review* 65: 647–65, 835–52.
Fustel de Coulanges, N. D. ([1864] 1956) *The Ancient City: A Study on the Religion, Laws and Institutions of Greece and Rome*, Garden City, New York: Doubleday.
Gooch, G. P. (1913) *History and Historians in the Nineteenth Century*, London: Longmans, Green & Co.
Isambert, F.-A. (1976) 'L'élaboration de la notion de sacré dans l'ecole durkheimienne,' *Archives de sociologie des religions* 42: 35–56.
Jones, R. A. (1977) 'On understanding a sociological classic,' *American Journal of Sociology* 83: 279–319.
—— (1981) 'Robertson Smith, Durkheim, and sacrifice: an historical context for *The Elementary Forms of the Religious Life*', *Journal of the History of the Behavioral Sciences* 17: 184–205.
—— (1986) 'Durkheim, Frazer, and Smith: the role of analogies and exemplars in the development of Durkheim's sociology of religion,' *American Journal of Sociology* 98: 596–627.
LaCapra, D. (1972) *Emile Durkheim: Sociologist and Philosopher*, Ithaca and London: Cornell University Press.
Lukes, S. (1972) *Emile Durkheim: His Life and Work: A Historical and Critical Study*, New York: Harper & Row.
Momigliano, A. (1970) 'La citta antica di Fustel de Coulanges', *Rivista storica italiana* 82: 81–98.
—— ([1970] 1982), 'The ancient city of Fustel de Coulanges,' in A. Momigliano (ed.), *Essays in Ancient and Modern Historiography*, Middletown, CT: Wesleyan University Press.

Pickering, W. S. F. (ed.) (1975) *Durkheim on Religion: A Selection of Readings with Bibliographies*, London: Routledge & Kegan Paul.

—— (1984) *Durkheim's Sociology of Religion: Themes and Theories*, London: Routledge & Kegan Paul.

Smith, W. R. ([1889] 1894), *Lectures on the Religion of the Semites*, second edition, London: Adam & Charles Black.

Thompson, J. W. (1942) *A History of Historical Writing. Volume II: The Eighteenth and Nineteenth Centuries*, New York: Macmillan.

2

THE ORIGINS OF CONCEPTUAL THINKING IN DURKHEIM

Social or religious?

W. S. F. Pickering

Most commentators agree that Durkheim's sociology of knowledge rests on two major texts. The first, the monograph 'De quelques formes primitives de classification: contribution à l'étude des représentations collectives' (1903; 1963) was published in 1903 with Marcel Mauss.[1] The second, published nine years later, was his greatest work, *The Elementary Forms of the Religious Life* (1912; 1915). Between the two works Durkheim published little on the subject, save an article which appeared in the *Revue de Métaphysique et de Morale* with the title, 'Sociologie religieuse et théorie de la connaissance' (1909). Except for the last section, the article was incorporated into *The Elementary Forms* as an introductory chapter. Further, it is generally held that Durkheim's final position regarding the sociology of knowledge is to be found in *The Elementary Forms* – a point no one can disagree with. What is to be contested, however, is that *Primitive Classification* is little more than an introduction to the final formulation. This is a position most commentators take. And if this position is not specifically stated by commentators, it is at least implied. For them there is no shift of emphasis, no turning in a slightly different direction, and certainly no radical change of goal or method. Such issues have seldom been raised, let alone debated, among scholars. One recent exception is Mary Hesse, who has remarked on the shift of thought in the two publications (1982). But the precise nature of that shift and its consequences have not been explored by her or by anyone else. What follows is an attempt to rectify the situation by focussing on two issues: the subject matter of the two works and the role of religion in each of them.

Before dealing with such issues, an introductory word about the importance of the monograph is not out of place. The article by Durkheim and Mauss of 1903 has been subject to many valid criticisms (Badcock 1975: 26–8; Needham 1963). Nevertheless the monograph has been grossly undervalued as an imaginative and innovative work in relating

52

classificatory concepts to forms of social organization. It is one of the foundation stones on which the sociology of knowledge has been built. David Bloor has supported this view by attempting to strengthen the main thesis with empirical evidence, not from preliterate societies, but from the state of science in the seventeenth century (Bloor 1982). Bloor has in turn been attacked, not so much for his evaluation of the monograph, but for the evidence he used in attempting to defend Durkheim's thesis (Hesse 1982; Lukes 1982).

CLASSIFICATION AND ABSTRACT CATEGORIES

It is generally assumed that the subject matter of the two works is the same: classificatory concepts or abstract categories. No distinction between the two is generally made. They may be the same. But before that conclusion is reached, it is necessary to look in more detail at each work, and in particular their starting points.

The monograph of 1903 has as its purpose an examination of the process of classifying and ordering experience. Durkheim and Mauss emphasize, at least initially, dichotomous classificatory systems such as male/female, left hand/right hand, and they seize on dichotomous social units, such as moieties. No one unit stands on its own; it is related to some contrasting unit of the same general kind or to some subdivision (hence Durkheim's frequent references to genus and species). Further, he suggests that classificatory concepts are hierarchically related, that some related concepts are held to be more important than others and that such a hierarchy is reflected in social organization.

In *The Elementary Forms* Durkheim refers to *Primitive Classification* and to an extension of that essay in the monograph by R. Hertz, 'La prééminence de la main droite: étude sur la polarité religieuse' (1909; 1960). Durkheim holds that *Primitive Classification* is evidence for the general thesis of the later book (1912: 16; 1915: 11–12). But there is a remarkable shift in what Durkheim is dealing with in *The Elementary Forms*. The subject matter in those sections connected with the sociology of knowledge is much wider than the notion of classification. It is concerned with abstract concepts, such as space, time, cause, totality and so on – the concepts at the center of Kant's epistemology, which Kant calls *categories*. Categories, in contrast to classifications, are not exclusively dichotomous or grouped terms. Indeed, categories are not really classificatory at all in the sense of putting 'things' and experience into classes or into opposite sorts of 'boxes'.

One can at least state unequivocally that both the book and the monograph are concerned with *représentations*.[2] The monograph has the subtitle, 'contribution à l'étude des représentations collectives.' But interestingly enough there is little about *représentations* as such in it

53

(quite in contrast to the essay of 1898; 1953). One infers that classificatory concepts are one type of *représentation*. This starting point is more clearly stated in the article of 1909 where Durkheim is seeking to show the importance of, and above all, the social origin of *représentations* (1909; 1982, especially pp. 238ff and 757ff). Four different terms thus confront us: *représentations collectives*, concepts, classificatory concepts, and categories. Some attempt must be made to differentiate them. This is particularly so because Durkheim never clarifies the differences between the terms.

'*Représentations collectives*' is a general term basic to Durkheim's sociology. They are mental 'photographic pictures' or mental entities designating people, groups, things, ideas and values held by society. Standing outside the individual, they are impersonal and are created by society. Indeed, they are the very basis of society (Lukes 1973: 6–9; Pickering forthcoming).

Durkheim refers on many occasions to 'concepts' broadly and contrasts them with 'abstract concepts'. It is quite clear that he holds 'concepts' in the more general sense to have the same meaning as *représentations* and that the two words are interchangeable (1912; 621; 1915; 435). He posits that there are both individual (*sensibles*) and collective concepts as with *représentations* (1912: 616ff, 431ff). But when he mentions 'concepts' he usually means 'collective concepts'. Individual concepts are in perpetual flux because they rest on sensations (1912: 619, 433). The characteristics of concepts are quite similar to those of *représentations collectives*: they are outside time, almost but not quite immutable, capable of being universal, the product of society, and are superior to and shape the concepts of the individual (1912: 625, 437).

'Classificatory concepts', as we have indicated, are a specific type of 'concept' or *représentation collective*. They are used to departmentalize personal and social experience.

'Categories', or, as Durkheim frequently calls them, 'abstract categories', are also within the general class of *représentations collective*. The word 'category' is open to various meanings ranging from the notion of class, division of things for the purpose of analysis, to any idea or concept fundamental to a system of philosophy, to any ultimate form. In examining the way Durkheim uses the word, one has to rely entirely on the context in which the word is found.

The importance of differentiating concepts from categories is apparent in the concluding sections of *Les Formes Elémentaires*. The first section relates specifically to concepts, their origin, the role of the community in creating and sustaining them. The second section deals with categories and with the role of society within the realm of thought. What applies to concepts in one section applies also in some measure to categories in the other. Yet the fact that Durkheim divides his conclusion in this way, and is prepared to be somewhat repetitious, suggests that in his mind categories are to be distinguished in some manner from concepts in general. To assume classificatory concepts and abstract categories are not identical types of *représentations collectives* allows us at least to suppose that the avowed subject matter of the article of 1903 and the book of 1912 are not the same. Let us press the case further.

Certain *représentations collectives*, such as causality, are surely not classificatory in the sense that male/female is a classificatory concept. Causality is an isolated term which exists on its own and does not possess an opposite – at least an opposite which has any meaning. To classify is to divide. As Ellen says, classifications 'attempt to divide up the real world' in accordance with patterns set by society or by investigators (Ellen and Reason 1979: 3). He rightly sees classification 'as the logical prerequisite of comparison, generalization and explanation' (1979: 2). Might it not also be right to see classification as a primitive form of abstract categories? By contrast, abstract categories are means of explanation – of getting behind data – which classification cannot do. Mary Hesse suggests the same idea when she writes, 'all kinds of cognitive categories are based on primitive classification of the natural and social worlds' (Arbib and Hesse 1986: 205). There is evidence that Durkheim sees that primitive classification has a continuity with modern scientific classification (1903: 66; 1953: 81). Quite rightly, and very fruitfully, he holds that in classification one connects ideas and relates facts one to another, social facts to social facts, symbols to structure.

Durkheim envisages categories as being superior concepts – the highest of the *représentations collectives* (1913a: 37; 1975: 172). 'They dominate and encompass all other concepts . . . they dominate the whole of logical activity' (1913a: 37; 1975: 172; and see also 1913a: 35; 1975: 171). Further, the reason they dominate thought is that 'they sum it up; the whole of civilization is condensed in them' (1909: 757; 1982: 238). These *sui generis* concepts, which Durkheim said 'we call categories,' are what Dennes saw as being at the top of the psychic scale (1924: 37). Durkheim was therefore prepared to speak of a hierarchy of *représentations collectives*. He said that the function of categories was 'to dominate and envelop all the other concepts; they are permanent molds for the mental life' (1912: 628; 1915: 440). In the last section of the 1909 article, 'Sociologie religieuse et théorie de la connaissance,' he stated unreservedly that some *représentations collectives* 'play a preponderant role', and these are categories (1909: 757–8; 1982: 238). Categories 'correspond to the most universal properties of things . . . they are like solid frameworks which enclose thought' (Bois 1914: 321). Durkheim wrote, 'The role of the categories is to envelop all the other concepts, the category *par excellence* would seem to be this very concept of totality' (1912: 629; 1915: 441). The notion of totality rivets Durkheim's attention because it is the most abstract of all the categories and therefore the chief. It leads him to apply it to society. It is not only that man cannot think without reference to *representations*, but he is so dependent on abstract categories that he cannot think of objects without reference to the categories of space, time and number (ibid.). But further, as he says, their importance rests on the fact that they 'dominate thought because they sum it up; the whole of civilization is condensed in them' (1909: 757; 1982: 238). This leads him to state that the system of categories is a synthetic expression of the human mind.

Categories do not originate and cannot be explained by reference to individual minds but are 'a result of history and of collective action' (1909: 758; 1982: 239). In the process each individual has only an infinitely small part (1909: 758; 1982: 239). Durkheim had sympathy with neo-Kantians, who saw as one of their chief tasks understanding and discovering laws about abstract categories and what unified them (1909: 758; 1982: 239). He held that concentrating on individual minds was a severe limitation. What was required was to see them in their historical and social modes and therefore to examine them through sociological reflection. He differed from neo-Kantians about categories in holding that categories summed up reality rather than shaped it (1909: 757n; 1982: 240n).[3]

One of the problems of Durkheim's approach to categories is that he does not attempt to enumerate categories, nor say a great deal about their characteristics other than that they are social. Here he is to be contrasted with Kant, many of whose ideas he accepts, who in *Pure Reason* posited four divisions of categories of understanding, those of quantity, quality, relation and modality, each of which had three subdivisions. As such, they are applied only to phenomena, not entities or things in themselves. Further, Durkheim's categories do not correspond to Kant's. Durkheim, therefore, dealt with categories only in a general way.[4]

In contrasting classificatory concepts with categories, we have looked at the problem in terms of Durkheim's logic. But might it not be argued that there are historical considerations which might enable one to employ a loosely evolutionary approach to the distinction? For example, one stage of thinking might have followed another in some sort of progression. First, people embarked on classifying their experience according to dichotomies which they derived from social organization, then they progressed to inventing more abstract concepts which helped them 'explain' the wider world. Durkheim wants to show a continuity in that they both 'make intelligible the relations which exist between things' (1903: 66; 1963: 81). But this could be said of all *représentations collectives*. Nevertheless *représentations*, for Durkheim, are subject to relatively slow historical change and to stages (*étapes*) (1903: 72; 1963: 88). Durkheim is to be contrasted in this respect with Lévy-Bruhl, who argues for discontinuity, and also differentiates the classificatory concepts discussed in the 1903 monograph from abstract categories. He wrote, 'There is nothing more significant than the primitive classifications I have already cited, to which Durkheim and Mauss have drawn attention, for in the primitive mentality these, to a certain extent, occupy the position held by categories in logical thought' (1926: 364). Yet this should not lead us to conclude that Durkheim does not make the same distinction. In the monograph, Durkheim is very much concerned with historical change in trying to account for the fact that various classificatory systems do not mirror the social organization of the society. This he sees as a key issue in his sociology of classification. Of necessity he must explain the lack of fit. No such effort is made in *The Elementary Forms*. There is no need for it because Durkheim, as we have argued, is not addressing himself to the same issues in this book as in *Primitive Classification*.

For the period of human existence which Durkheim is considering, there is no historical information. The very notion of 'primitive' classification suggests development *to* abstract categories, which are of a 'higher order' than the former. If documented this would refute the Kantian *a priori* approach to epistemology. But without historical knowledge, it is just as legitimate to suggest that classificatory concepts emerged socially, parallel with abstract categories. And this is also implied in Durkheim (Lévy-Bruhl 1926: 364). Much of his thinking is nevertheless based on historical assumptions, not least his consideration of religion (see infra; the last page of [1903] is full of references to historical matters). The ambiguity in Durkheim rests on the interplay between logical argument and appeal to historical data.

Durkheim slides easily from classificatory concepts and their function to abstract categories. Both appear side by side in the monograph and the book. For example, notions of time and space are referred to in the monograph (1903: 70; 1953: 86). And there is also reference to classificatory concepts in *The Elementary Forms* (1912: 16; 1915: 11). There is thus in the texts themselves no absolute line of demarcation between the subject matter of *Primitive Classification* and *The Elementary Forms*. But it cannot be denied that there is a shift of focus from the more particular to the general, from classificatory processes to the existence of *représentations* in a more abstract sense. And this shift is directly associated with Durkheim's concern with a theory of knowledge in the book, which in turn is associated with Kantian problems of epistemology.

The conclusions are also different. In *Primitive Classification* the basic explanatory factor is social organization; in *The Elementary Forms* abstract categories are seen to be the outcome of religious thinking. By extension one would expect that in examining other types of *représentations collectives*, different social bases would emerge as their point of explanation: N number of types would be associated with N number of different explanatory factors. Hence, there should be no surprise that since the subject matter was different, the outcome was also different.

CLASSIFICATION, EMOTION AND THE SACRED

Whereas religion assumes a place of ultimate importance in *The Elementary Forms* it is virtually absent in *Primitive Classification*. There is no reference to religion as such but only to religious emotion (1903: 70; 1953: 86). All is derived from the isomorphic relation between what we have called social organization (or perhaps better, social structure) and classificatory concepts. As with religion, so with the sacred, to which there is only a passing reference (1903: 70; 1963: 86).

Only in the conclusion of the article is much made of the emotional halo which stands over some classifacatory systems. Durkheim wrote: 'a species of things is not a simple object of knowledge but corresponds above all to a certain sentimental attitude' (1903: 70; 1963: 85–6). This injection of emotion at the end of what seemed a purely cerebral or 'cold' approach to classification has given rise to considerable criticism. The strident note was further exacerbated when Durkheim went on to suggest that such a characteristic prevented 'critical and rational examination' (1903: 71; 1963: 88). To most, this has represented the abandonment of faith in the possibility of a scientific approach to the data which are at the heart of social life. Durkheim associates the emotional element with religious emotions, which attribute to species their most essential properties (1903: 70; 1963: 86). And as he continues: 'Things are above all sacred or profane, pure or impure, friends or enemies, favorable or unfavorable' (1903: 70; 1963: 86). The point to be noted is that the emotional/religious/sacred element seems tangential to his main argument and is added as an appendix to demonstrate why he has not been more successful in making a thoroughly rational analysis of classification. Let it not be forgotten that his main argument is dependent neither on religion as a concept or phenomenon, nor on its basic characteristics. Religion is not, therefore, the key to understanding.

The emotional component of certain *représentations* is also overtly stated by Durkheim in *The Elementary Forms*. The obvious example relates to the notions of the sacred and the profane which are very much surrounded by an affective element (see Pickering 1984: Chs 7, 8). He wrote: 'there is perhaps *no représentation collective* which is not delirious [*delirante*] in some sense or other' (1912: 325; 1915: 227). But one thing is certain: Durkheim does not state that because they are so affectively charged, they are beyond scientific analysis. When he deals with the abstract concepts of time, space and totality he does not treat the emotional aspects as central. Sacred time has no doubt existed in many societies but not necessarily in all. Of course, sacred concepts lose their sacred, and therefore emotional, canopy through the process of secularization (Pickering 1984: Ch. 24).[5] So Durkheim appears to use the emotional component differently in the monograph and the book. Understanding the sacred in emotive terms does not raise any deep 'scientific' difficulties. Many happily accept what he postulates about the sacred, but the claimed emotional element surrounding classificatory concepts and above all the support of its refraction to scientific analysis is not so easy to defend.

The notion of the emotional element in classificatory concepts was developed by Lucien Lévy-Bruhl (1857–1939) – and between Lévy-Bruhl and Durkheim there was mutual respect, even admiration. In his provocative book of 1910, *Les Fonctions Mentales dans les Sociétés Inférieures*, Lévy-Bruhl attempted, among other things, to show that in creating classificatory concepts, and in generalized statements, primitive people did not employ rational criteria, but ones associated with emotion. Later he wrote:

> the primitive mind does not arrange its concepts in a regular order. It perceives preconnections, which it would never dream of changing, between the *représentations collectives*; and these are nearly always of greater complexity than concepts, properly so called. Therefore what can its classifications be? Perforce determined at the same time as the preconnections, they too are governed by the law of participation, and will present the same prelogical and mystical character.
>
> (1926: 128)

And he goes on to say that the 'emotional force fully compensates, even goes beyond, the authority which will be given to general concepts by their logical validity at a later stage' (1926: 128). That a highly emotional aura surrounds primitive classificatory concepts many would accept, and see the emotional element as a crucial mark of differention. Lévy-Bruhl, in an anti-evolutionary spirit, does not account for the change from a primitive mentality to a modern, rational, scientific one. Here he is in contrast to Durkheim, who tried to show in a more evolutionary vein that the one led to the other.

RELIGION AND COSMOLOGY: KEYS TO EPISTEMOLOGY

In *The Elementary Forms* Durkheim attempts to solve epistemological problems through an analysis of religion. In it he wrote that religion had the dual characteristics of being concerned with material things as well as those of a moral kind, and added: 'It is this double nature which has enabled religion to be like the womb from which come the leading germs of human civilization' (1913: 319; 1915: 223). Durkheim's contention is

59

that religion first taught people how to think, that is, to think abstractly. Mythologies demonstrate how originally people were confused and believed that even rocks had a sex, for example. Religion clarified a great deal of this, for 'religion was the agent which brought about this transfiguration. Religious beliefs were responsible for substituting a different world from that perceived by the senses' (1913: 388; 1915: 235; for the role of religion in the development of thought, see also 1913: 336; 1915: 230–9). More specifically it was through the use of *représentations* that religion helped people to think. Durkheim wrote in *The Elementary Forms*:

> When I learn that A regularly comes before B, my consciousness is enriched by a new knowledge; my intelligence is not all satisfied by a statement which does not in itself give a reason for itself. I only begin to *understand* if I am able to imagine B in such a way that I can see that it is connected with A, as if it were linked to A by some tie of kinship. The great service which religions have rendered to thought is to have constructed a first *représentation* of what these relations of kinship between things might be.
>
> (1912: 340; 1915: 142)

Again, earlier in the book:

> To a greater or less extent, all known religions have been systems of ideas which tend to embrace the universality of things, and to give us a complete *représentation* of the world.
>
> (1912: 200; 1915: 141)

In short, what religion was able to do was 'to liberate the mind from its enslavement to tangible appearances, indeed, to teach it to dominate them and to connect what is separated by the senses' (1912: 340; 1915: 237).

The special contribution which religion has made in this respect is in its cosmological component, that is, in seeing the world, human existence or a social group as a whole, and visualizing the forces at work in it – in more modern parlance, trying to discover its laws. To primitive people, such a world was inhabited by gods and spirits, and the way they were said to act gives rise to the notion of force. Durkheim wrote, at the beginning of *The Elementary Forms*, that 'Every religion proclaims a cosmology, as well as speculating about the divine' (1912: 12; 1915: 9). So he holds that the role of religion in helping people to create abstract concepts is derived from one particular characteristic of religion, its cosmological component, where cosmology is seen as the understanding of the universe as a whole. By being able to visualize the world in terms of spirits, gods and forces, people are able to go a stage further and conceive of concepts such as wholes, classes, totality. Referring to the human ability to think conceptually, Durkheim wrote that:

He [man] has no more conceived the world in his own image than he has conceived himself in the image of the world; he has done both at one and the same time. In his idea of things, he has undoubtedly included human elements; but in his idea of himself, he has included elements derived from things.

However, there is nothing in experience to suggest to him these comparisons. It is therefore obvious that some exceptionally powerful cause must have intervened and transfigured reality in such a way as to give it an appearance which is not really its own.

(1912: 337–8; 1915: 236; cf. 1913a: 35; 1975: 171)

In Durkheim's thinking, religion emerges as a result of people living in groups. This gives rise to cosmology which in turn generates conceptual thinking. Later, it gives rise to scientific thought. But even in so simple a position there is ambiguity. Religion gives rise to *représentations* but at the same time *représentations* give rise to religion (see in particular 1913a: 35; 1975: 171). Of course it is possible to argue, at another theoretical level, that there could have been a third force at work which promoted both religion and *représentations* and which subsequently disappeared. This would solve everything, but what such a third force might have been no one has ever dared to postulate.

One issue turns on the problem of logical development. Did people in fact learn to think conceptually as a result of inventing cosmological ideas? Durkheim held that this was precisely what happened. In L. H. Gray's article on cosmogony and cosmology in the *Encyclopedia of Religion and Ethics*, written about the time when Durkheim was working on *The Elementary Forms*, the point is reversed. Gray suggests that the reason why some societies do not have cosmogonies (myths relating to the beginning of the world) is probably because they did not have 'the amount of abstract thought required for the development of a cosmogony' (1911: 125). Where people could not think in this way they spoke of the creation of human society by people and not through cosmic stories. Thus, people could only speak about the origin of the world after they had accounted for the origin of human society itself. This both confirms and denies what Durkheim implied (see 1912: 337–8; 1915: 236). But Gray suggests that abstract thought precedes cosmogonies, not vice versa. Cosmogonies have extended human powers to use concepts, but that they cause people to think in concepts *ab initio* is beyond the possibility of proof. The same would apply to cosmologies. Thus, one is back at the old problem. There seems to be a consensus amongst scholars that there exists a correlation between cosmogony and cosmology on the one hand, and abstract thought on the other, but which is the cause and

61

which is the result remains unresolved. And is it important, like the eternal issue of the chicken and egg? There is no answer and, with our limited historical knowledge, it is futile to search for one. The call for an answer is the demand of the old-fashioned rationalist. Durkheim's contribution was in strengthening the connection; it is impossible to go beyond this.

It might be argued that the focus on religion in *The Elementary Forms* was not really important for the sociology of knowledge. The main thesis in the book is that what is crucial to the understanding of the emergence of categories is the role of the social – society itself and the social component of human experience. That is certainly the case in *Primitive Classification* where social organization is, as we have seen, the telling factor and is really one one degree removed from reality *par excellence*, that is, society. To clinch the argument one might point to Durkheim's concept of religion as a social force. He held that religion exerted real and observable forces over individuals and society. In Durkheim the notion of force is used in many different ways but one thing is evident, and that is that religion seems to have 'invented' the notion of force, which becomes developed by modern science (Pickering 1984: 170–5, 209–16). Religion, therefore, not only provided people with a method of thinking but itself gave them knowledge – real knowledge, though crude and limited.

There is much in Durkheim's focus on religion as a key to the sociology of knowledge that is reminiscent of Comte's notion of the three stages, with the first being the religious. As Vogt has observed, the notion that religious ideas were the primitive form of all thought was common in the positivist tradition (1979: 116). Durkheim, however, went further and showed how religion helped to form the mind itself and itself provided knowledge (Vogt 1979: 116).

So is Durkheim saying anything about the sociology of knowledge in *The Elementary Forms* which he has not said before? Those who would answer in the negative would doubtless point to the fact that for Durkheim the all-important element in religion is its social component, as for the sphere of knowledge generally. No real change occurred in the book with respect to this central thesis: the main thesis of the book is that what is crucial to the understanding of the emergence of categories is the role of the social – society itself. That is certainly the case in *Primitive Classification* which social organization is, as we have seen, the telling factor. Those who hold this view might point to this quotation from the review by Durkheim himself of *The Elementary Forms*: 'It is society which taught men there was a point of view other than that of the individual and which made him see things under the form of totality' (1913a: 37; 1975: 172).

This is too simple a way of dealing with the issue. One cannot reduce religion just to its social dimension and make religion identical to the social. But do not forget that Durkheim had said elsewhere with regard to the quotation just mentioned that it was religion which gave people a sense of totality. Is Durkheim's mind completely muddled?

WHY TURN TO RELIGION?

In the Introduction to *The Elementary Forms*, Durkheim wrote: 'the study of religious phenomena provides a means of reviving the problems which, until now, have only been discussed amongst philosophers' (1912: 12; 1915: 9). No such claim was made in *Primitive Classification*. The question which has to be faced is why he turned in such a direction. There are two possible but not mutually exclusive explanations. One relates to Durkheim's intellectual outlook and the other to the weaknesses of the monograph itself.

In *Durkheim's Sociology of Religion: Themes and Theories* (Pickering 1984) I tried to demonstrate the crucial role that religion came to play in Durkheim's intellectual life. For him it became the key to the understanding of the foundations of social life. It was the *fons et origo* of all things social. Everything that people were able to achieve in their social and cultural life has stemmed from religion. It was impossible to understand people as social beings without having a scientific knowledge of their religion. Durkheim held that in the beginning people were essentially religious beings. If that is accepted, then people's later accomplishments – their civilization – must logically have been derived from religion. Therefore, not only do art, medicine, philosophy and mathematics have their roots in religion but the ability to think abstractly itself had its roots there. As Horton says: 'For Durkheim the moment at which religion is born is the moment at which the possibility of all higher forms of thought is also born' (1973: 260). Not only is religion the location of abstract categories together with the means of creating them, but it possesses an authority over individuals. It had a selecting process whereby the multitude of *représentations* which people had in their minds were so divided that the truly individual ones could be filtered out or down-graded, and the collective ones thereby strengthened. It taught people what to accept and what to reject. It can, therefore, be argued that for Durkheim to try to solve long-standing problems in the theory of knowledge, he journeyed to the source of knowledge, to religion itself. He wrote of his own book in a review that 'the most essential of human ideas, ideas of time, space, genus and species, force and causality, and personality, in short those to which philosophers have given the name categories and dominate the whole of logical activity, were developed at the very heart of religion' (1913a: 35; 1975: 171).

The change in Durkheim's thinking might also be understood from a different angle. We have already referred to the many weaknesses of the 1903 monograph (Needham 1963). In particular there are the problems of negative examples, the issues of historical change, and the intrusion of an affective element into what might be seen to be initially a purely cerebral process. Were such criticisms expressed when the article was published and was Durkheim aware of them? Alas, no answers to these questions have so far emerged. But it does seem plausible to suggest that he was not ignorant of the internal and empirical weaknesses of the monograph. One thing is certain: he never doubted that classificatory systems and abstract categories were derived from social sources. The problem was to prove the point. If a more all-embracing, more consistent positive approach could be found than that of the monograph, his position would be all the more sure. The answer was to be found in turning to primal social conditions, not necessarily those of social organization but to the primal institution, religion itself. Here there is no plague of exceptions or poor fits or negative cases. The starting point is the basic characteristics of religion. All that is required is to demonstrate that 'in the beginning' religion taught people to think abstractly through religious *représentations*, through cosmology. If that can be demonstrated the problem of the emergence of abstract categories is solved.

There is another issue which we have already touched on. In *Primitive Classification* Durkheim referred to changes which take place in classificatory concepts. The explanation of how and why changes occur is very far from satisfactory, not least because of its reliance on the notion of a social soul. The term *âme collective* does not appear in the conclusion of *The Elementary Forms*. In the book Durkheim makes a great deal of the notion of effervescent assembly (Pickering 1984: Chs 21, 22; Bois 1914: 322). His interest in the subject occurs only in the third period of development in his analysis of religion, and is limited largely to the discussion in *The Elementary Forms* (Pickering 1984: 382), where effervescence is put forward as a means of showing the techniques and processes of change – processes which originally were totally religious. In gatherings marked by frenzy and excitement new ideas – new *représentations* – emerge. There are plenty of problems in the notion of collective assembly. For example, no attempt is made to show why particular new forms come into being and are accepted. There is no 'social cause'. They just happen socially. Nevertheless, there is more merit in focussing on effervescent assembly than some critics have allowed. One has to face the fact of the emergence of the novel and whether it can be rationally accounted for. The point is that once again Durkheim has turned to religious institutions to provide answers to age-long problems, and, in particular, to one form which is the progenitor or at least the potential progenitor of categories.

IS IT POSSIBLE TO DISENTANGLE THE RELIGIOUS FROM THE SOCIAL?

From what has just been said, it is evident that one of the most problematic and unresolved issues in Durkheim's sociology of religion is to see precisely the relation between the social and the religious – what he meant by a 'religious society' and how it is 'explained'. The issue is acute with respect to preliterate societies. For example, he wrote: 'This [creative] influence of society is felt most strongly through religious *représentations*' (1910: 42–3). Yet as was pointed out earlier, religion creates *représentations*. In the same piece of writing, he commented that it was right to 'determine a few of the sociological conditions of knowledge' to discover what religious factors have entered into people's *représentation* of the world. Much of what he says appears to be paradoxical or ambiguous and is difficult to resolve rationally. We refer to only a few of the issues.

Durkheim does not in fact equate religion with society (Pickering 1984: Ch. 14). The social is more than the religious. He said in a discussion: 'the religious can be social without everything social being religious' (1913b: 8; 1984: 8). Durkheim's well-known definition of a religion in *The Elementary Forms* is that it is a system of beliefs and practices around sacred things to form a moral community (1912: 47; 1915: 65). This would also imply that Durkheim differentiates religion from society. Nemedi underlines this by asserting that for Durkheim the sacred is not identical with society (1989: 15).

When Durkheim declares that religion has primacy over all other social components, and that they are religious, what does he mean? He has at the back of his mind, of course, pre-literate or primitive societies and that such societies are in their totality religious. But what does that mean? Does religion pervade everything? It would seem so, and he clarifies the issue in a review of 1913. 'The ideas which at that time controlled the movement of the *représentations* originated at the very heart of religion' (1913a: 35; 1975: 171). Thus, a religious society is one where religious *représentations* dominate that society. On the other hand, he often implies that religion is a separate entity within society itself. This is apparent when, as stated above, he defines religion as a system, as a separate institution within society which nevertheless extensively influences other institutions. This latter possibility also becomes evident in the idea that religion gives rise to such components of civilization as science, art, philosophy and so on. To say that these components just evolved from society would not make a notable contribution to sociological thought. The idea becomes more striking if they are supposed to emerge not just from society itself, but from religion, seen as a distinctive social institution. Durkheim means just this when he refers to religion

as 'the womb from which come all the leading germs of human civilization' (1912: 319; 1915: 223). Thus, religion as a distinct social institution
is the primal source of ideas, of all *représentations collectives* – therefore
of society itself.

Yet as every student of Durkheim knows, religion is not the creation
and certainly not the invention of individuals, though Durkheim admits
they have a role to play (1919: 143; 1975: 189). Religion is not dependent
on individual leaders. It is derived from and supported by society.
Religion gives rise to society but society gives rise to religion. Durkheim
said that religious categories 'were even made in the image of social
things' and 'that they were pregnant with social elements' (1913a: 35;
1975: 171).

The paradox is most sharp when it is a question of seeing things 'in
the beginning'. In historical times, with relatively clearly differentiated
institutions, Durkheim's argument becomes more convincing and less
ambiguous. One can imagine the various components of civilization shak-
ing themselves free from their religious roots – how secular *représentations* have come into being. Durkheim's procedure is to read back into
primitive societies what he saw happening in modern ones. Thus, when
he turns to simple forms he encourages his readers to imagine how
societies, even earlier than the Arunta, functioned. Yet he denies this
when he writes that origin does not mean a first beginning. There is no
moment when religion began (1912: 11; 1915: 8). Instead, he looks at
what he claims are ever-present 'causes'.

In one sense Durkheim is right. There can be no knowledge of how
'it all began'. Nor can one hope to solve in a rational way the sequence
of events – the egg before the chicken. That religion is closely entwined
with the social no one can deny – and we now accept that largely through
Durkheim's influence. But a paradox emerges for Durkheim when he
attempts to 'explain' religion solely in terms of the social. The logic of
his basic positions leaves him no alternative. In the last analysis the
problem is to know whether Durkheim is arguing along the lines of logic
or whether he is basing his stand on some alleged evolutionary/historical
evidence. He is apt to slip very easily from one type of argument to
another.

CONCLUSION

Durkheim's sociology of knowledge stems directly from problems set by
Kant. His theory 'is explicitly a socialization of Kantian rational categories' (Hesse in Arbib and Hesse 1986: 205; cf. Vogt 1991). Although his
sociology was based on the antinomies and dichotomies of Enlightenment
thought, he attempted to transcend these by the discipline of sociology,

at the heart of which was his concept of society as *sui generis* – rejected by many rationalists.

But he failed to meet the rationalist criteria in other ways, notably by making religion crucial to understanding the nature of *représentations* and, more crucially, abstract categories. At first he set out quite 'scientifically' to relate 'primitive categories', that is, classification, to social structure. By taking such a leap and seeing that what he held was a real connection between classification and the social, he showed great originality and took a most fruitful path. A sociology of classification could be established without any reference to religion. Why did he not continue along that path and try to show how categories were similarly related to social structure? Surely, it would have been the 'Kantian thing' to do. Instead, he turned to religion as *the* factor in understanding not only how early people began to think, but how they came across abstract concepts. Thus, he abandoned the obvious rationalist path. The 'solve-all' key, religion, is inserted to unlock an age-long problem. Admittedly it is the social component of religion which is crucial; but to assume that borders on circularity.

It is clear from Durkheim's writings that the sociology of knowledge, which is concerned with *représentations*, stands at the center of his sociology (Vogt 1979: 102). So it is possible to see that, in the last analysis, 'all Durkheimian sociology was a theory of knowledge', which logically becomes a sociology of belief (Vogt 1979: 102). A great deal turns on his sociology of religion, which is to a very large extent portrayed in *The Elementary Forms*.

As I have had occasion to say elsewhere, there seems little doubt that his enormous concern with things religious, which emerged in so much that he wrote, not least in his final book, proved to be something of an embarrassment to his followers (Pickering 1984: Ch. 27). Many felt that he had gone too far in seeing religion as the *clef de voûte* of social life. And when it comes to the sociology of knowledge and his use of religion in explicating it, the same kind of criticism emerges: he claims too much for religion, and does not supply sufficient empirical evidence. This has tended to make scholars forget, quite conveniently, what he has to say about the role of religion in epistemology.

Durkheim's contribution to the sociology of knowledge is essentially an evolutionary or anthropological one. This is not to say that he does not have a great deal to contribute to the discipline, in ways which have been raised here. But his concern with religion as the vehicle which taught people how to think and derive abstract categories means that he concentrated on 'how it all began', that is, on evolutionary issues. A parallel case for another period and for another subject is Max Weber's concern with the relation of the ethic of Protestantism to the spirit of capitalism. Durkheim sought ever-present causes within society itself, but in seeing religion as the one factor which provides the answer, the notion of ever-present causes ceases to be valid, as religion changes its character with the passing of time, and today it is coming close to disappearing in many societies. Categories go their way without being modified by religion, much as capitalism no longer rests on the Protestant ethic.

NOTES

1 Although the article bears the names of both authors, we shall frequently refer to it as being written by Durkheim.
2 In accordance with common practice among many English-speaking scholars, the French word, *représentation* is retained since it defies a precise English equivalent. The English word, representation, is quite inadequate. (For the French meaning, see below and Lukes 1973: 68.) The adjectives commonly associated with Durkheim's use of the word, such as *collective* and *individuelle*, are also retained.
3 Durkheim went further. We have seen that categories and concepts are socially derived, for they are 'the work of the collectivity'. But 'categories are in contradiction with simple concepts'. These quotations come from a 1913 discussion on *The Elementary Forms* in which Durkheim also said that categories but not all concepts 'are collective in another sense'. This second sense holds only for categories because they 'represent social realities' (1913b: 90; 1984: 22). This means that categories stand at the heart of society and are its most important *représentations*.
4 Peter Worsley, who in his article of 1956 on Durkheim's sociology of knowledge makes no reference to *Primitive Classification*, holds that, according to his study of Australian totemism, there are two types of classification. One consists of proto-scientific classifications, which we would see as being close to abstract categories, and which are based on collective experience of the environment, and the other are derived from totemism, as in *Les Formes Elémentaires* and from other religious phenomena. These are basically religious and have no scientific value (Worsley 1956: 60–1).
5 Rodney Needham, in his introductory remarks to the English translation of *Primitive Classification*, held that the insertion at the end about the emotive quality of classificatory concepts was 'a profoundly important feature of all human thought, and few propositions could be of more consequence' (1963: xxii). But he admits that no evidence for the assertion was presented in the monograph. Neither is there much evidence for Needham's contention that the authors' statement is of such consequence. It is abundantly clear that some cognitive concepts – some classificatory concepts – are associated with emotion, such as those concerned with the sacred. Today, relatively fewer concepts are so associated in the face of the growth of secular and scientific thinking.

REFERENCES

Arbib, M. A. and Hesse, M. (1986) *The Construction of Reality*, Cambridge: Cambridge University Press.
Badcock, C. R. (1975) *Levi-Strauss. Structuralism and Sociological Theory*, London: Hutchinson.
Bloor, D. (1982) 'Durkheim and Mauss revisited: classification and the sociology of knowledge', *Studies in the History and Philosophy of Science* 13: 267–97.

Bois, H. (1914) 'La sociologie et l'obligation', *Revue de Théologie de Montauban* 23: 193–250, 320–79.

Dennes, W. R. (1924) *The Method and Presuppositions of Group Psychology*, Berkeley, CA: University of California Press.

Durkheim, E. (1898) 'Représentations individuelles et représentations collectives,' *Revue de Métaphysique et de Morale* VI: 273–303. (Translation in [1953] *Sociology and Philosophy*, trans. D. F. Pocock, London: Cohen & West.)

—— (1909) 'Sociologie religieuse et théorie de la connaissance', *Revue de Métaphysique et de Morale* XVII: 733–58. (Translation in part in [1915] *The Elementary Forms of the Religious Life*, trans. J. S. Swain, London: George Allen & Unwin; translation in [1982] *The Rules of Sociological Method and Selected Texts on Sociology and its Method*, trans. W. D. Halls, London and Basingstoke: Macmillan.)

—— (1910) Review, 'Jerusalem, Wilhelm, *Sociologie des Erkennens*', *Année Sociologique* XI: 42–5.

—— (1912) *Les Formes Elémentaires de la Vie Religieuse. Le Système totémique en Australie*, Paris: Alcan. (Translation in [1915] *The Elementary Forms of the Religious Life*, trans. J. S. Swain, London: George Allen & Unwin.)

—— (1913a) Review, 'Lévy-Bruhl – *Les Fonctions Mentales dans les Sociétés Inférieures*, Paris, 1910', 'Durkheim (Emile) – *Les Formes Elémentaires de la Vie Religieuse. Le Système Totémique en Australie*, Paris, 1912', *Année Sociologique* XII: 33–7. (Translation in [1975] *Durkheim on Religion*, trans. J. Redding and W. S. F. Pickering, London: Routledge & Kegan Paul.

—— (1913b) Contribution to discussion: 'Le problème religieux et la dualité de la nature humaine', séance du 4 février 1913, *Bulletin de la Société Française de Philosophie* XIII: 63–75, 80–7, 90–100, 108–11. (Translation in [1984] 'The problem of religion and the duality of human nature,' trans. R. A. Jones and P. W. Vogt, *Knowledge and Society* 5: 91–121.

—— (1915) *The Elementary Forms of the Religious Life*, trans. J. S. Swain, London: George Allen & Unwin. (Translation includes part of [1909] 'Sociologie religeuse et théorie de la conaissance', *Revue de Metaphysique et de Morale* XVII: 733–58.)

—— (1919) Contribution to discussion in F. Abauzit *et al.*, *Le Sentiment Religieux à l'Heure Actuelle*, pp. 97–105, 142–3, Paris: Vrin. (Translation in [1975] *Durkheim on Religion*, trans. J. Redding and W. S. F. Pickering, London: Routledge & Kegan Paul.)

—— (1953) *Sociology and Philosophy*, trans. D. F. Pocock, London: Cohen & West. (Translation of 'Représentations individuelles et représentations collectives', *Revue de Métaphysique et de Morale* VI: 273–303.)

—— (1963) *Primitive Classification*, trans. R. Needham, London: Cohen & West. (Translation of Durkheim and Mauss, M. [1903] 'De quelques formes primitives de classification', *Année Sociologique* VI: 1–72.)

—— (1975) *Durkheim on Religion*, trans. J. Redding and W. S. F. Pickering, London: Routledge & Kegan Paul. (Translations of various items, including [1912] *Les Formes Elémentaires de la Vie Religieuse. Le Système Totémique en Australie*, Paris: Alcan; [1913], Review, 'Lévy-Bruhl – *Les Fonctions Mentales dans les Sociétés Inferieures*, Paris, 1910', 'Durkheim (Emile) – *Les Formes Elémentaires de la Vie Religieuse. Le Système Totémique en Australie*, Paris, 1912,' *Année Sociologique* XII: 33–7. [1919] Contribution to discussion in F. Abauzit *et. al. Le Sentiment Religieux à l'Heure Actuelle*, pp. 97–105, 142–3, Paris: Vrin.)

—— (1982) *The Rules of Sociological Method and Selected Texts on Sociology and its Method*, trans. W. D. Halls, London and Basingstoke: Macmillan. (Translations include, in part [1909], 'Sociologie religieuse et théorie de la connaissance,' *Revue de Métaphysique et de Morale* XVII: 733–58.)

—— (1984) 'The problem of religion and the duality of human nature', trans. R. A. Jones and P. W. Vogt, *Knowledge and Society* 5: 91–121. (Translation of [1913] Contribution to discussion: 'Le problème religieux et la dualité de la nature humaine', séance du 4 février 1913, *Bulletin de la Société Française de Philosophie* XIII: 63–75, 80–7, 90–100, 108–11.)

Durkheim, E. and Mauss, M. (1903) 'De quelques formes primitives de classification', *Année Sociologique* VI: 1–72. (Translation in Durkheim [1963] *Primitive Classification*, trans. R. Needham, London: Cohen & West.)

Ellen, R. F. and Reason, D. (1979) *Classifications in their Social Context*, London: Academic Press.

Flew, N. (1985) *Thinking about Social Thinking: The Philosophy of the Social Sciences*, Oxford: Blackwell.

Gray, L. H. (1911) 'Cosmogony and Cosmology,' *Encyclopedia of Religion and Ethics*, New York: Scribner's.

Hertz, R. (1909) 'La préeminence de la main droite', *Revue Philosophique* 68: 553–80. (Translated in [1960] *Death and the Right Hand*, trans. R. and C. Needham, London: Cohen & West.).

—— (1960) *Death and the Right Hand*, trans. R. and C. Needham, London: Cohen & West.)

Hesse, M. (1982) 'Comments on the papers of David Bloor and Steven Lukes', *Studies in the History and Philosophy of Science*, 13, 4: 325–31.

Horton, R. (1973) 'Lévy-Bruhl, Durkheim and the scientific revolution', in R. Horton and R. Finnigan (eds), *Modes of Thought*, London: Faber.

Lévy-Bruhl, L. (1910) *Les Fonctions Mentales dans les Sociétés Inférieures*, Paris: Alcan. Translated in [1926] *How Natives Think*, trans. A. Clare, London: Allen & Unwin.)

—— (1926) *How Natives Think*, trans. A. Clare, London: Allen & Unwin.

Lukes, S. (1973) *Emile Durkheim. His Life and Work. A Historical and Critical Study*, London: Allen Lane; New York: Harper & Row.

—— (1982) 'Comments on David Bloor', *Studies in the History and Philosophy of Science* 13: 313–18.

Needham, R. (1963) 'Introduction' to E. Durkheim, *Primitive Classification*, trans. R. Needham, London: Cohen & West.

Nemedi, D. (1989) 'Durkheim and the strong programme in the philosophy of science', (unpublished manuscript) Institute of Sociology, Eötvös University, Budapest, Hungary.

Pickering, W. S. F. (1984) *Durkheim's Sociology of Religion: Themes and Theories*, London: Routledge & Kegan Paul.

—— (forthcoming) *Durkheim's Sociology of Knowledge: A Study of Representations*. (The British Centre for Durkheimian Studies, Oxford.)

Vogt, W. P. (1979) 'Early French contributions to the sociology of knowledge', *Research in the Sociology of Knowledge. Science and Art* II: 101–21.

—— 1991 'Political Connections, Professional Advancement, and Moral Education in Durkheimian Sociology', *Journal of the History of the Behavioral Sciences* 27, 56–75.

Worsley, P. M. (1956) 'Emile Durkheim's theory of Knowledge', *Sociological Review* 4 (NS): 437–62.

3

DURKHEIM'S SOCIOLOGY OF LAW

Morality and the cult of the individual

W. Paul Vogt

Any complete general social theory must deal with legal institutions, for these are the main formally organized normative structures of modern societies. Durkheim's general social theory certainly meets this test of completeness. The sociology of law was an essential component of his work, so much so that his sociology cannot be fully understood without considering it. A particular interpretation of legal phenomena was a central part of the Durkheimians' disciplinary consensus and the focus of much of the research not only of Durkheim, but of many of his most important students and colleagues as well (Vogt 1983).

Durkheim emphasized the study of legal phenomena more in the early than in the later stages of his career. He wrote no major work on the subject following his 1901 article on 'two laws of the evolution of punishment' ([1901] 1969), but he always continued to include the law in his later discussions of the science of sociology and its mission. Thus, in a 1909 work on 'sociology and the social sciences', he repeated the basic point that he had been making for two decades:

> There is no need to demonstrate the social character of legal institutions. They are studied by the sociology of law, which is, furthermore, closely tied to the sociology of morality, since moral ideas are the soul of the law. A legal code gets its authority from the moral ideal that it incarnates and that it translates into precise formulae.
>
> ([1909] 1970: 149–50)

If one adds to this formulation Durkheim's thesis that moral and legal phenomena were clothed in religious garb in most societies, particularly societies in comparatively early stages of social evolution, we arrive at Durkheim's 'trinity' of law, morality and religion as the three faces of social solidarity. Law, morality and religion are, in Durkheim's sociology, all forms of social control – of social regulation and integration. They are the means by which rules of conduct are established and internalized, rules that make it possible for individuals to live together in groups. Without such rules societies could not exist. Sociology can study no more fundamental phenomena than these, which are constitutive of its very subject matter. Law, religion and morality are, Durkheim said in his critique of Simmel's formalism, 'the very framework of social life'; they are 'society itself, living and acting; for, it is by its law, its morality, its religion, etc. that a society is characterized' (Durkheim and Fauconnet 1903: 481).

While law, morality and religion have separate identities and may be studied by separate branches of sociology, each, Durkheim maintained, is the expression of the same basic set of social forces. Law is, in brief, merely the most institutionalized, codified or 'crystallized' version of the same social facts that give rise to religion and morality. Law is the more important form of social solidarity in higher societies; religion imbues moral ideas in lower, or primitive, societies.

Upon these basic insights Durkheim built his entire sociology, now stressing one 'person' of the Trinity, then another, when constructing his general theory of society and of social evolution, and when formulating his basic ideas about social integration and social regulation. He pursued studies of a wide range of legal phenomena including crime and punishment, the State and forms of government, the law of contract and the organization of economic life, and, most significantly, the place of the individual and of individualism in modern society. The central theme in Durkheim's sociology of law was the emergence in modern society of a form of secular humanism based on respect for, indeed a 'cult' of, individual human dignity. Every one of his particular studies of law in society, from his analyses of the functions of punishment to his lectures on the evolution of the law of contract, are shaped by the conclusion that the 'religion' of the individual is the main ligature of modern society.

While the great majority of Durkheim's publications have at least some indirect relevance to his sociology of law, our key texts will be four of Durkheim's works which contain his fullest and most systematic treatments of legal issues. The most significant of these texts is comprised of a course of lectures he delivered several times at the Universities of Bordeaux and Paris between 1890 and 1912. The manuscript we have probably dates from 1899–1900,[1] but it was published only posthumously in 1950 as 'sociological lessons on the physiology of mores and the law' (in English as *Professional Ethics and Civic Morals* [1957].

Durkheim's most systematic monograph of the sociology of law was his 'Two laws of the evolution of punishment', which dates from the same period as *Professional Ethics*. These two works are the pinnacle of Durkheim's achievement in the sociology of law, but they are much less well known and less controversial than two of his earlier works dealing with legal phenomena, *The Division of Labor in Society* (1893) and *The Rules of Sociological Method* (1895).

Speaking solely from the standpoint of the sociology of law these last two are comparatively marginal works. In *Division of Labor* Durkheim used the history of criminal and civil law as an index to or as evidence about the evolution of different sorts of social solidarity, but he focussed more on forms of solidarity than on forms of law; legal history had more methodological than substantive importance in *Division*. Similarly in *The Rules*, Durkheim discussed the nature of crime more to illustrate what he meant by the concept of a 'normal' social fact than to discuss crime *per se*. Yet the fact that Durkheim chose to use legal phenomena for important methodological and illustrative purposes in the period 1893–5 (in *Division* and *Rules*) foreshadows his more systematic and substantive studies of the period 1899–1901 (in *Professional Ethics* and 'Two laws').[2] And, taken together, these four texts can give us Durkheim's full analyses of the main topics in his sociology of law: the definition of crime; the social functions of punishment; the changing character of laws and punishment in modern society; the definition of the State and of forms of government; the need to regulate by law modern society's economic functions; and the evolution of the idea of the just contract. The main theme Durkheim stressed in each of these topics is the centrality of the individual in modern society and the concomitant decline of repressive, religiously dominated forms of social organization.

THE FUNCTIONS OF LAW AND PUNISHMENT

Durkheim's first major discussion of legal phenomena, in *Division of Labor*, contains his only extensive analyses of the *general* nature of law in society, rather than of particular aspects of the sociology of law. In these analyses, the 'trinity' of law, religion and morality is most evident. By including the lesser 'deities' Durkheim mentioned, we are able to form a sort of hierarchy of six sets of rules of conduct ranging from the least to the most formal – in ascending order of intensity and organization: etiquette, custom, convention, morality, religion and law. In the simplest societies, these were all one. Even in more advanced societies where they have become differentiated, they remain versions of the same social forces. They usually support one another; seldom do they clash. For example, Durkheim said that conflict between custom (*moeurs*) and law 'arises only in rare and pathological cases that cannot endure without danger'. Not all customs are backed by the force of law, of course, yet 'acts which custom alone must repress are not of a different nature than those the law punishes; they are only less serious' ([1893, 1902] 1969: 65, 301).

In the preface to the first edition of *Division of Labor* Durkheim

73

claimed that law and morality are inseparable: 'Continual exchanges take place between them; now there are moral rules which become juridical, and now juridical rules which become moral.' Given Durkheim's conclusion here, it is not surprising that he defined the two sorts of rules by the same criterion: legal rules and moral rules can be distinguished from other rules of conduct by the fact that when they are violated they are punished. The main difference between moral and legal rules is in the way the punishments are applied or administered. Legal punishments or sanctions are 'organized' while solely moral sanctions are 'diffuse'. In practical terms this means that infractions of legal rules are condemned by legal tribunals, while infractions of moral rules are condemned by the 'court' of public opinion. Normally, these two 'courts' render the same judgment. What is illegal is usually considered to be immoral by public opinion, which thus supports the law; conversely, without the support of the law 'morality . . . remains as a sort of dead letter, as a pure abstraction, instead of being an effective discipline of wills' ([1893, 1902] 1969: 426–7).

Connections between law, morality and religion are particularly close in the case of criminal or penal law. Other forms of law Durkheim discussed – such as constitutional, administrative, commercial and procedural law – have less direct ties to religion and morality ([1893, 1902] 1969: 126–7, 132n). Durkheim was much less concerned with these in his earlier works in the sociology of law. This was no doubt partly because, according to his theory, criminal law was the original form. Also, criminal law was especially receptive to his approach to definition and classification. Durkheim's reasoning here paralleled that of the nineteenth-century English legal positivist, John Austin, and the twentieth-century American jurists Benjamin Cardozo and Oliver W. Holmes. Austin defined a law as a command backed by a sovereign force; Cardozo and Holmes defined it as the rules the courts enforce. Similarly, Durkheim defined crime by punishment and kinds of crime by the different sorts of punishment to which they give rise.

If religion and morality were strong enough, if socialization to society's values were perfect, and if these religious and moral values were perfectly known, everyone would always behave correctly. There would be no challenge to the society's dominant values and hence no need for law. But, as Durkheim maintained, 'such a universal and absolute uniformity is utterly impossible' ([1895] 1982: 100). Therefore, crime will exist in all societies. What is labelled crime will vary from one society and social type to the next, but it is impossible for any society to be free of crime. In other words, since it is in the very nature of social life that individuals will 'diverge to some extent from the collective type, it is also inevitable that among these deviations some assume a criminal character' ([1895] 1982: 101). Not only is crime inevitable, Durkheim said in a phrase that shocked his contemporaries and subsequent generations of social theorists, but 'crime is normal'. He went even further; crime is not only inevitable and normal, 'it is a factor in public health, an integrative element in any healthy society' ([1895] 1982: 98).

These assertions, offered as an illustration of his 'Rules for the distinction of the normal from the pathological' are among the most controversial conclusions in all of Durkheim's work. Gabriel Tarde responded indignantly in the pages of the *Revue Philosophique*. Durkheim's reply, which contains some useful clarifications of his original statements, was published in a subsequent number of that journal. It is important to take some pains to be exact about what Durkheim said here since it has often been misconstrued and since it introduces us to a key element of his theory of criminal law and punishment.

Crime is normal, according to Durkheim, because it is inevitable; a crime-free society is a contradiction in terms. Crime is not only necessary, 'it is useful, for the conditions to which it is bound are themselves indispensable to the normal evolution of morality and law' ([1895] 1982: 101). While many might concede the point that crime is inevitable, few commentators at the time or subsequently found it easy to imagine that crime was useful.

There are, Durkheim held, both frequent indirect benefits of crime and infrequent direct benefits. The indirect benefits have to do with the intensity of social control. If social control were strong enough to prevent all crime, the resulting regime would constitute an intolerably (as well as impossibly) repressive society, one that would be destructive of all individuality. Only in a pathologically repressive society could crime rates drop below a 'certain' level, the 'normal' level for a society of that social type. While Durkheim's attempts to specify what such rates and levels should be were utter failures, this does not vitiate the main point, that it is impossible to have social control that dampens only undesirable deviation from the norm.

In addition to the indirect usefulness of crime as a sort of by-product of the social conditions that permit individuality, crime occasionally has a more direct function. Sometimes a crime is also 'an anticipation of the morality to come' ([1895] 1982: 102). Socrates and other 'heretics' who made possible freedom of thought were criminals in their day and were legitimately punished – but we nonetheless owe them a great debt. Improvement can come only through the efforts of pioneers. How, after all, can one 'change morality except by departing from it' (1895: 521)?

Durkheim's position on the normality and functionality of crime has raised considerable controversy, mostly because it is easy to misinterpret. Durkheim must share some of the blame for the misinterpretations since he did not always make it clear that his conclusions applied only at a very high level of generality – that of comparisons of societies and societal types. It is normal for all societies to have crimes, but criminals in a particular society are not normal. They may be serving a useful social function, but they are not normal individuals in their society. While crime is normal at the comparative societal level it is not normal behavior for the individuals in a particular society. As Durkheim put it in an attempt to clarify his views in response to Tarde's criticisms, 'it is thus socially normal that in all societies there are individuals who are psychologically abnormal' (1895: 523).

In his debate with Tarde, Durkheim found himself in an unusual position. Generally known for arguing that modern societies were lacking in their amplitude of social regulation, and that this lack led to anomie, Durkheim here left himself open to the accusation of being indifferent to violations of social regulations. Tarde claimed that Durkheim had allied himself with 'the disastrous progress of the most abusive indulgence on the part of judges as well as of juries' (Tarde, 1895: 152). This is a somewhat understandable misconstrual of Durkheim's views on the matter, but as far as one can tell from his works and from biographical evidence, Durkheim was never a particularly strong advocate of leniency in criminal sentencing.

Tarde also claimed that Durkheim portrayed criminals as geniuses who, like Socrates, expand the boundaries of human freedom. Durkheim replied that he believed that only occasionally does a criminal anticipate the future course of moral development. Most criminals provide their social usefulness in less direct ways. While crime has social uses, most crimes are in fact injurious to society, but 'the social evil caused by the crime is compensated for by the punishment' (1895: 521). Thus, while it is normal for there to be crime, it is also normal for crime to be punished.

This last point is wholly typical of Durkheim's treatment of crime. Most generally Durkheim discussed crime only when linking it closely with punishment. His interest in crime (and in criminals) was wholly overshadowed by his interest in punishment. In other words, his theory led him to have a greater interest in the social reactions to crimes (that is, punishments) than in the crimes themselves, to say nothing of criminals, in whom he expressed virtually no interest. Durkheim was a penologist, not a criminologist.

It is not unfair to say that for Durkheim one of the main benefits of crime was that it gave righteous people an opportunity to punish wrong-doers. The function of punishment is to reinforce the community's belief in the rule that has been broken and thereby challenged. Crime, and especially the reaction to crime that is punishment, brings good people together. In so doing, punishment fulfills 'its true function' which is 'to maintain social cohesion intact' ([1893, 1902] 1969: 108). Punishment is not then focussed mostly on the criminal, but rather is directed toward the rest of society. The rest of society demands 'vengeance', which has always been the essence of punishment. What we avenge, Durkheim concluded, 'is the outrage to morality' ([1893, 1902] 1969: 89).

The outrage can reach great levels of intensity, an intensity that stems ultimately from the religious origins of penal law. But, today, in nations where the law is wholly secular and where justice demands that the punishment fit the crime, the situation, said Durkheim, is no different. Indeed, 'there is no society where it is not the rule that the punishment should fit the crime' ([1895] 1982: 103). The fact that we have a different sense of justice today than in earlier eras and that this sense of justice puts limits on how far we will carry vengeance, so that we no longer engage in the more violently repressive punishments common in earlier eras, in no way invalidates the general proposition that we punish to get revenge and that we proportion our vengeance to what we perceive as the gravity of the crime.

Durkheim's most extensive discussion of these ideas occurs in what at first blush might seem an unlikely source: lectures he gave in the academic year 1898–9[3] on moral education. Although Durkheim's context was the functions of punishing those who broke school rules, he made it quite clear that the same principles applied to the punishment of crimes in the adult world.

The reason the punishment must fit the crime is to make the disapproval communicated by the punishment as clear as possible. We punish to show our disapproval. This demonstration is partly for the edification of the criminal, but mainly for ourselves. Were our punishments random, sometimes very harsh, at other times very lenient, we would risk miscommunication about the gravity of the offense. A punishment would be too lenient if it failed effectively to express blame, and the essence of the punishment, Durkheim said in these lectures, is the sense of blame it arouses. We should punish not in order to deter the would-be criminal, since the *direct* deterrent powers of punishment are quite minimal. Rather we should, indeed we must, punish a wrongdoer because his or her crime weakens faith in the rightness and the authority of the law. The law is built on this faith; it is this faith, this commitment to what is right, that deters individuals who might otherwise break moral and legal rules. If infractions went unpunished, the moral authority of the rules would be eroded. Thus, we punish to restore respect for the violated rule. The punishment is an expression of repugnance toward the wrongdoer and thus a reaffirmation of the community's commitment to the broken rule.

Punishments do not have to be viciously repressive to accomplish the goal of restoring our faith in moral rules; indeed, overly harsh punishments can be counterproductive. Such reasoning led Durkheim to oppose corporal punishment in schools; that kind of punishment violated human dignity. Human dignity, Durkheim believed, was the chief value schools in modern societies should be promoting, not violating through their methods of discipline. Corporal punishment may have been appropriate in other eras, but not in a society whose principle moral belief was respect for human beings' individual worth. In sum, although the punishment always has to fit the crime, in different societies at different stages of social evolution, different punishments could be fitting for the same crime ([1924] 1961: Chs 11–13).

STAGES OF SOCIAL AND LEGAL EVOLUTION

The main goal of Durkheim's sociology of law was to gain a better understanding of the stages of societal evolution. In his efforts to uncover the character of different social types, he never deviated far from the procedures laid down in *Division of Labor:* types of society may be classified by types of solidarity; types of solidarity may be determined by studying societies' dominant types of law; types of law can be classified by the types of sanctions attached to them. Hence, social evolution could be studied via the evolution of sanctions or punishments.

Types of society	Primitive	Modern
Types of solidarity	Mechanical	Organic
Types of law	Criminal/religious	All others
Types of sanction	Repressive	Restitutive

Two basic types of sanction are found in all societies. A *repressive* sanction (the only kind we have discussed thus far in this chapter) expresses the moral outrage of the community and functions to reaffirm its commitment to challenged values. A *restitutive* sanction is designed to right a wrong, but not to punish a wrongdoer; it merely 'consists of a simple return in state' ([1893, 1902] 1969: 111). Examples include resolving conflicts over the terms of contracts, invalidating elections in which proper balloting procedures have not been followed, determining the taxes owed on various sorts of income, and so on.

These two main categories of sanction enable us to distinguish the two categories of law. Repressive sanctions are used in the case of violations of criminal or penal law; and 'all penal law is more or less religious' ([1893, 1902] 1969: 141). Restitutive sanctions are used in the case of violations of all other sorts of law – civil, commercial, procedural, constitutional, administrative, etc. The two different categories of sanction and law then provide us with the means to distinguish between the two main types of social solidarity. 'Since law reproduces the principal forms of social solidarity,' Durkheim maintained, 'we have only to classify the different types of law to find therefrom the different types of social solidarity which correspond' to them ([1893, 1902] 1969: 68). The types of solidarity in question are the now famous 'mechanical' and 'organic' solidarity. (Durkheim abandoned these terms after 1893, but the ideas behind them remained directing concepts in his works.) Mechanical solidarity arises from the similarity of members of society; it is collective and functions to produce conformity. It predominates in primitive societies where the only law is criminal/religious. Organic solidarity, on the other hand, is a social bond arising from social and individual differences produced by the division of labor. When there is a decline of criminal law, relative to the growth of other forms, this shows that a society is becoming more modern. For example, 'adminstrative law', by which Durkheim mainly meant government bureaucracy, 'is as much more developed as societies approach a more elevated type' ([1893, 1902] 1969: 221).

Thus, one of sociology's earlier and more influential 'modernization' theories was built upon an evolutionary model of the sociology of law. Like many other authors of such theories, Durkheim was more interested in differentiating between extreme versions of the primitive and modern types than he was in intermediate stages, in historically concrete mixed types, or in the process of how societies moved from the one to the other. Durkheim's theory of social change, here and elsewhere, was not elaborate. According to Durkheim, social change is, in a word, slow; it happens little by little.

> Originally . . . everything social is religious; the two words are synonymous. Then, little by little, political, economic, scientific functions free themselves from the religious function, constitute themselves apart and take on a more and more acknowledged temporal character.
>
> ([1893, 1902] 1969: 169)

Durkheim's best elaboration of this theory occurs in his 'Two laws of the evolution of punishment'. The first law was quantitative; it had to do with the *amount* and *severity* of retributions exacted. The second was qualitative and dealt with the *kinds* of penalties inflicted.

The first law had two parts. It is important to state them separately since Durkheim explicitly said that they involved phenomena that could vary independently of one another.

[a.] *'The intensity of punishment is greater the more societies belong to a less advanced type.'*

[b.] The intensity of punishment is greater the more *'the central power has an absolute character'* ([1901] 1969: 245).[4]

Durkheim spent more time defining the characteristics of absolutism (part [b.] of the first law), no doubt because he had done very little previous work on governmental forms. Absolutist governments, he wrote, have relations with the rest of the society that are 'unilateral' and not 'reciprocal'. Governmental absolutism is not simply related to the size and number of governmental functions; this can be seen by comparing the democratic governments of the late nineteenth century with the monarchies of Europe in the seventeenth century. The monarchies were much smaller and provided far fewer services, but were much more absolutistic. It is also important to note, Durkheim said, that there is no necessary relationship between the evolutionary stage a society has reached and the degree of absolutism of its government. Governmental types are relatively independent of, and can change faster than, social types. It is thus possible for the two facets of the first law to work in opposite directions. For example, the tendency to milder punishments that came with the advance in social complexity and organization between the twelfth and seventeenth centuries in Western Europe was completely overwhelmed by the simultaneous advance in governmental absolutism which led to an era of unusually severe punishments.

The second, qualitative, law states that

Punishments that take away liberty and liberty alone for periods of time that vary according to the gravity of the crimes tend increasingly to become the normal type of repression.

([1901] 1969: 256)

Durkheim was referring here, in a manner that anticipates later and better-known works,[5] to the rise of imprisonment as the chief method of punishment. It became the main form of penal sanction only in the nineteenth century. Prior to that time prison was more often used as a pre-trial administrative measure designed to keep the accused from fleeing before sentencing.

Durkheim noted that societies needed a certain level of permanence, organization and wealth before the second law could come into effect – nomadic bands could hardly have prisons. But the main explanation of the second law was the first law, which is to say that the rise of imprisonment can best be understood as part of the general trend toward 'the progressive weakening of legal punishments'. As more and more of the brutal forms of punishment (dismemberment, stoning, etc.) faded into desuetude, other forms developed 'to fill the gaps produced by this withdrawal' ([1901] 1969: 262). In explaining the second law by the first, Durkheim had in fact subtly changed its terms. The first law was not originally stated as a trend over time in the direction of more leniency, but was rather a statement of the (atemporal) conditions under which punishment would be more severe. While Durkheim suggested that the evolution of societies toward ever higher social types was by no means inevitable, and while he explicitly stated that political change was to a large degree independent of social evolution, his underlying assumptions appear to have been otherwise.

In any case, the validity of the explanation of the second law rests upon the validity of the first, and it was, thus, to the explanation of the first law that Durkheim turned. As societies evolve from primitive to modern types, he said, there is a parallel evolution in the nature of the crimes typically found in them. Crimes in primitive societies are mainly against religious and collective entitites. In modern societies they are mostly human and individual. In the primitive/collective/religious type of crime the feelings of indignation and the sense of the odiousness of the transgressor are enormous; punishments are correspondingly harsh. Any pity one might feel for the criminal undergoing a hideous punishment is overwhelmed by the intensity of the collective/religious emotion: 'What does an individual's pain matter when it is a question of appeasing a god?' ([1901] 1969: 266).

Conversely, when it is a matter of a crime by one individual against another, the moral balance is much closer. While we have much sympathy for the victim of a crime as a fellow human being, and our desire for retribution is stimulated, the criminal is also a human being for whom we may have some sympathy – not as much as for the victim, certainly, and not enough that we would forego punishment altogether, but enough perhaps that we might oppose torturing the criminal's family, gouging out his or her eyes, and then roasting him or her over a slow fire. Only a transcendental crime against a superior being could be thought to justify such punishment. (Another way to change the balance so as to allow for harsh punishment, one might add, is to portray the person to be punished as subhuman.)

Today, in modern societies, collectivities such as the state or the society have been largely desacralized. Crimes against them have become human wrongs committed against secular, human institutions. 'We no longer hypostatize the famiy or the society under the form of transcendent and mystical beings' ([1901] 1969: 270). That is why we no longer need to tear limb from limb those who transgress collective rules.[6] It is quite otherwise under absolutist governments and theocracies, however. In a description meant to refer mostly to seventeenth-century absolute monarchs, but one that could apply more broadly as well, Durkheim said that by raising the individual ruler so high above ordinary persons, absolutism always evokes religiosity; crimes of lèse-majesté quickly enough become acts of 'lèse-divinité' and are punished accordingly.

But when crimes can be committed only against humans and when criminals are also seen as humans, those who would punish are faced with an inevitable contradiction.

It might seem completely natural to sacrifice without reserve the human dignity of one guilty of outraging the divine majesty. On the other hand, there is a real and irremediable contradiction in avenging the human dignity offended in the person of the victim by violating it in the person of the criminal. The only way, not to

EMILE DURKHEIM

eliminate the antimony (for strictly speaking it is not soluble), but
to lessen it, is to reduce punishment as much as possible.
([1901] 1969: 268)

Thus, the decline in the intensity of punishment is due in part to greater
pity for those who undergo suffering and to greater respect for their
individual human dignity – even if they are criminals. However, the
decline in the severity of the average punishment is also, Durkheim
concluded, due to the evolution of societies and their cognate types of
crime. With the elimination of the types of crime which in the past
received the harshest penalties (heresy, sacrilege, lèse-majesté, etc.) the
average level of punishment will naturally decline, but, Durkheim predicted, when such archaic forms of crime are totally gone, the rate of
decline in the average intensity of punishment will be greatly slowed, if
not altogether eliminated.

THE STATE, INDIVIDUAL RIGHTS AND SOCIAL JUSTICE

Durkheim devoted most of his analyses to forms of law he believed to
predominate in primitive societies, that is, penal, religious and repressive
law. He spent less time on types of law that occurred more frequently
in modern societies. The main exception is his course of lectures on the
'physiology of mores and the law' (1957). Here he elaborated on topics
in the sociology of law discussed only briefly in his other works. In the
paragraphs that follow, we will pay particular attention to constitutional
questions concerning the nature of forms of government and of the State
and the law of contract, especially Durkheim's understanding of the
concept of the just or equitable contract. Durkheim's account of the
modern State and of the just contract were inseparably linked to his
conclusion – which we have already seen to be one of the root ideas of
his sociology of law – that the cult of the individual (which entails respect
for the dignity of human rights) is the single most important moral
principle in a healthy modern society.

Individual rights are not threatened by the growth of the modern state.
Indeed, there is a direct 'relation of cause and effect between the progress
of moral individualism and the advance of the State' (1957: 57).[7]
Although this conclusion about the contribution of the state to individualism is one of Durkheim's least well-known theories, it is central to his
sociology of law, which in turn forms the basis of his understanding of
modern society. Durkheim defined the state conventionally enough by
sovereignty: 'we apply the term "State" . . . to the agents of the sovereign authority and "political society" to the complex of which the State
is the highest organ' (1957: 48). Unlike in some of his earlier works,
Durkheim emphasized here that the State has considerable autonomy

82

from the society; legislation is not simply a sort of translation of social opinion. The State does not merely reproduce 'the collective conscious- ness' in laws; rather it carries the ideas found there to a 'higher degree of consciousness and reflection'. The State is not the society's autonomic nervous system; it is its brain; 'its essential function is to think' (1957: 50–1).

The State is a constituent part of the political society, but differs from other such constituents in that they are subordinate to it. By tolerating no superiority of other groups (religious, family, ethnic, local, etc.), the State keeps other groups weak enough that they cannot tyrannize over the individual. Individual liberty is only possible in a society with a multiplicity of groups *and* only if no one of those groups is strong enough to exercise exclusive authority over the individual. The State limits the power of the *paterfamilias*, the local priest, the village elders, etc., and thus it reduces their control over the individual. Of course the State then tends to become despotic itself, and its despotism can be worse than that of smaller groups, which at least may be in touch with the particularities of individual needs. Unchecked, the State can become a massive leveller. If individual liberty is to survive, the State also needs to have its despotic tendencies counterbalanced. So while it is true that without the State other social groups would become tyrannical, it is also true that without intermediate groups the State would be. Thus, 'it is out of this conflict of social forces [between the State and intermediate groups] that individual liberties are born' (1957: 63).

Durkheim believed that European societies were lacking in the sort of intermediate groups needed to check and to complement the State. We cannot study in any detail his proposals to remedy the situation, but we need to look at them briefly to see what role the law was to play in the needed social reforms. Like Weber, Durkheim stressed that the economy was at the root of the most fundamental social changes that had resulted in modern society. What in pre-industrial societies had been a fairly insignificant institutional sector, the economy, had become the main determinant of modern social life. Durkheim maintained that this main facet of modern life was as yet unregulated by moral discipline. Until the seventeenth and eighteenth centuries in Europe moral regulation of the economy had been provided by the occupational guilds. But the guilds proved incapable of controlling the activities of large-scale industry. The State was equally incapable of exerting controls. Hence, by the nineteenth century, the economy was in a condition of insufficient regulation, that is, of anomie.

What was needed, Durkheim argued in his lectures, as well as in the better-known preface to the second (1902) edition of *Division of Labor*, was the revival of suitably modernized guilds. Only such professional groups would have the ability to generate the moral standards necessary to regulate economic life. Durkheim said that these standards cannot come from the outside; they 'can be established neither by the scientist in his study nor by the statesman; it has to be the task of the groups concerned' (1957: 31). But the groups did not exist. Durkheim was more than a little vague about how they could be established. Even had some rudimentary forms been developing, some sort of legal provision would have had to have been made for them to exercise the full range of powers Durkheim thought necessary. Durkheim did not explicitly say, but he seemed to imply that initially the groups would have to be established by legislation. Then, 'once the group is formed, nothing can hinder an appropriate moral life from evolving' out of it (1957: 23–4).

In one respect Durkheim's prediction was correct. Modern industrialized societies have developed much more governmental regulation of economic life, including regulation based on notions of morality and equity. But the agent of that regulation has been the State, not occupational groups. In addition to underestimating the ability of the State to regulate economic life, Durkheim also underestimated the lasting power of more traditional intermediate groups (religious, ethnic, regional, etc.). Durkheim doubted their ability, in the face of an expanding central authority, to counterbalance the actions of the State. He thought that only more modern social groups could fulfill this crucial function. In any case, according to Durkheim, individual rights required both a strong central State and intermediate groups that could check the State's tendency to subject individuals too closely to its power.

Just as Durkheim thought that some kinds of intermediate groups were more suited to modern society, he also believed that some forms of government were more appropriate to it than others. Durkheim thought that the one governmental form most supportive of the growth of individualism and thus most closely tied to the fundamental moral principle of modern society was the democratic State.

As we have seen above, Durkheim viewed the State or the central government as the social brain. For him, the same relation exists between morality (which is diffuse) and law (which is organized) as exists between public opinion (which is society's diffuse mental life) and the government (which is the organized expression of the society's ideas). Since the State is the deliberative organ of the society, to distinguish various forms of government we need to look to the characteristics of that deliberation. In contrast with some ordinary notions of what democracy was, for Durkheim the number of persons directly involved in decision making was not a key issue. Those politicians and scholars who would define the degree of democracy by the proportion or by the number of those governing are, Durkheim thought, logically compelled to see the highest form of democracy as a stateless anarchy. This he believed was a negation of all government, not a way to describe one of its chief forms. Since the government is always in the hands of a minority, what matters is how that minority conducts its business. A democracy does so in a manner that is open to the scrutiny and to the influence of the rest of society.

This criterion recalls the distinction, discussed above, that Durkheim made between absolutism, which had unilateral relations with the rest of society, and democracy (not specifically so named), which had a reciprocal relationship with other members of the society. Unlike in 'Two laws', where these distinctions were made, the course of lectures we are examining not only discusses parliamentary democracy in detail and by name, it contains a spirited defense of that form of government. Durkheim often said, in the most uncompromising terms, that a social scientist should do nothing that could be interpreted as propagating his personal political views under the guise of scholarship; perhaps his standards were somewhat different in his teaching than his scholarly monographs. On the other hand, Durkheim clearly considered his conclusions in *Professional Ethics and Civic Morals* to be serious, scientific ones that arose from systematic analyses of evidence, not mere propaganda. He thought he could demonstrate something he only hinted at in the 'Two laws' monograph, that is, that the character of modern societies makes them likely to adopt a democratic form of government: 'it is the form that societies are assuming to an increasing degree' (1957: 89). How did Durkheim arrive at his dual conclusion that democracy is more suitable for modern societies and, therefore, that it is a form of government we are likely to see more of in the future?

Durkheim contended that a government is its society's consciousness, where deliberations take place concerning the policies the society will follow. The character of a government is determined by the extent to which its deliberations and decision making are open to view and in communication with the rest of the society. Since no form of government is ever wholly isolated from the rest of society, nor is communication between the populace and the government ever perfect, the criterion of openness is a matter of degree. At the lowest levels of openness were absolutist governments (common in seventeenth-century Europe, for example) where the State was seen as 'a kind of mysterious being to whom the ordinary man dared not lift his eyes and which he even, more often than not, represented to himself as a religious symbol' (1957: 81–2). Such mystification is impossible in a democracy where the openness and visibility of the processes of deliberation and governing insure that the government will be seen for what it is – a human creation in the service of human ends. A democracy must follow practices that institutionalize open communication between the State and the rest of society, such as parliamentary procedures with open debates and publicly available records of legislative activity. None of this means, however, that parliaments and other devices of the democratic State are merely ways to organize plebiscites. Durkheim insisted that the State, even the democratic State, is no mere echo of public opinion. To be effective a democratic State must be autonomous from diffuse, amorphous public opinion, at least in the short run, so as to fulfill its function of systematic deliberation and conscious decision making.

Since democracy is a governmental system based more upon reflection and conscious decision making than upon habit and tradition, Durkheim concluded, change is easier to institute. In a democracy, 'everything may for ever remain open to question . . ., everything may be examined' (1957: 84). Thus democracy is not only more open to public scrutiny, but it is also a form of government where a greater range of subjects is open to discussion. Democracy is a system rooted in thought; this is what gives it its 'moral superiority' (1957: 91), and it is also what makes it the governmental form of the future in modern societes. The reason is simple: 'the more societies grow in scope and complexity, the more they need reflection in conducting their affairs. Blind routine and a uniform tradition are useless in running a mechanism of any delicacy' (1957: 89–90).

The reason modern societies are complex and delicate mechanisms, Durkheim believed, is because the division of labor has fostered differentiation and individuation in them. As societies become more complex there grow up a multiplicity of social groups that compete with one another and with the State for influence over the individual. This situation fosters individual liberty and the moral values – particularly the cult of the individual – that make it possible and that are its expression. To be the object of such a cult and to have true liberty, the individual requires 'some physical sphere of action within which . . . [he can] exercise a kind of sovereignty' (1957: 172). That sphere is individual property; the cult of the individual depends directly upon it.

While Durkheim believed in the sacredness of the right of property, this belief by no means led him to a laissez-faire individualism of the sort advocated by classical economists and political conservatives of his day. As we shall see, he was clearly an advocate of what was called at the time 'the new liberalism' – a kind of liberalism that was perfectly willing to accept state intervention in social and economic life in order to strengthen individual rights and liberties (cf. Hobhouse 1911).

Durkheim's focus was always on the *individual* in individual property. He claimed that when we say that individual property is sacred, what we are really expressing is our belief that the individual is sacred; the only reason that violating property is morally wrong is that to do so is to violate the individual to whom it belongs. Durkheim's analyses of the right of individual property are revealingly parallel to his discussion of human dignity and punishment. Just as he believed that we cannot effectively promote human dignity by punishments that violate the dignity of those we punish, he concluded that we cannot reasonably expect to foster individualism by the social and economic policies of classical economics, which are so devastating to weak individuals. For Durkheim, property was not a natural right, nor was it an immutable right. Like the individualism which it supports, property is a social creation and one that developed only slowly in the course of societal evolution. In all societies, 'the range of persons qualified to own is decided by the laws . . . as is the range of things qualified to be owned' (1957: 138). In a modern democracy, property rights are not matters of blind tradition, but are open to conscious deliberation – and change if this seems more efficient or just. The main function of property laws (and, as we have seen, the main function of the State) as far as Durkheim was concerned was to foster individualism. He always viewed property law from that perspective. He concluded that if individual property is to fulfill its social function of protecting individuals, property law must be structured in such a way that it does not violate the moral principle of individualism.

Durkheim pointed out that in modern societies there are two ways to come into possession of something: by inheritance and by exchange or contract. Since inheritance of wealth is an archaic survival which Durkheim believed (or hoped) was destined to disappear, he focussed most of his analyses of modern property law on contract. He discussed inheritance only to argue for its abolition. He based his opposition to inherited wealth on meritocratic arguments of a fairly unambiguous sort: individual advantages and disadvantages should not be based on something as arbitrary as inheritance, for 'the distribution of things amongst individuals can be just only if it be made relative to the social deserts of each' (1957: 214). Unlike many of the French solidarist theorists of his era, with whom he had much in common, Durkheim did not emphasize how difficult it might be to measure 'social merit' with any precision. The main problem with inheritance, he believed, is that 'by creating inequalities amongst men from birth, that are unrelated to merit or services, [it] invalidates the whole contractual system at its very roots' (1957: 213). To explain how this was so and why it posed a serious problem for modern societies, Durkheim examined the nature and origins of the modern, just contract.

As the division of labor and specialization become more pronounced in society, people become increasingly dependent upon exchange for survival, and exchange involves, explicitly or implicitly, contractual relations. Hence, 'the contractual law of civilized peoples becomes ever more voluminous' ([1893, 1902] 1969: 381). While many theorists of his day saw contract law essentially as a business convenience, Durkheim stressed that, like other forms of law, it was mainly a source of social/ moral bonds. Contractual law, no less than penal law, must conform to the moral values of the society. Contracts in fact always rest on a bed of customary notions of equity, and this customary basis is often explicitly recognized in law.

The contract, Durkheim pointed out, appeared relatively recently in the course of social evolution. That is because at least the rudiments of individualism had first to make their appearance for it to be possible for individuals to bind their wills merely by agreeing to do so.[8] Social guarantees of individualism and of contractual law have tended to evolve together. If modern contracts are to conform to today's moral ideals, Durkheim said, they must have three characteristics. First, they must be good faith or *bona fide* contracts, or contracts in which the legal consequences are exclusively determined by the intent of the contracting parties. Second, a contract has to be made by mutual consent: no party to a contract may be compelled (directly or indirectly) to enter into the agreement. Sometimes a contract may meet these two criteria, but be nonetheless revised by the courts if unintended consequences of the contract are patent violations of customary notions of justice and equity. Thus, the third characteristic: the contract must be objectively equitable, which is to say that 'things and services are exchanged at the true and normal value, in short, at the just value' (1957: 211). If this is not the case, the contract does injury to one of the parties and is therefore objectively unjust. Society no longer gives its recognition and sanction to contracts if they are unjust, if they are merely a way of exploiting one of the contracting parties.

Since weaker parties to a negotiation leading to a contract will often be constrained by their subordinate status to agree to terms they would otherwise reject, and since constraint is one of the marks of an unjust contract, a main barrier to just contracts, Durkheim concluded, is inequality. Inequality based upon inherited wealth is particularly blameworthy in this respect since there is no sense in which the beneficiaries could be said to have earned their wealth. Over the decade or so that Durkheim wrote about such matters, his position remained firm. Thus in *Division of Labor* he said that 'there cannot be rich and poor at birth without there being unjust contracts' ([1893, 1902] 1969: 384); and in *Professional Ethics* that 'as long as such sharp class differences exist in society . . . the system operates in conditions which do not allow of justice' (1957: 213).

In general Durkheim's position was a meritocratic one. Inequality was acceptable, and even efficient for society, as long as opportunities were equal and as long as those who had more wealth had earned it. But these conditions could never obtain when wealth was inherited. This is why he felt legislation was needed to institute a system that would better conform to modern notions of morality and justice. In the closing paragraphs of his lectures, Durkheim went further – to suggest that his preference was to go beyond meritocracy toward a social system based more heavily on charity and fellow feeling. He concluded that if we calculate too strictly and reward persons only according to what merit and hard work would justify, some individuals would be left to suffer more than modern sensibilities will ordinarily countenance. Even if some individuals do little to merit a decent standard of living – that is, if they do not generate wealth equivalent to what they need to consume – compassion and respect for the dignity of even 'unworthy' individuals means that we want for them a decent minimum. Finally, Durkheim predicted that since respect for the individual was so integral a part of modern society, 'feelings of human fraternity' (1957: 220) will continue to increase; this will temper more and more the strict demands of meritocracy and lead to an increasingly humane society.

CONCLUSIONS

In several respects Durkheim's analyses as described in the preceding pages are uncharacteristic of his *oeuvre*. The emphasis on, and frank advocacy of, individualism and modern social institutions are not the dominant themes in his work as a whole. But they are important themes. And they are much more visible when focussing on his sociology of law than when studying his other major contributions to social theory. His sociology of law gives us a window onto Durkheim's optimistic and liberal side, a side that did not predominate in his published works following *Division of Labor*, but one that is quite evident in the works of several of his students (Vogt 1983). The sociology of law in Durkheim's work was generally part of his attempt to understand the stages of social evolution; it was his main means of defining social types, a crucial problem in his general sociological theory. In other words, for Durkheim the sociology of law was part of a theory of modernization. He used it to specify the characteristics of modern versus primitive societies. After his research interests turned away from modern societies, where the most important moral rules are expressed in legal terms, and towards primitive societies (Vogt 1976), where those rules are religious in nature, he wrote very little directly on the sociology of law. But even his later works on primitive religions were informed by the social typology he devised using legal phenomena as a defining criterion. Thus when assessing Durkheim's contribution to the sociology of law the first issue to consider is the adequacy of that typology.

Durkheim's method for drawing the typology can still be used with profit. The evolution of law may indeed provide a useful index of the evolution of morality, that is, of predominant attitudes about right and wrong. In the absence of public opinion polls, it is one of the better indices available. Durkheim's chief mistake was to exaggerate the similarity between forms of morality (or solidarity) and types of law. He insisted that the law must follow morality – except in pathological circumstances, which is to say, when it did not. Morality in its turn must follow morphology, that is, the basic facts about the size, density and complexity of the society in question. Durkheim left little room for slippage, gaps, leaks, or resistance in the causal chain that led from morphology to law:

Morphology → Morality → Law

In the case of primitive societies Durkheim apparently assumed that the links in the causal chain were so firm that he could abandon his ordinary method of studying law to uncover forms of morality. Rather, he took the assumed facts of the morphology of simple societies and deduced from those their forms of morality and law. While the laws of literate societies provided easily available evidence for studying moral beliefs and attitudes, in primitive, pre-literate societies this methodological advantage, which was the whole point of studying law, was lost. For primitive societies Durkheim simply assumed that the simplicity of their morphology was enough to speak decisively about their morality and law. In some respects he had little choice. The ethnographic literature available to him was comparatively undeveloped at the time. Today, ethnographic research has challenged many of Durkheim's beliefs about the inflexibility, emotionality and repressiveness of pre-literate societies. Even in societies without legal institutions properly so called (that is, where there is no permanent third party to resolve disputes even when the parties do not request such intervention), there is a great deal of 'restitutive' law and negotiated conflict resolution (Aubert 1983). We can see today that Durkheim's ideal types of primitive and modern society border on being stereotypes. This was in large part because his conception of social evolution was unilinear; his work contains but few hints that there might be different kinds of primitive societies or different kinds of modern societies.

Although Durkheim discussed the study of legal phenomena mostly in terms of its methodological uses, his works also clearly implied substantive claims about the nature and strength of the links between legal and moral phenomena. Durkheim thought that the law was institutionalized morality, but did not analyze in any depth the legal systems that did the institutionalizing. He had little to say about the courts, judges, juries, attorneys, legislatures, legislators, notaries, police and administrative officials that actually make up a modern legal system. Thus he was ·ceptionally vague about the processes by which forms of morality and ¹arity are translated into law. He came close to implying that legal ⸳ns could be made by what Max Weber ridiculed as the vending ⸳udge: 'an automaton into which legal documents and fees are ⸳he top in order that it may spill forth the verdict at the bottom along with the reasons read mechanically from codified paragraphs' (Weber 1978: 979). Because Durkheim was convinced that law making was a fairly unproblematic activity, there was little room in his theory for the idea that modern law is characterized by the logical analysis of the meaning of abstract legal concepts and rules, and therefore that jurisprudence, interpretation and discretion are key elements of moden systems of law. Durkheim's law and morality formed a system that Weber dismissed as a 'law without gaps'.[9]

The basic weakness in Durkheim's sociology of law is not what he said, but in what he did not say. The idea that a society's law usually parallels its moral values seems indubitable. But law, morality and the connections between them are all vastly more complex than Durkheim's works would lead one to believe. We can refer here only to a few of the complexities passed over by Durkheim by way of illustrating the scope of his errors of omission.

Legislators and other law makers could not simply codify and enforce normal moral standards even if they wished to do so. The reason is that law makers have no systematic means of discovering exactly what morality in fact is. For obvious reasons they cannot employ Durkheim's method of using the law to find out what morality is so that they could then use morality to decide what the law should be. In even the simplest cases, where consensus within a society is very high, norms of conduct can be quite complicated. For example, in modern societies murder is usually thought of as the worst crime and the gravest violation of moral norms. But there can be very great debates about the *definition* of murder. Which acts of killing constitute murder – abortion, self-defense, mercy killing, suicide, negligence that leads to another's accidental death? Even assuming agreement on a definition of murder, that is, on a particular kind of wrongful death, sharp conflict may erupt over the proper punishment. Should the wrongdoer be executed, imprisoned for life, imprisoned for from twenty-five years to life with the possibility of being released on parole after one-third of the sentence has been served? The severity of sentencing by judges and juries has routinely been a highly controversial issue in modern societies, including in France at the time Durkheim wrote. (Consider the Dreyfus Affair or Durkheim's debate with Tarde, reported above.) In sum, even where there is widespread agreement on general 'diffuse' moral principles (for example, murder is the greatest wrong and we should reserve our most harsh punishments for it), exceptionally sharp conflicts commonly occur over the correct legal implementation of the moral principles. Durkheim discussed none of this. Rather he claimed that except in pathological circumstances 'all ordinary consciences' agree on what is right and wrong, on the gravity of particular wrongs, and therefore on what ought to be a crime and what its punishment should be.

EMILE DURKHEIM

Even when legislation is very clear about a tort, precise in the stipulation of the punishment, and fully supported by the general population, legal officials may still remain faced with complicated decisions involving the interpretation and application of moral principles. Very often courts have to determine not only whether an individual committed an act but whether that act, in the circumstances in which it was committed, violated the law. Was the defendant 'inciting to riot' or 'exercising a right to free speech'? Is the accused 'guilty of child abuse' or 'a parent with very strict methods of child rearing'? 'Hard cases' (Dworkin 1977) such as these may be the exception rather than the rule, but hard cases are 'normal social facts', just as crimes are. In such cases courts are expected to make decisions not as automatons or vending machines but by applying the moral principles of justice and equity to particular cases.

A *range* of moral opinion will always be present in any reasonably complex society. As we have seen above, Durkheim was well aware of this when he pointed out that moral uniformity is absolutely impossible. But he did not systematically apply this insight to moral opinions about the justness of laws. With modern survey techniques it is fairly easy today to be quite empirical in our studies of the range of moral opinion on an issue. We can specify with some precision what percentages of a population believe that a particular act is very wrong and ought to be a felony, that it is wrong but should be only a misdemeanor, that it is wrong but ought not to be illegal, or that it is perfectly acceptable behavior. Consider, for example, the debates that have raged in various nations over abortion, divorce, homosexuality or the use of cannabis. While it is clear that Durkheim would agree that a 'certain amount' of such disagreement is perfectly normal, it is also clear that the amount he had in mind was much smaller than has been characteristic of Western societies in the nineteenth and twentieth centuries.

Durkheim admitted, indeed he *insisted*, that different societies at different stages of evolution will be strikingly different in their morality and law. But when it was a question of societies at the same stage of evolution, and even more so when the discussion shifted to what was normal within a particular society, Durkheim saw much less room for latitude. His position can be characterized as 'relativistic absolutism', that is, relativism among societies, absolutism within them (Vogt 1982). This means that Durkheim was unwilling to focus on the normal social facts that in any given society agreement will not be total on *any* issue and that on some issues disagreement will be very extensive. The range of opinion on any particular issue may be narrow or wide, but there will always be some range of opinion on every issue. When disagreement leads to deliberation (rather than, say, to terrorism) moral evolution may occur in a manner Durkheim believed to be consonant with the nature of modern democratic society.

Except in some lectures not published in his lifetime and in some early works, Durkheim paid but little attention to what in his own theory were the defining characteristics of modern society. While that constitutes a weakness in his sociology of law and in his theory of modernization, his contribution was nonetheless major. In modern societies, he pointed out, morality is increasingly expressed in a new form – law. As societies, driven by the division of labor, move from an amorphous, diffuse state to a more complex and consciously organized state, the morality appropriate to such societies will tend to become ever more consciously organized, that is, expressed as law. Things that in simpler societies can be accomplished by habit, custom, tradition or religion must be achieved in more highly differentiated societies by legal means. Durkheim's only failing was to describe the laws of modern societies as relatively direct and uncomplicated expressions of moral values. He described modern legal systems in terms more suggestive of mechanical solidarity than of the complex, organic social relationships institutionalized in contemporary legal practices.

NOTES

1 The editor states that according to Marcel Mauss, the text was written between November 1898 and June 1900. Internal evidence also supports this dating; for example, Durkheim's reference to 'our recent law on industrial accidents' – the first of several pieces of legislation on industrial accidents was passed in France in 1898.

2 During this later period, Durkheim was also preparing the second editions of *The Rules* (1901) and *Division of Labor* (1902).

3 This text has commonly been dated to 1902–3, but Besnard's arguments (1987: 124–5) that 1898–9 is correct are decisive.

4 The characteristics of a social type that was primitive or 'less advanced' were, Durkheim said, relatively unproblematic, particularly as defined in opposition to advanced, modern societies which are more 'complex' (*'composées'*) and more 'organized'.

5 Foucault's work (1977) on the subject is in many ways parallel to Durkheim's. But Foucault criticized Durkheim for studying too broad a range of general social types. This, he claimed, led Durkheim to misinterpret the rise of the prison and the reduction in the severity of punishment as a sign that individual freedom was increasing. In fact, Foucault believed, prisons and physically mild punishments were new tactics for maintaining power over individuals.

6 Similar arguments can be found in Ch. 5 of *Division of Labor*, Ch. 3 of *The Rules*, and Ch. 10 of *Professional Ethics*.

7 This link between individualism and the State is also one of the main themes in the work of Durkheim's colleague, C. Bouglé (1899).

8 For an extension of this analysis by one of Durkheim's students see Davy (1922).

9 Weber was not directly referring to Durkheim's work here, nor even indirectly to Durkheim's idea of a nearly automatic conversion of moral rules and social forms into an uncontroversial legal order. The principle of the 'gaplessness' of the law has a very intricate history and one quite distinct from the issues

discussed in this chapter. The basic point is simply the instructive contrast between Weber, who thought that cases 'where the statute fails to provide a clear rule' (1978: 886) were central to understanding modern law, and Durkheim, who had little room for such complications in his theory.

REFERENCES

Aubert, V. (1983) *In Search of Law: Sociological Approaches to Law*, Oxford: Martin Robertson.

Besnard, P. (ed.) (1983) *The Sociological Domain: The Durkheimians and the Founding of French Sociology*, Cambridge: Cambridge University Press.

—— (1987) *L'Anomie: Ses Usages et ses Fonctions dans la Discipline Sociologique depuis Durkheim*, Paris: Presses Universitaires de France.

Bouglé, C. (1899) *Les Idées Egalitaires: Etude Sociologique*, Paris: Alcan.

Davy, G. (1922), *La Foi Jurée: Etude Sociologique du Problème du Contrat*, Paris: Alcan.

Durkheim, E. ([1893, 1902] 1969) *The Division of Labor in Society*, trans. G. Simpson, New York: Free Press.

—— ([1895] 1982) *The Rules of Sociological Method*, trans. W. D. Halls, New York: Free Press.

—— (1895) 'Crime et santé social', *Revue Philosophique* 39: 518–23.

—— (1898) 'Note sur la morphologie sociale', *Année Sociologique* 2: 521–2.

—— ([1901] 1969) 'Deux lois de l'évolution pénale', in J. Duvignaud (ed.), *Journal Sociologique*, Paris: Presses Universitaires de France.

—— ([1909] 1970) 'Sociologie et sciences sociales', in J.-C Filloux (ed.), *La Science Sociale et l'Action*, Paris: Presses Universitaires de France.

—— ([1924] 1961) *Moral Education: A Study in the Theory and Application of the Sociology of Education*, trans. E. K. Wilson and H. Schnurer, New York: Free Press.

—— (1957) *Professional Ethics and Civic Morals*, trans. C. Brookfield, London: Routledge & Kegan Paul.

Durkheim, E., and Fauconnet, P. (1903) 'Sociologie et sciences sociales', *Revue Philosophique* 55: 465–97.

Dworkin, R. (1977) *Taking Rights Seriously*, Cambridge, MA: Harvard University Press.

Foucault, M. (1977) *Discipline and Punish: The Birth of the Prison*, New York: Pantheon Books.

Hobhouse, L. ([1911] 1930) *Liberalism*, London: Williams & Norgate.

Tarde, G. (1895), 'Criminalité et santé sociale', *Revue Philosophique*, 39: 148–62.

Vogt, W. P. (1976) 'The uses of studying primitives: a note on the Durkheimians, 1890–1940', *History and Theory* 15: 33–44.

—— (1982) 'Relativistic absolutism in moral education', *New York University Education Quarterly* 13: 29–33.

—— (1983) 'Obligation and right: the Durkheimians and the sociology of law', in P. Besnard (ed.), *The Sociological Domain: The Durkheimians and the Founding of French Sociology*, Cambridge: Cambridge University Press.

Weber, M. (1978), *Economy and Society*, Berkeley, CA: University of California Press.

4

DURKHEIM'S POLITICAL SOCIOLOGY

Hans-Peter Müller

Institutional analyses of government, parliament, parties, elections, legislation and bureaucracy – the classical topics of political sociology in the narrow sense – are absent from Durkheim's writings. The subject was given no place in his classification of sociology, and no independent heading in the *Année Sociologique*.[1] But the questions Durkheim asks about the interrelation between social structure, politics and culture provide the beginnings of a political analysis. He seeks to establish a social configuration capable of securing the social structure of dynamic industrial capitalism within social and political organizations. And he seeks to achieve this in such a way that the modern ideal of justice – 'moral individualism' – becomes a reality.

Durkheim believed that rapid technological and economic progress had driven modern society into a crisis of anomie, which needed to be eliminated by means of institutional reform. Durkheim's political analysis of professional groups, State and democracy, was a response to the crisis. He adopted a normative standpoint, namely the search for a dynamic *and* just social order, from the outset.

In this essay, I will consider Durkheim's analysis of social structure and the State in its contemporary context of political and social crisis. Following this, his writings on politics in the *Leçons de Sociologie* will be discussed and critically evaluated.

THE POLITICAL CRISIS

Like many nineteenth-century thinkers, Durkheim traced the widespread unease felt in European societies to the rapid change in social structures from an agrarian-corporate society to an industrial-capitalistic society. According to his diagnosis, rapid change led to a *moral crisis* with specific historical and national features (Bellah 1973: 9–55; Filloux 1977; König 1975; Müller 1983: 1–60; 1988: 129–58; Tiryakian 1978: 187–236). Although the French Revolution had established a binding normative framework in 1789, epitomized by the slogan 'Liberty, Equality, Brotherhood', it had as yet proven impossible to realize these values in appropriate institutions. The succession between revolution and restoration in France underlined this failure. The Third Republic was the eighth regime since 1789, after three monarchies, two empires and two republics. Between 1789 and 1870, fourteen different constitutions had been tried. The double shock of the defeat in the Franco-Prussian War of 1870–1 and the Paris Commune had seriously dented the self-image of the 'grande nation,' and various ways of coming to terms with this trauma were found.

The Third Republic's extreme fragmentation and its division into three irreconcilable political camps were an expression of this. The *conservatives*, backed by the Catholic Church, the military, certain sections of the bureaucracy and the industrial elite, were thoroughly anti-democratic, anti-parliamentary, anti-intellectual and anti-semitic. They wished to put an end to the moral and intellectual anarchy which they thought resulted from rampant rationalism, self-centred, godless individualism and mass democracy through the restoration of the monarchy. The *radicals*, including the working classes and parts of the critical intelligentsia, favored a socialist revolution. Their supporters, who were undemocratic and anti-parliamentary, held capitalism responsible for the 'social question' and economic anomie. Between these two poles, which can be summed up in the twin battle cries of 'terminer la Révolution' and 'continuer la Révolution', were the *Republicans*, supported by the bourgeoisie and the intelligentsia. They were anti-clerical, anti-military and hostile to Bourbons and Bonapartists alike, and sought to eradicate economic and moral anomie through the 'modernization' of all areas of social life. For them, neither restoration nor revolution but properly planned reforms alone could realize the values of the French Revolution and end the crisis.

Ending the crisis required the solution of three questions: the national question, the social question and the education question. For Durkheim, as a convinced supporter of the Third Republic, the solution to the national question was for the irreconcilable political camps to swear allegiance to republicanism. Only in this way could the problem of legitimacy and loyalty, the Achilles' heel of the Third Republic, be overcome, France's tattered self-image as a 'grande nation' be restored, and an appropriate place in the concert of European powers be won back. To achieve this, all social groups must participate in political life; only then could the enfeebled 'spirit of collectivity regain . . . its organic unity' (1888: 47). The social question could be solved only when social inequality in the economy had been eliminated and social justice created in the relations between employers and workers. The solution of the education question required restraining the conservative influence of the Catholic Church in the schools and validating the democratic spirit and individual morality through a wholly secular education.

BASIC PREMISES

Durkheim addressed these questions in terms of some basic sociological ideas about the structure and function of modern societies. The central structural principle is the *division of labor*: Durkheim's 'Etude sur l'organisation des sociétés supérieures' (the revealing and subsequently abandoned title of the first edition) remained his frame of reference throughout his life (1893; the tenth [1978] edition is cited here). He discussed the dominant problems of modern society in terms of it, and it is fundamental to his political writings (Allardt 1968: 1–16; Giddens 1978; Müller 1983: 117ff). In the eighteenth and nineteenth centuries, the change from traditional to modern society was, generally speaking, conceived in terms of the division of labor. Various schools of social thought were distinguished from one another only in their assessment of its consequences.

The *individualistic-utilitarian tradition*, from Smith's 'classical political economy' to the sociology of Spencer, stressed progress in productivity, with its beneficial influence upon the wealth of nations and the welfare of their citizens. The *collectivist-socialist tradition*, from Marx to Schmoller, stressed the costs of the division of labor, such as the creation of classes, exploitation and alienation. The *French tradition* is fragmented: Saint-Simon welcomed industrial society, which was to do away with the parasitic feudal State in favor of an economic association of producers and to promote technical progress; Comte saw the division of labor as a source of social fragmentation which can only be eliminated by a strong State and by philosophy providing strict collective ideals. Durkheim's central theme is neither the relation between the division of labor and productivity nor the relation between the division of labor and the class system; it is the link between the division of labor and solidarity, a noted theme in the French tradition. Solidarity, he thought, prevails when a society's social structure and its system of values closely correspond. 'Solidarity' is a *moral phenomenon*, for social institutions will radiate *moral authority* and attain legitimacy only when they at least approximately reflect the values of a society. Thus for Durkheim the question is whether, as the central structural characteristic of modern societies, the division of labor is a source of morality or whether instead it is responsible for their crisis of values.

The potential effects of the division of labor on the creation of morality are demonstrated in his contrast of archaic and modern societies. Archaic societies consist of small, segmentally differentiated units, in which a strong collective conscience creates solidarity out of similarities between members. This *'mechanical' solidarity directly* integrates the individual within the community. Modern societies, by contrast, consist of large, functionally differentiated spheres of life. The division of labor creates a network of interdependencies between them. *Organic solidarity* thus consists of differences, and binds the individual *indirectly* to society by integrating him or her into whatever fields of activity he or she is involved in. Differentiation and specialization favor the development of the individual personality because different special activities require different abilities. As the individualization of the members of society advances, they can no longer be integrated within one single collective conscience. Instead, the collective conscience itself also becomes differentiated into a plenitude of function-specific codes or norms, which nevertheless retain their moral character. There is, consequently, a link between the division of labor, solidarity and morality: 'In a word, since the division of labor becomes the prime source of social solidarity, it also becomes the basis of the moral order' (Durkheim 1978: 396).

But the precise link between the division of labor and organic solidarity is notoriously unclear (Luhmann 1977: 17–34; Lukes 1973: 137–78; Müller 1983: 128ff; Parsons 1967: 166–91; Pizzorno 1963: 1–36; Poggi 1972: 165ff; Pope and Johnson 1983: 681–92; Sirianni, 1984: 449–70; Tyrell 1985: 181–250). Only in the concluding chapters of *The Division of Labor in Society*, on the *abnormal* forms of the division of labor, does one learn about *normal* emergence of organic solidarity. Durkheim distinguished three pathological forms: the anomic, the enforced division of labor, and 'another abnormal form', which might be termed lack of internal organizational coordination. *Anomie*, which is expressed in economic crises, the antagonism between capital and labor, and anarchy in science, arises at times of rapid change, during which new organs and functions develop without a corresponding development of rules of cooperation and therefore of social ties. *Normally*, Durkheim assumes, rules develop *spontaneously* in the course of social intercourse, as part of a gradual process of *habitualization* in which the exchange is first regulated provisionally, then as a habit and last of all legally. This hypothesis of the self-regulation of social life therefore relies on the factors of 'time' and 'continuous contact' between the various bodies concerned. In the long term, organic solidarity 'normally' but mysteriously arises from functional interdependencies. Anomie, the lack of regulation or deregulation of social life, is the result of rapid and radical social change. But anomie does not mean a fundamental *crisis of the system*, but rather a *crisis of adaptation*, and continuous contact will eventually produce new rules and a new functional equilibrium between the divided functions, thus assuring social integration.

Though anomie can be eliminated by the gradual development of new rules, in the case of the *enforced division of labor* it is 'these very rules themselves which are the cause of the ills' (Durkheim 1978: 367). Rules come to be felt as oppressive and unjust when they represent a social order which no longer corresponds to the developed moral conscience and can therefore only be maintained by force. Class conflict and anger over unjust contracts are products of the discrepancy between traditional social structure and the feeling of social justice. The traditional allocation of status according to the privileges of birth flies in the face of the natural distribution of talents and is antithetical to modern professional society, which must assign status according to performance, not social origin. Durkheim therefore champions formal equality of opportunity, freedom to choose a profession. Force points to a crisis in the system, a constitutive defect in a society's system of rules, which can only be eliminated by radical changes in the rules themselves and can by no means be left to the healing power of time. Revolutionary change of this kind would necessarily have to alter property rights, control over the means of production, and the distribution mechanism for scarce goods and resources, which is to say a radical transformation of the social order such as Marx had foreseen.

Anomie therefore indicates a *transitional* state of absence of rules; *force* indicates an illegitimate order, whose unjust rules *systematically* create an asymmetrical division of power which favors a small elite at the expense of the mass of society. Which type of crisis is held to be dominant is of decisive importance as regards both the theory of society in general and political sociology in particular (Horton 1964: 283–300; Lukes 1967: 134–56). Marx traces the origins of the enforced division of labor to the laws of capitalist production, which necessarily lead to exploitation and alienation. In so doing he provides the premises of the German tradition, according to which the division of labor is always seen in the context of the development of classes. For Durkheim, on the other hand, the anomic division of labor is the dominant fact. He regards force as a temporary phenomenon, associated with anomie, which disappears when new rules for the coordination of functions and the cooperation of groups have been institutionalized.

Since, according to Durkheim's diagnosis, modern societies are in a state of transitional anomic crisis, though not a fundamental crisis of the system, the 'cure' lies not in a radical transformation, but in subjecting social relations to planned social change. In this respect, Durkheim is a typical representative of the French tradition, which stresses the 'moral value of the division of labor':

> It is wrong therefore to contrast the society that derives from a community of beliefs with one based on cooperation, ascribing only a moral character to the former and seeing in the latter no more than an economic grouping. In reality, cooperation also has its own intrinsic morality.

> (Durkheim 1978: 208)

Like Saint-Simon, Durkheim hails the 'great transformation' unreservedly and with evolutionary optimism. In the industrial revolution and the implementation of the capitalist economic order, in the political revolution and the emergence of democratic relations, and also in the ethical revolution and the emergence of individualistic morality, he sees the outlines of a 'new framework', which appears to hold out the promise of a reconciliation between the social order and individual freedom.

Yet the connection between the division of labor and organic solidarity ultimately remains unexplained. There were three particular problems which Durkheim was never able to solve:

1 The role of *collective actors*: since he bases his argument largely on the antithesis between the individual and society, the vehicles of organic solidarity are not dealt with in detail.[2]
2 The role of the *State*: Durkheim's appraisal in the *Division of Labor* is ambiguous. Against Comte's collectivist appeal for a strong State, he suggests that the modern State itself is only a by-product of social differentiation. His objection to Spencer's liberal 'night-watchman' State is that the State has already become a central regulating body.
3 The role of the *modern collective conscience*: on the one hand, he gives the impression that the division of labor is taking the place that the collective conscience formerly held as the source of solidarity and that the collective representations are being diluted by the 'cult of the individual'; on the other hand he considers the cult of the individual to be the ultimate and supreme collective ideal of modern times.

THE POLITICAL ANALYSES

These unsolved problems from the *Division of Labor* are the subject of Durkheim's political writings. In the *Leçons de Sociologie*, he discusses the role of professional groups as the vehicles of organic solidarity, the functions of the State and democracy, and also the significance of 'moral individualism' as a modern collective ideal. He reasons that if it is possible through institutional reforms to achieve smooth coordination between professional groups, the democratic State and the individualistic ideal, the division of labor will create organic solidarity and ensure social integration. In *Leçons de Sociologie*, he therefore outlines the *nomos* of a functionally differentiated society and sketches a normative picture of a dynamic and just social order.

Durkheim's announced 'étude spéciale sur le régime corporatif et les lois de son évolution' was never completed (1960: 451). His ideas on social groups remained vague. Nevertheless, social groups are at the heart of his view of institutional reform. He considers the establishment of social groups to be of central economic and socio-political importance. They are the appropriate vehicles for economic and political organization alike. *Professional* groups are supposed to eliminate anomie in the economy. Industry and trade, according to Durkheim, have been deregulated and freed from political control for over a hundred years, and no organizational network has taken over the essential tasks of regulation. The trade unions were crushed at the time of the 1871 Commune and it was not until 1884 that the workers regained the right to form trade unions. But no successful solution was found to the 'social question' through a system of industrial relations. The 'bosses' steadfastly refused even to negotiate with workers' representatives. It is this paradoxical development – increasing autonomy and deregulation of the economy on the one hand and the primacy of the economy in modern societies on the other – that is the source of the oppressive anomie which finds expression in the social question.

Durkheim's solution was a particular institutional reform. He outlined a remarkable vision of the future of corporate bodies, modern analogues to the medieval guilds, in the regulation of economic life (cf. Filloux, infra). The proposal to make economic groupings the basis of political organization contains a strong element of corporativism. Once again it is the French experience of the failure of all intermediate bodies which lies behind this. The result of the abolition of 'intermediate bodies' during the French Revolution, and the subsequent centralization, was a structure in which a centralized State and a mass of individuals stood face to face. 'A society composed of an infinite mass of unorganized individuals, which an hypertrophied State seeks to limit and restrain, is a veritable sociological monstrosity' (1969: 129). In Durkheim's view, the root cause of the anomie in the economy and in society is therefore a parallel structural weakness: 'Our political malaise therefore has the same origin as our social malaise: the lack of secondary organs intercalated between the individual and the State' (1969). Durkheim's conclusion was that the professional groups should serve as intermediate authorities between the State and the individual and act as counterweights to State power. The political reorganization of society and the establishment of a system of checks and balances to the State are the necessary minimum prerequisites for transforming the values of the French Revolution into an institutional reality.

In demonstrating the feasibility of this reform Durkheim is compelled to re-examine the concept of the *State* and State power. In *The Division of Labor in Society* the concept of the State fluctuates between a view of the State as a mechanical product of social differentiation and as an independent central body. In a later study on the development of criminal law, Durkheim suggested that the connection between the state of social differentiation and the degree of centralization of political power is historically contingent (1901: 65–95). The absolutism of State power depends not on the number and scope of the State's functions, as Spencer had wrongly assumed, but on the existence of opposing forces. This important insight suggested to Durkheim the idea of drawing a conceptual distinction between the State and political society. He defines the State as the representation of sovereign power. But the State itself is no more than the supreme legislative body encompassing all the other secondary groups in society which make up 'political society'. Durkheim elaborates his conception of the State by defining it as:

> a group of *sui generis* officials, within which representations and volitions are worked out which commit the collectivity, even though they are not the product of the collectivity. . . . The State is a special organ, whose task it is to work out certain representations which are valid for the collectivity. These representations are distinguished from the other collective representations by their greater degree of consciousness and reflection.
>
> (1969: 86, 87)

The State therefore consists of a group of officials, who represent a kind of articulation, information and decision-making center which seizes diffuse collective representations in society, systematizing and transforming them into collectively binding decisions.

Together with this controlling function, the State has integrative functions. It is the 'protector of the collective ideal'. In traditional society, it stood guard over the *cult of the State*. Under archaic collectivism, in which the individual counted for little, the State was everything. In modern societies the relation between the State and the individual is reversed and the individual becomes sacrosanct, yet without the State thereby losing any of its functions:

> The fact that history actually provides a justification for this relation of cause and effect between the progress of moral individualism and the progress of the State is clearly shown by the facts. Leaving aside abnormal cases which we will discuss later, the stronger the State, the more the individual is respected.
>
> (1969: 93)

But this argument is only valid in specific circumstances. In their absence, despotism develops: 'every society is despotic, that is provided nothing from without intervenes to contain its despotism' (1969: 96). Durkheim distinguishes two pathological forms, collective particularism and State tyranny. In *collective particularism* the State is weak and the dominant groups rule. For example, in the Middle Ages the guilds ruled the individual and tied him wholly to local authority. *State tyranny* arose when no other powers opposed the State. There must therefore always be a system of opposing forces, which are counterbalanced. 'And it is from this conflict of social forces that individual freedoms are born' (1969: 99).

From the analysis of pathological forms, Durkheim draws the following conclusions: *balance of power* and *communication* are the two decisive minimum conditions which must characterize the relation between secondary groups and the State so that individual autonomy may develop. *Democracy* is the political form which combines these two properties within itself and thus minimizes pathological developments. Both the conceptions of *direct democracy* and of *liberal democracy*, as embodied in the Third Republic, are inadequate. They underestimate the significance of such a balance of powers for the realization of the essential legacy of the French Revolution: moral individualism. So a balance of power between the professional groups and a democratic State is the central structural prerequisite for ensuring the development of the 'cult of the individual.'

But is not moral individualism also a kind of secular religion, a *civil religion* in the sense used by Rousseau?[3] Durkheim assumes that the central values of a society, regardless of whether it is secular or religious, always tend to be seen as 'sacred' in the eyes of its members. The question of its strength is a question of whether it is binding. The Dreyfus Affair provided empirical evidence of the binding character of moral individualism (1898: 7–13). In the attacks of Dreyfus' opponents against 'godless individualism' and the championing of individual freedom by his supporters, Durkheim recognized the first signs that, however open to dispute it might be, the 'cult of the individual' was the supreme yardstick for evaluating social relations. Beyond all the heated disputes, there stands the religious nature of the ideal, for moral individualism represents the *sacredness of the individual*:

> This human individual . . . is considered to be sacred, in the ritual sense so to speak. He has something of the transcendent majesty ascribed by the Churches in all ages to their gods. . . . And this precisely is the origin of the respect bestowed upon it. . . . This morality is therefore not simply a hygienic discipline or a prudent economy of existence; it is a religion of which man is both the disciple and the God.
>
> (1898: 264, 265)

The religious aspect which Durkheim ascribes to moral individualism explains the strong reaction of public opinion to the Dreyfus sentence. The judgment was seen as a sacrilege against the sacred collective ideal, the freedom and inviolability of the individual. The public outcry therefore was not only an expression of sympathy for the victim; it also served to purify and restore the religious ideal of individualism.

Durkheim was confident that the development of the legacy of 1789 under a State which is the supreme guardian of the individualistic collective ideal, professional organizations which are the regulating bodies of economics and politics, and a rational system of upbringing and education is the best way of safeguarding the development of autonomous personalities and will lead to a truly democratic society. He was therefore not afraid to advocate peaceful *patriotism*. This is to be distinguished from aggressive nationalism in that cosmopolitan values at the national level will serve as a model for the other nations of Europe. Of course, even in Durkheim's time, this ideal conception was in striking contrast to the aggressive imperialism of the Third Republic. And it was to become completely nonsensical on the outbreak of World War I, at the height of nationalist war fever. Durkheim's wartime writings note the growth of mechanical solidarity, but lament the high price that has to be paid for it, namely moral regression into archaic collectivism (Denis and Durkheim 1915; Durkheim 1915). He seeks to explain the violent outburst of German nationalism by reference to the war mentality, as expressed above all in the writings of Treitschke. He can do no more than register the fact that it is a sociological monstrosity, which is pathological and therefore can only be transitory: 'A State cannot maintain itself when it has humanity against it' (Durkheim 1915: 45).

THE CORPORATIVE SOCIETY AND THE STATE

Durkheim's institutional program amounts to corporativism, an idea whose origins go back to Saint-Simon. The *project for a corporative society* appears to him to have three advantages:

1 It makes it possible for the economy to be controlled by the regulatory bodies of the State. The aim of control is to eliminate the individual struggle for existence: 'it is neither necessary nor even possible for social life to be free from struggle. The role of solidarity is not to eliminate competition, but to moderate it' (1978: 357). This 'moderation' would improve social relations and thereby contribute to *organic solidarity*.
2 The political control of the economy increases opportunities for democratic State intervention in favor of the individual, because in principle all areas of social life are now subordinated to the State (*social justice*).
3 The prospects for the achievement of *moral individualism* appear to him to be most favorable if these two socio-structural and institutional prerequisites are met.

The model of a corporative society also serves to overcome the irreconcilable *theoretical* positions of economic utilitarianism and socialism (Mauss 1971: 27–31; Neyer 1960: 32–76; Pels 1984: 309–29). In common with the *utilitarians*, such as Spencer, Durkheim accepts the primacy of the economy, though without feeling bound thereby to see society as an economic association. However, utilitarianism, applied to modern State and professional organizations, underestimates the need for political organization and coordination. It completely overlooks the socio-cultural framework within which economic and political action are confined, and which lays down standards of legitimate behavior as well as social aspirations and therefore makes for a genuine increase in organic solidarity.

Although Durkheim's program concurs with various trends in *socialism* with respect to the social question, social justice and the political regulation of the economy, with respect to means and methods it diverges sharply. Neither violent revolution nor the socialization of the means of production appears to him to be necessary for social change. Moreover, socialism in his eyes is not merely the question of the workers or of particular groups or classes, but concerns the society as a whole.[4]

The intellectual reception of Durkheim's model of professional groups points to its links with both traditional corporatism and Mussolini's corporate fascism (Mitchell 1931: 87–106; Ranulf 1939: 16–34). But the connections with both of them are somewhat superficial. Although the function of 'intermediarity' does indeed display analogies with the 'intermediate bodies' of the *Ancien Régime*, these were based on a hierarchical society with legalized inequality and privileges apportioned on the basis of birth. The corporativist model of fascism makes professional groups subordinate to the dictates of the totalitarian State and in this respect does not share the advantages of relative autonomy and individual freedom that are part of Durkheim's model. Finally, there is a parallel between Durkheim's and Hegel's conception of the State, civil society and the family. The State conceived as the repository and guardian of the collective ideal, as the body which helps society towards awareness of itself and which plays the role of custodian of the general interest, might well have come from Hegel's philosophy of law. However, Durkheim sharply criticizes Hegel, who represents for Durkheim the renaissance of archaic collectivism and mysticism (1969: 90). The central difference between the two conceptions, however, resides in the fact that, according to Hegel's conception, the State itself is the object of the collective ideal, whereas in Durkheim's model it is the individual that is so.

Durkheim can be described as a typical protagonist of the *normative theory of democracy* (Prager 1981). Representatives of this tradition first devise an ideal system and then enquire about the conditions for its realization. However important this normative approach may be to the task of appraising institutions, discussing constitutions and devising utopias, it displays a central weakness, from which Durkheim's political writings also suffer (Kern and Müller 1986). It remains unclear how and in what structural and functional conditions the State and professional groups can actually perform the tasks normatively ascribed to them. Under what conditions does the group of officials comprising the State

105

advance to the common good? Durkheim says that the State officials *should* renounce the pursuit of their own selfish interests in favor of the common interest; they should not establish trade unions of officials, for example. But if they nevertheless act according to their own interests, which is empirically probable, Durkheim can do no more than interpret this as a pathological phenomenon. These 'pathological' forms of behavior, however, correspond to the 'normal' conception of the state of other classical sociological theorists. The Marxian conception, for example, according to which the ruling State in certain circumstances represents only the State of the ruling class, constitutes the typical case of *State despotism*. Weber's conception, according to which political institutions are the preferred arena for the ceaseless struggle between rival status groups for power in a State, is Durkheim's pathological case of *collective particularism*.

A similar situation obtains where the corporations are concerned: professional groups and not trade unions *should* regulate industrial relations. Durkheim ascribes a moral value only to professional groups. Trade unions are dismissed as purely combative interest groups. However, historically speaking, it was precisely their readiness to engage in conflict – such as strikes and wage disputes – that enabled the implementation of the workers' demands that achieved Durkheim's goals: moderating the effects of economic struggles, thereby preventing radical conflicts (anomie) and maintaining social peace (moral order).

What this shows is that Durkheim lacks an account of the relationships between ideas and institutions, values and interests, groups and stratification, and power structure. The imbalance which results in his sociological writing from the excessive weight given to moral regulation and the undervaluing of power and group interests is also responsible for the curious relationship in his political writings between normality and pathology, and for the paradoxical result that the 'normal' is, in empirical terms, rare and exceptional, while 'pathological' developments are, empirically, typical.

Durkheim avoided these topics out of a deep aversion for the intrigue-ridden everyday political life of the Third Republic and his conviction that scientific sociology was not the province of the ideologue. But his awareness of the crises around him compelled him to develop a political standpoint which linked social structure, politics and culture together. This political standpoint was not an expression of the conservative longing for collective order (Coser 1960: 211–32; Nisbet 1967). Rather it was a reformist attempt to link the dynamic of the socio-structural development of the division of labor to the advance of an individualistic morality, through an institutional framework capable of resolving the problem of social order and individual freedom. It is a subtle irony of history, and perhaps no coincidence, that neither Marx's socialist society as the 'kingdom of freedom' nor Weber's sombre vision of bureaucratic ossification in a new 'cage of servitude' has become a reality. But the elements of Durkheim's reformism, including regulated economics, modern welfare States and individualistic morality, became the institutional reality of almost all the industrial societies of Western Europe, and have come to be seen as Durkheim saw them: the fulfillment of collective obligations (Alber 1984: 225–51; Bendix 1960: 181–210; Janowitz 1976; Müller 1983: 175ff).

NOTES

1 This is the general trend of the secondary literature on Durkheim's political writings; cf. M. Bach (1990), H. E. Barnes (1920), P. Birnbaum (1976), T. Bottomore (1981), S. Fenton (1984), J. C. Filloux (1970), A. Giddens (1977a), M. J. Hawkins (1981), F. Hearn (1985), I. L. Horowitz (1982), B. Lacroix (1981), K. Meier (1988), H.-P. Müller (1983), M. Richter (1960) and K. Thompson (1982).
2 This shortcoming forced Durkheim to add a further preface on the professional groups to the second edition.
3 For Durkheim's 'Cult of the Individual', see R. N. Bellah (1973), A. Giddens (1977b), C. E. Marske (1987), M. Mitchell (1976), H.-P. Müller (1986) and E. Wallwork (1972).
4 Cf. his reviews of A. Labriola (1897) and of S. Merlino (1899). See also his contribution to the discussion *Sur l'Internationalisme et Lutte des Classes*, the *Libres Entretiens* (1905–6), partly reprinted in *La Science Sociale et l'Action* (1970), as well as his lecture on *Le Socialisme* (1971).

REFERENCES

Alber, J. (1984) 'Versorgungsklassen im Wohlfahrtsstaat', *Kölner Zeitschrift für Soziologie und Sozialpsychologie* 36: 225–51.
Allardt, E. (1968) 'Emile Durkheim: sein Beitrag zur politischen Soziologie', *Kölner Zeitschrift für Soziologie und Sozialpsychologie* 20: 1–16.
Bach, M. (1990), 'Individualism and legitimation: paradoxes and perspectives on the political sociology of Emile Durkheim', *European Journal of Sociology* 37: 187–98.
Barnes, H. E. (1920) 'Durkheim's contribution to the reconstruction of political theory', *Political Science Quarterly* 35: 236–54.
Bellah, R. N. (1973) 'Introduction', in E. Durkheim, *On Morality and Society*, Chicago: University of Chicago Press.
Bendix, R. (1960) 'Social stratification and the Community', *European Journal of Sociology* 1: 181–210.
Birnbaum, P. (1976) 'La conception durkheimienne de l'Etat: l'apolitisme des fonctionnaires', *Revue Française de Sociologie* 17, 2: 247–58.
Bottomore, T. (1981) 'A Marxist consideration of Durkheim', *Social Forces* 59, 4: 902–17.
Coser, L. A. (1960) 'Durkheim's conservatism and its implications for his sociological theory', in K. H. Wolff (ed.), *Emile Durkheim*, Columbus, Ohio: Ohio State University Press.

Denis, E. and Durkheim, E. (1915) *Qui a Voulu la Guerre? Les Origines de la Guerre d'après les Documents Diplomatiques*, Paris: Colin.

Durkheim, E. (1888) 'Cours de science sociale. Leçon d'ouverture', *Revue Internationale de l'Enseignement* 15: 23–48 Also in [1970] *La Science Sociale et l'Action*, ed. and intro. J. C. Filloux, Paris: Presses Universitaires de France.

—— (1897) Review of A. Labriola, *Essais sur la Conception Materialiste de l'Histoire*, *Revue Philosophique* 44: 645–51.

—— (1898) 'L'individualisme et les intellectuels', *Revue Bleue*, 4e serie, 10: 7–13. Reprinted in [1970] *La Science Sociale et l'Action*, ed. and intro. J. C. Filloux, Paris: Presses Universitaires de France.

—— (1899) Review of S. Merlino, *Formes et Essences du Socialisme*, *Revue Philosophique* 48: 433–9.

—— (1901) 'Deux lois de l'evolution pénale', *Année Sociologique* 4: 65–95. Reprinted in *Journal Sociologique* (1969), Paris: Presses Universitaires de France.

—— (1905–6) Contribution to discussion *Sur l'Internationalisme et Lutte des Classes*, *Libres Entretiens*, 2: 17, 27, 30–3, 35, 39–42, 45, 56–7, 147–8, 150, 412, 420–36, 480–4. Partly reprinted in [1970] *La Science Sociale et l'Action*, ed. and intro. J. C. Filloux, Paris: Presses Universitaires de France.

—— (1908) 'Sur l'Etat, les fonctionnaires et le public; le fonctionnaire citoyen; syndicats de fonctionnaires', *Libres Entretiens*, 4. Partly reprinted in V. Karady [ed.] [1975] *Textes*, Vol. 3, Paris: Miniut.

—— (1915) *L'Allemagne Au-dessus de Tout: la Mentalité Allemande et la Guerre*, Paris: Colin.

—— (1960) *Le Suicide. Etude de Sociologie*, new edn, Paris: Presses Universitaires de France.

—— (1969) *Leçons de Sociologie. Physique des Moeurs et du Droit*, 2nd edn, Paris: Presses Universitaires de France.

—— (1970) *La Science Sociale et l'Action*, ed. and intro. J. C. Filloux, Paris: Presses Universitaires de France.

—— (1971) Lecture on *Le Socialisme*, 2nd ed, Paris: Presses Universitaires de France.

—— (1973) *On Morality and Society*, ed. and intro. R. N. Bellah, Chicago: University of Chicago Press.

—— (1978) *De la Division du Travail Social*, 10th edn, Paris: Presses Universitaires de France.

Fenton, S. (1984) *Durkheim and Modern Sociology*, Cambridge: Cambridge University Press.

Filloux, J. C. (1970) 'Introduction', in E. Durkheim, *La Science Sociale et l'Action*, Paris: Presses Universitaires de France.

—— (1977) *Durkheim et le Socialisme*, Geneva/Paris: Librairie Droz.

Giddens, A. (1977a) 'Durkheim's political sociology', in *Studies in Social and Political Theory*, London: Hutchinson.

—— (1977b) 'The "individual" in the writings of Emile Durkheim', *Studies in Social and Political Theory*, London: Hutchinson.

—— (1978) *Durkheim*, Glasgow: Fontana.

Hawkins, M. J. (1981) 'Emile Durkheim on democracy and absolutism', *History of Political Thought* 2, 2: 369–90.

Hearn, F. (1985) 'Durkheim's political sociology: corporatism, state autonomy, and democracy', *Social Research* 52, 2: 151–78.

Horowitz, I. L. (1982) 'Socialization without politicization. Durkheim, Emile, theory of the modern state', *Political Theory* 10: 353–77.

Horton, J. (1964) 'The dehumanization of anomie and alienation: a problem in the ideology of sociology', *British Journal of Sociology* 15: 283–300.

Janowitz, M. (1976) *Social Control of the Welfare State*, New York: Elsevier.

Kern, L. and Müller, H.-P. (ed.) (1986) *Gerechtigkeit, Diskurs oder Markt? Die neuen Ansätze in der Vertragstheorie*, Opladen: Westdeutscher Verlag.

König, R. (1975) *Kritik der historisch-existentialistischen Soziologie*, Munich: Piper.

Labriola, A. (1897) 'Essais sur la conception materialiste de l'histoire', *Revue philosophique* 44: 645–51. Reprinted in E. Durkheim [1970] *La Science Sociale et l'Action*, ed. and intro. J. C. Filloux, Paris: Presses Universitaires de France.

Lacroix, B. (1981) *Durkheim et le Politique*, Montreal: Presses de la Fondation Nationale des Sciences Politiques.

Luhmann, N. (1977) 'Arbeitsteilung und Moral. Durkheims Theorie', in E. Durkheim, *Über soziale Arbeitsteilung*.

Lukes, S. (1967) 'Alienation and anomie', in P. Laslett and W. G. Runciman (eds), *Philosophy, Politics and Society. Series 3*, Oxford: Blackwell.

—— (1973) *Emile Durkheim. His Life and Work*, Harmondsworth: Penguin.

Marske, C. E. (1987) 'Durkheim's "cult of the individual" and the moral reconstitution of society', *Sociological Theory* 5, 1: 1–14.

Mauss, M. (1971) 'Introduction', in E. Durkheim, *Le Socialisme*, 2nd edn, Paris: Presses Universitaires de France.

Meier, K. (1988) *Emile Durkheim's Konzeption der Berufsgruppen*, Berlin: Duncker & Humblot.

Merlino, S. (1899) 'Formes et essences du socialisme', *Revue Philosophique* 48: 433–9. Reprinted in V. Karady (ed.) [1975] *Textes*, Vol. 3, Paris: Minuit.

Mitchell, M. (1931) 'Emile Durkheim and the philosophy of nationalism', *Political Science Quarterly* 46: 87–106.

—— (1976) 'The individual and individualism in Durkheim's, *Sociological Analysis and Theory*' 6: 257–77.

Müller, H.-P. (1983) *Wertkrise und Gesellschaftsreform. Emile Durkheims Schriften zur Politik*, Stuttgart: Enke.

—— (1986) 'Gesellschaft, Moral und Individualismus', in H. Bertram (ed.), *Gesellschaflicher Zwang und moralische Autonomie*, Frankfurt: Suhrkamp.

—— (1988) 'Social structure and civil religion. Legitimation crisis in a later Durkheimian perspective', in J. C. Alexander (ed.), *Durkheimian Sociology*, New York: Cambridge University Press.

Müller, H.-P. and Schmid, Michael (1988) 'Arbeitsteilung, Solidarität und Moral', postscript to 2nd edn of E. Durkheim, *De la Division du Travail Social*, Frankfort: Suhrkamp.

Neyer, J. (1960) 'Individualism and Socialism in Durkheim', in K. H. Wolff, *Emile Durkheim*, Columbus, Ohio: Ohio State University Press.

Nisbet, R. A. (1967) *The Sociological Tradition*, New York: Basic Books.

—— (1975) *The Sociology of Emile Durkheim*, London: Oxford University Press.

Parsons, T. (1967) 'Durkheim's contribution to the theory of integration of social systems', in Parsons (ed.) *Sociological Theory and Modern Society*, New York/ London: Free Press.

—— (1968) *The Structure of Social Action*, Vol. 1, New York: Free Press.

Pels, D. (1984) 'A fellow traveller's dilemma: sociology and socialism in the writings of Durkheim', *Acta Politica* 19, 3: 309–29.

Pizzorno, A. (1963) 'Lecture actuelle de Durkheim', *European Journal of Sociology* 4: 1–36.

Poggi, G. (1972) *Images of Society*, Stanford: Stanford University Press.

Pope, W. and Johnson, B. D. (1983) 'Inside organic solidarity', *American Sociological Review* 48: 681–92.
Prager, J. (1981) 'Moral integration and political inclusion: a comparison of Durkheim's and Weber's theories of democracy', *Social Forces* 59: 918–50.
Ranulf, S. (1939) 'Scholarly forerunners of Fascism', *Ethics* 50: 16–34.
Richter, M. (1960) 'Durkheim's politics and political theory', in K. H. Wolff (ed.), *Emile Durkheim*, Columbus, Ohio: Ohio State University Press.
Sirianni, C. (1984) 'Justice and the division of labour: a reconsideration of Durkheim's division of labour in society', *Sociological Review* 17: 449–70.
Thompson, K. (1982) *Emile Durkheim*, London/New York: Tavistock.
Tiryakian, E. A. (1978) 'Emile Durkheim', in T. Bottomore and R. A. Nisbet (eds), *A History of Sociological Analysis*, New York: Basic Books.
Tyrell, H. (1985) 'Emile Durkheim – Das Dilemma der organischen Solidarität', in N. Luhmann (ed.), *Soziale Differenzierung*, Opladen: Westdeutscher Verlag.
Wallwork, E. (1972) *Durkheim: Morality and Milieu*, Cambridge, MA: Harvard University Press.

5

DURKHEIM AND SOCIAL MORPHOLOGY

Howard F. Andrews

A variety of problems faces the researcher attempting to assess the significance of Durkheim's thinking about social morphology. Coming to grips with his thought is made difficult by the absence of any sustained development of his ideas on this particular topic, which therefore requires reassembling from numerous separate sources, usually written with different objectives than those of clarifying the subject matter and purpose of social morphology. There are indeed a number of passages in the corpus of Durkheim's writings in which 'morphology', 'morphological facts' and 'social morphology' are referred to or discussed explicitly. But the passages show a good deal less consistency than might be desired for a straightforward exegetical account of the place of social morphology in his sociology. Indeed, this very state of affairs serves as an important reminder, in itself easily overlooked but nonetheless of considerable significance, that Durkheim's thinking on social morphology changed markedly as his views on other areas of sociology developed over time (Andrews 1984; Lukes 1973).

The most important change in his thinking, to be described below, concerns the revision of his early claims for a close explanatory connection between the facts of social morphology and the nature of social life and collective beliefs. After the late 1890s, the latter, *les représentations collectives*, are viewed increasingly as largely autonomous elements. It is religion, rather than morphological facts, which acquires a pre-eminent explanatory status (Durkheim 1897: 645–51; 1898a: 273–302). Somewhat ironically, at the same moment that Durkheim diminishes the direct explanatory priority of morphological facts in this way, in papers written in 1897–8, he establishes 'social morphology' as a distinct and concrete sub-field of sociology by introducing a separate rubric for it, as Section VI of the *Année Sociologique* (from Volume 2 on). This apparent paradox has been viewed by Jean Duvignaud as an indication of Durkheim's indomitable search for scientific explanation in sociology:

Might this not be seen as a token of the richness of Durkheim's

111

EMILE DURKHEIM

explanatory thinking? For in outlining the reduction of social facts such as exogamy to religious psychological beliefs, he recovers his epistemological "conscience" to the full, broadening the scope of sociology by defining social morphology.

(Duvignaud 1969:133)

There may be other explanations for this seemingly contradictory turn of events, however. To fashion such an explanation will require drawing a distinction between, first, Durkheim's discussions of the nature and significance of social morphological facts in explaining social organization and social institutions, and, second, his conceptualization of the domain of sociology and its sub-fields, particularly as these relate to adjacent (pre-existing) disciplines (Besnard 1983).

My aims in this chapter are hence twofold. First, I plan to describe in summary form the evidence of Durkheim's thinking on social morphology up to approximately 1897–8, when the topic took on the status of a distinct sub-field of sociology in the *Année Sociologique*. This will necessitate a return to several of Durkheim's earliest analyses and reviews, as well as a consideration of his three substantial book-length works published before the launching of the *Année Sociologique* (Durkheim 1893; 1950; 1897). In this earlier period of Durkheim's work, the emphasis is placed more squarely on a consideration of the nature and scope of *morphological facts* – their definition, their explanatory significance – although the phrase 'social morphology' is certainly to be found (for example, 1950: 81, 89, 11).

My second aim is to examine the development of this idea of social morphology during the period of the publication of the *Année Sociologique*, to approximately 1913. In this later period of his work, it seems that Durkheim was less concerned with the theoretical status of morphological facts within sociology, and far more interested in establishing social morphology as a distinct sub-field of his discipline vis-à-vis contiguous disciplines. If the pre-*Année* period may be characterized as one during which social morphology evolved as an 'end in itself', then this later period, between 1898 and 1913, might be characterized as one in which social morphology instead served as a 'means to other ends', these being the clarification of the core and boundaries of sociology and the advancement of sociology's claims to independent scientific status.

PRE-*ANNÉE* ORIGINS OF SOCIAL MORPHOLOGY

It is convenient to begin with an extract from Durkheim's introductory statement defining social morphology, for Section VI of the *Année Sociologique*. This statement represents, of course, the end-point of the development of ideas I hope to trace in this section: placing Durkheim's comments at the beginning of this account provides us with a clear notion of where his earlier discussions were leading, as well as with a useful summary of the kinds of phenomena he conceived to be properly the concern of social morphology:

> Social life is based on a substratum whose size and form alike are determined. It is made up of the mass of individuals which constitute society, the manner of their geographical distribution and the nature and configuration of the whole range of phenomena which affect collective relations. The social substratum varies in relation to the size or density of the population, to whether it is concentrated in towns or scattered in rural areas, to the layout of the towns and houses, to whether the space occupied by the society concerned is large or small, to the kind of frontiers by which it is bounded, to the transport links which run the length and breadth of it, etc. On the other hand, the makeup of this substratum directly or indirectly affects all social phenomena, in the same way as all psychic phenomena are in mediate or immediate relation to the state of the brain. So these are all problems which are patently concerned with sociology and which, as they all refer to the same object, must be part of one science. It is this science we propose to call *social morphology*.
>
> (Durkheim 1899: 520)

As a sub-field of sociology, therefore, this newly constituted 'science' was to embrace questions dealing with the material aspects of society; the physical parameters of the territory it occupied; its population size and structure, density and spatial distribution; the varying modes of transportation and communication networks; the size and nature of human settlements; in short, anything which differentiates 'le substrat social' of one society from another, since all social phenomena and collective life are affected, directly or indirectly, by the nature of this substratum. Delineated in this way, Durkheim's social morphology is at once both broad in scope and deep in empirical research possibilities. In proposing this new field of enquiry, however, Durkheim obviously did not conjure it entirely out of the air. We may find the formative discussions of varying aspects of social morphology scattered in his earlier writings.

A common procedure at this point, in seeking pre-*Année* roots of social morphology, is to turn to statements in *Rules of Sociological Method* and especially in his doctoral thesis, *De la Division du Travail Social* (Duncan and Pfautz 1960; Halbwachs 1938; Schnore 1958). Without denying the importance of these sources for the question at hand, there is much to be found in Durkheim's writings predating these works, and they provide considerable evidence that several of his key ideas

113

relating to the nature of morphological facts and their place in sociology were formulated at a relatively early stage in his intellectual development (cf. Giddens 1970).

Not the least of these ideas concerns the obvious natural science origins of the term 'morphology' itself, and the transference of this and many other biological terms and concepts to the idea of society. Organismic theories of society can of course be traced back to roots far earlier than Durkheim, but the effect of Darwin's writings on social thought towards the end of the nineteenth century was to greatly expand the extent to which apparent similarities were noted between society and the structure and functioning of living organisms. The numerous discussions of these analogies and references to Spencer's work scattered throughout the *Division* and elsewhere in his earlier writings provide ample evidence of the influence of this line of thought for Durkheim (Lukes 1973). In his very first published review of Albert Schäffle's *Bau and Leben der sozialen Körpers* we find signs of a cautious acceptance of Schäffle's use of organismic analogies and the earliest published indication of the attraction that some of these analogies possessed for Durkheim (1885: 84–101). In discussing different types of social 'tissue' binding together the members/cells of the social organism, Durkheim paraphrased part of Schäffle's description as follows:

> Each organ occupies a site which it adapts to its own functions. Towns, villages, farms and roads thus form a sort of vast web which runs the length and breadth of society, somewhat in the manner of our *bone structure*. Bereft of its inhabitants, a capital city resembles the cranium, with the secondary towns strung out at intervals like vertebrae. [emphasis added]
>
> (1885:90)

The analogy being drawn here is echoed reasonably clearly some twelve years later in the *Rules* when, having defined the nature of social facts, Durkheim draws the basic distinction between facts of social physiology (ways of functioning) and facts of social morphology (ways of being):

> He asks whether [his] definition (of social facts) is a complete one. For the facts which have provided us with the basis of it are all *ways* of doing, which lie within the realm of physiology. There are also collective *ways* of being or social facts, which lie within the realm of anatomy or morphology.
>
> (1950: 12–13)[1]

The question of the influence of 'le milieu social' on social life was not readily answered. It took Durkheim several years to clarify his position on the significance of the individual's surroundings for social organization and social change, the significance, that is, of the facts of

114

social morphology. In his earliest writings he argued forcibly for the active role of the individual, downplaying the possible influence of 'le milieu social'.[2] In reviewing a work by Ludwig Gumplowicz in the same year, Durkheim argued strongly against the position that the social milieu provided any external influence shaping social life:

> Since there are nothing but individuals in society, it is they and they alone who are the makers of social life . . . But the individual is an effect, not a cause, people say; he is a drop in the ocean; he does not act but is acted upon and it is social life which governs him. But what does this environment consist of, if not of individuals?
>
> (1885: 632)

The physical environment, on the other hand, is taken as a given, although recognized by Durkheim as one of the principal factors in the development of morality in the work of Wilhelm Wundt (Durkheim 1886: 659; 1887: 116).[3]

There seems to have been much in Wundt's work that excited Durkheim and, with respect to the development of his ideas concerning morphological facts, it is possible that his reading of Wundt gave him cause to reassess the views on the significance of 'le milieu social' that he had asserted earlier in his review of Gumplowicz (Lukes 1973: 90–1; Giddens 1970: 176–7). Not only was 'le milieu social' now to be viewed as something *in addition* to the individuals composing it, but, in his discussions of Wundt, we find the conceptualization of the social environment as a cluster of independent variables involving population size, growth and density. Thus, in discussing the origins and the later diffusion of ideas of morality in primitive society, Durkheim noted as follows:

> history teaches us that this original tendency has become increasingly differentiated in tune with the corresponding differentiation of the social settings within which it has manifested itself . . . Yet this dispersion of moral ideas is not the last word in this process, and a long time ago now a trend towards concentration began which is continuing before our eyes. As societies have increased in size, the bond connecting men one with another has ceased to be a personal one. What this concrete affinity has been replaced by is a more abstract though no less powerful attachment to the actual community one is part of, in other words, to the material and ideal possessions which are common property, namely art, literature, the sciences, morals etc. Hence, the members of a particular society have loved and helped one another not because they knew one another and because of the extent to which they knew one another, but because they were all substrata of the collective conscience.
>
> (1887: 122–3)

Similar views were being expressed in the same year (1887) in his inaugural lecture series at Bordeaux for which he had selected the topic of 'la solidarité sociale'. Summarizing the content of the course the following year, he began by describing sociology's initial problem as the basic question to be addressed in the course: 'what are the bonds that unite men to one another, that so to speak determine the formation of social aggregates?' (1888a: 257–81). The historical transition in the nature of social solidarity from traditional (pre-industrial) societies to contemporary (industrial) societies, a transition marked by the increasing development of the division of labor, formed a central issue in confronting this question. The explanation of this historical transition took on more and more of the morphological language and themes that would appear eventually in greater detail in *De la Division*:

> we have seen that, whereas in places where societies occupy a small area and by dint of the more intimate contact between their members, the more complete community of their lives, the virtual identity of what they think about, the similarities are greater than the differences and the whole is thus greater than the parts. On the other hand, as the various elements constituting the group grow more numerous, yet without at the same time ceasing to be closely connected, individuals can only hold their own if they become differentiated, if each chooses a task and a lifestyle of his own in this enlarged battlefield, where the intensity of the struggle grows in keeping with the number of the combatants. The division of labor thus becomes the primary condition of social equilibrium. And indeed, this simultaneous increase in the volume and density of societies is the major new element distinguishing the nations of today from those of former times; this is probably one of the principal factors dominating history as a whole; at any rate, it is the cause which explains the transformations which social solidarity has undergone.
>
> (1888a: 258–9)

Here, Durkheim identified more clearly than before the key morphological variables that would play such a central role in his subsequent writing – the variables of population size, density and social interaction. Although the idea of 'social morphology' as a distinct sub-field of sociology is yet to find expression, by 1887 its major elements have thus already been identified and ascribed a fundamental explanatory role.[4]

The causal or explanatory significance of morphological facts was given further support by Durkheim's empirical study of suicide rates and birth rates (1888a), in part a prologue to his longer study, *Suicide* (1888b: 446–63). Variations in both of these rates and the inverse relationship found between them were accounted for by characteristics of 'the social milieu'. The pace of population growth, the 'density of families' and household size, rural to urban migration, and the intensity or strength of social interaction were all cited as elements of the social milieu bearing upon the problem (1888b: 462–3; 1889: 416–22; 1930). 'Family density' as a morphological variable received greater elaboration in *Suicide*, but also in Durkheim's Bordeaux lectures of 1891–2 (1930: 208–14; 1921: 1–14).[5] Durkheim used this term to refer not simply to numbers of children, which in the absence of further data could be used as its surrogate, but to household size and composition as well. Hence the variable is conditioned less by the birth rate *per se* than by the numbers interacting with each other within the family unit. The key characteristic to which family density related was the 'intensity of collective life', and this is one of those primitive concepts which serves to mediate the causal sequence connecting the facts of social morphology with those of social physiology.

The historical evolution of the family is clearly associated with morphological variables in Durkheim's final lecture for the 1891–2 academic year. As the social environment of the family expands in size, the family unit becomes progressively smaller, and this is part of a morphological process with far broader ramifications:

> our examination of the patriarchal family has shown that the size of the family must necessarily shrink as the social milieu every individual is in immediate contact with expands. . . . If there is one fact which dominates history, it is the gradual extension of the social milieu each of us is part of. The village system is superseded by that of the city; the milieu formed by the city and the towns and villages subject to it is superseded by the nations incorporating various different cities; nations still small, such as the Germanic peoples, are superseded by the vast societies of today. At the same time, the different parts of these societies have forged closer and closer links as a result of the increasing multiplicity and speed of communications, etc.
>
> (1921: 6–7; cf. 1893: 287–8)

But the morphological explanation for changes in the size of the family unit accounts for other changes affecting the family as well:

> The same reasons which have led to a gradual reduction in the size of the family circle, mean also that the personality of the family members becomes more and more sharply delineated. As we have said, the greater the size of the social milieu, the less the development of the private divergences is contained. But among these divergences, thére are some which are special to each individual,

117

to each family member; and they even become more and more numerous and marked as the scope of social relations expands.

(1921: 8)

Although it is later that we find his famous assertion that the facts of social morphology play 'a preponderant role' in collective life and in sociological explanations (1950: 111), the most elaborate discussion of the explanatory priority he accorded morphological variables is to be found in Book II, Chapters 2–3, of *Division du Travail* (1893: 282–337). Since his arguments in this section are well-known and discussed extensively elsewhere, we need not describe them here in great detail (Lukes 1973: 147–78; Poggi 1972: 165–89). Essentially, social morphological characteristics – population size, territorial extent, population density ('material density') and socio-spatial interaction ('dynamic or moral density') – are all presented as independent variables, seen as explaining a wide variety of institutional outcomes of social organization, occupational differentiation and patterns of regulation of distinct areas of social activities. These latter, dependent variables are either directly explained by the morphological characteristics, or are indirectly affected through the mediation of intervening solidarity variables. In summary form, Durkheim was proposing a distinct causal sequence here for the historical development of societies from those characterized by organic solidarity to those dominated by bonds of mechanical solidarity, a sequence in which morphological variables are given explanatory priority (Poggi 1972: 185–6). See Figure 5.1.

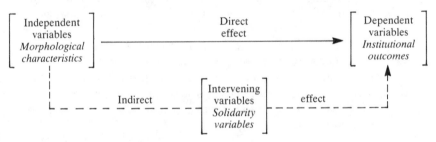

Figure 5.1 The explanatory structure of social morphology

The morphological characteristics seen as particularly important in this schema were those of population size, or the 'volume' of society, and of 'dynamic density', or the 'degree of concentration of the mass' (1950: 112), by which Durkheim meant the extent of socio-spatial interaction of all kinds.[6] Indeed, these two characteristics were seen as so dominant that although not claiming to have found *all* the morphological characteristics of importance in the social milieu, Durkheim asserted that he had not been led to seek out any others (1950: 114; 1895: 705). It should not be assumed that Durkheim was here proposing the facts of social morphology as some kind of ultimate, determining set of causes, since he specifically discounted this as a possibility (1950: 114).[7] Nonetheless, the point is reached where to discard the explanatory scope of characteristics of the social environment is tantamount to denying the possibility of sociology as an explanatory science:

> This conception of the social milieu as the determining factor in collective development is of the utmost importance. For if it is rejected, sociology is unable to establish any causal link whatever.
>
> (1950: 115)

At the time the *Rules* was being written and published, Durkheim was giving his first lecture course on religion.[8] To judge from his own testimony, the experience of organizing his thoughts to tackle this topic made a profound impact on him, impelling a review of his previous ways of thinking:

> Not until 1895 did I have a clear sense of the vital role played by religion in social life. It was in that year that, for the first time, I found a way of approaching the study of religion through sociology. It was a revelation. This lecture course of 1895 marks a dividing line in the development of my thinking, so much so that all my previous research had to be re-evaluated to be brought into line with these new views.
>
> (1907: 613)

What was particularly challenged as a result of this initial attempt to view religion sociologically was Durkheim's previous position, which assigned a pre-eminent role to morphological factors for the explanation of collective beliefs and practices (Bouglé 1951: ix-x; Wallwork 1972: 81-5).

His reassessment of the relationship of collective representations to the morphological base of society was first elaborated at length in a paper published in 1898 (1898a: 273-303). In essence, the morphological characteristics of the social substratum are reduced from providing a necessary *and* sufficient explanation for collective representations, to providing a necessary (primitive) condition only. Once institutionalized, collective representations and practices could become 'partially autonomous reality', undergoing changes and subsequent modifications *independent* of their original morphological base. It was in the study of the history of religion that Durkheim found the most striking examples of this phenomenon:

> Perhaps it is impossible to understand how the Greek or Roman pantheon came into being unless one knows how the city grew up, the way the primitive clans gradually intermingled with one another,

119

how the patriarchal family developed, etc. But, on the other hand, this lush vegetation of myths and legends, all these theogonic, cosmological etc. systems which religious thought constructs, are not directly linked to specific features of social morphology.

(1898b: 43–4)

Thus, although one must *begin* with a clear understanding of the morphological base, this alone is not sufficient to account for those collective ideas and practices – myths, legends and rituals, for example – which are themselves a *sui generis* outcome of social activity, with their own coherent and internally consistent systems of development and change.

In fact, Durkheim published a paper in the same year as this discussion of individual and collective representations which provided a case-study in analyzing the relative autonomy and evolution of a particular collective belief (1898b: 1–70). Although a good deal of speculation was included in his discussion of the historical sequence of ideas regarding incest, his purpose was to demonstrate how a set of contemporary beliefs and practices evolved from the merging or grouping of antecedent beliefs, which themselves may have long since disappeared:

> Indeed, it cannot be stressed too often that everything which is social consists of representations and is thus a product of representations. However, this emergence of the collective representations, which is the very stuff of sociology, does not consist in a progressive realization of certain fundamental ideas which, initially obscured and veiled by adventitious ideas, gradually cast these aside in order to become more and more completely themselves. If new states are produced, it is *in large measure* because former states have grouped together and combined. [emphasis added]

(1898b: 69–70)

This final sentence must be qualified, however. If, 'in large measure', new states of beliefs and practices are formed from the combination of former states, this is not, Durkheim adds as a footnote, the only way they may occur, since changes to the morphological base can bring about a similar effect.[9] Thus, while he argues the existence of real social phenomena largely independent of the original matrix of morphological characteristics, the latter are never entirely dismissed and they retain a fundamental place in his thinking. Without doubt he found the less 'crystallized' social facts of institutionalized beliefs and practices more intellectually exciting and challenging than the more 'concrete' facts of social morphology, but he never denied the importance of the latter:

> religious, legal, moral and economic facts must all be handled as their nature dictates, in other words, as social facts. Whether we wish to describe or to explain them, they must be related to a

specific social milieu, to a definite type of society, and it is to the characteristic features of this type that one must look for the determining causes of the phenomenon under consideration. . . . One does not know social reality if one has only seen it from the outside and has no idea of its underlying structure.

(1899b: ii, v)

SOCIAL MORPHOLOGY DURING THE YEARS OF THE *ANNÉE SOCIOLOGIQUE*

As noted earlier, the phrase 'social morphology', implying a separate branch or sub-field of sociology, occurs in Durkheim's writing before its introduction in the *Année Sociologique*, where it is construed very clearly as a field of study concerned with problems of 'le substrat social'. Several years earlier, in the *Rules*, we find a field of study termed 'social morphology' being proposed by Durkheim, whose task would be 'to constitute and classify social types':

without going into the facts in great detail, it is not hard to surmise where to look for the characteristic properties of the social types, for we know that societies are composed of separate parts added one to the other. Since the nature of every resultant necessarily depends on the nature and number of its constituent elements and the manner of their combination, it is clearly these characteristics which we must take as our basis and, as we shall subsequently see, it is on them that the general facts of social life depend. Moreover, as they are essentially morphological, *Social Morphology* might be described as that part of sociology whose task it is to fashion and classify the social types.

(1950: 80–1)

In fact, these two separate proposals are not as far apart as they first appear. Both are obviously concerned with facts 'of a morphological order', namely, the number and nature of the elements actively co-participating in social life, forming the base of societies (social types) with differing degrees of organization. However, social morphology as a primarily classificatory exercise was not seriously pursued by Durkheim in the *Rules*. It surfaces more or less in this form in *Suicide*, as a possible mode of classifying sample observations of individual suicides (1930: 139ff, 312ff).

This is nonetheless quite some distance from the spirit and purpose of 'social morphology' as Durkheim proposed it in the *Année Sociologique* for 1897–8:

Social morphology is not . . . a mere science of observation, describing these (material) forms (of societies) without accounting for them; it can and must be explanatory. It must investigate what the conditions are which cause variations in the political areas occupied by peoples, in the nature and characteristics of their borders, the varying density of their populations. It must ask how urban groupings arise, what the laws of their development are, how their numbers increase, what their role is, etc., etc. So it does not merely weigh up the social substratum as it is now, in its present, complete form, in order to make a descriptive analysis of it. It observes the social substratum in the process of its development in order to shed light on how it is formed. It is not a purely static science; yet it naturally embraces the trends from which the states it studies arise.

(1899a: 521)

Indeed, given the evolution of Durkheim's ideas about the significance of morphological facts as outlined in the previous section, it is certainly legitimate to raise the question as to how and why, at this particular juncture, a relatively well-defined sub-field of sociology, with a mandate as described above, could be proposed. At the same time that Durkheim was retreating markedly from a position of attributing real and significant explanatory power and priority to morphological facts, he appears to be advancing an entirely new sub-field to study them. Of course, this apparent paradox must not be exaggerated: although Durkheim was certainly placing a greater emphasis on the importance of *représentations collectives*, he was not about to (nor did he ever) discount the morphological base or assign to it a trivial role only.

At least part of the reason for the sudden appearance of social morphology as a practically ready-made field of study is to be found in developments taking place in adjacent disciplines, notably geography, history and demography, at the same time that Durkheim and his co-workers were attempting to establish the new science of sociology as an independent field of study amongst the social and human sciences. This is a large topic, whose adequate treatment lies far beyond the scope of the present chapter. Research into these developments has already been described elsewhere, and need not be repeated here (Andrews 1984; Besnard 1983). An argument can be made, however, that Durkheim's thinking on social morphology during the span of the *Année Sociologique* hardly developed at all from the outcomes of his own research, but perhaps entirely in reaction or response to the work of other (non-Durkheimian) authors. Such an argument does not rest only on examining the contexts in which Durkheim wrote about social morphology in the 1898–1913 period, but is entirely consistent with the proposition that, during this period, his over-riding preoccupation was with the progressive clarification, refinement and elaboration of the status of his sociology and the internal coherence of its sub-fields. If this describes Durkheim's major objective for the period, then the principal means at his disposal were the systematic critique of the arguments and positions of other sociologists with whom he disagreed, and, importantly, the critique and rebuttal of the 'sociologizing' tendencies he detected in neighboring disciplines. The *Année Sociologique*, of course, was the major vehicle through which these means could be utilized: a year-by-year, cumulative process of defining his sociology through the critique and rebuttal of contrary positions, and the 'salvaging' or refocussing of ideas deemed useful from contemporary studies.

In Volume I of the *Année* there were a number of books reviewed in a 'miscellaneous' section which were, in fact, closely concerned with morphological considerations. These included a monograph by the German geographer Friedrich Ratzel, as well as a number of works on demographic topics. The review of Ratzel's work contained the central criticisms that Durkheim would level against the work of human geographers for the next dozen years or so (1898c).[10] It seems quite likely that Durkheim's reaction to Ratzel's monograph and to the latter's earlier work, *Anthropogeographie*, was an important stimulus to his clarification of the nature of social morphology as a sub-field of sociology, in introducing the rubric in the *Année* the following year.

The basis for the Durkheimian critique of Ratzel – extended perhaps too readily to embrace the entire discipline of (human) geography – is not difficult to find in the lexicon of Durkheim's methodological writings. In discussing the distinctions to be drawn between the psychological and the social, and the impossibility of explaining the latter by the former, Durkheim provided in the *Rules* the key to our understanding of his critique of Ratzel and the work of other geographers, provided we substitute in that discussion the 'geographical' for the 'psychological' (1950: 103–6). In essence Ratzel was criticized for purporting to explain social facts by those of physical geography, and for claiming far too much for geographical factors which at best could provide conditions for the subsequent development of social phenomena, but could in no way provide anything approaching a sufficient explanation for them. Ratzel, and later other geographers, could thus be accused of dealing with the problem superficially, of dealing with it in a one-sided way, because it went far beyond the scope of their discipline, and hence at the same time of possessing unrealizable ambitions for the explanatory significance of their studies.

But it was not only (Ratzel's) geography which tackled these important topics of social morphology in an unsatisfactory fashion: demography and history also, undertaken properly and working in concert, had much to contribute to the study of morphological facts. Thus, the statement introducing social morphology in Volume 2 of the *Année* reveals the true agenda for the new section to be something more than an intellectual exercise alone:

> The studies which deal with these matters [i.e. social morphology] currently lie within different disciplines. It is geography which studies the territorial forms of States; history which traces the development of rural or urban groups; demography which deals with all matters related to population distribution, etc. There is, in our view, everything to gain from drawing these fragmentary sciences out of their isolation and bringing them into contact, grouping them all together under one heading. They will thus develop a feeling of their unity . . . a school of geography is currently attempting to achieve just such a synthesis under the heading *political geography*. However, we fear this title may generate confusion. The point is to study not the forms or shape of the land, but the forms taken on by societies when settling on the land, which is quite a different matter. Rivers, mountains etc. are no doubt some of the elements from which the social substratum is made up, but they are not the only nor indeed the most essential ones. The term geography almost inevitably entails ascribing to them an importance they do not possess, as we will subsequently have occasion to see. The number of individuals, the way they are grouped together and the form of their dwellings are not geographical facts by any means. Why then adhere to a term which is so far divorced from its original meaning? For these reasons there seems to us to be a need for a new heading. The one we are proposing has the advantage of clearly highlighting the unity of aims common to all these investigations, namely the tangible, material forms of societies, in other words, the nature of their substratum.
>
> (1899a: 520–1)

It has been argued here that the appearance of social morphology as a separate sub-field in the *Année* can be related to Durkheim's reaction to the work of Ratzel and of other geographers. His reaction to Ratzel was entirely consistent with his established views on the characteristics of morphological facts and especially with his position on the explanation of social facts. What is important about this introductory statement on social morphology is that it not only spelled out the nature of the sub-field for the first time, providing a preliminary synthesis of his previous comments about morphological facts, but also marked a new stage in the process of clarifying the internal subdivisions of sociology, and supporting its mission as a broadly synthetic though nonetheless scientific discipline.

On the next occasion that we find Durkheim elaborating his views on social morphology, it was not the work of a geographer that provided the stimulus, but that of another sociologist, Georg Simmel (1900a: 127–48). Durkheim had, in fact, translated a short memoir by Simmel for inclusion in the first volume of the *Année* and it was principally to the ideas expressed in this memoir that Durkheim was responding (Simmel 1898). He first took issue with the conclusion of Simmel's main thesis, that society is made up of two elements comprising, first, the 'content' of social life produced by individuals in association with each other, and, second, the 'container' for these diverse activities, the association itself which formed the framework for observing the various social phenomena. This led Simmel to propose that, since the various other sciences already studied the 'content' of social life, so described, then sociology should concern itself with studying the container or the 'form' of association which made social life possible. Thus, wrote Durkheim in paraphrasing and quoting Simmel:

> The association is the only truly social phenomenon, and sociology is the science of the association *in abstracto*: 'Sociology must not seek its problems in the content of social life, but in its form.'
>
> (in Karady 1975: 15)

As one might have anticipated, Durkheim found such a restricted definition of sociology too limiting by far, and Simmel's assertion that it was only the 'container' that possessed a social nature while the 'content' did not, or did so only indirectly, clearly threatened to emasculate sociology from Durkheim's perspective. Moreover, to pursue Simmel's apparent objective of equating sociology with the study of social form and forms of association in general would effectively reduce the subject to social morphology, the investigation of the social substratum alone:

> what do the expressions *social forms* and form of association generally mean? Were one solely to discuss the relation of individuals one to another within an association, its dimensions, its density, in short its external, morphological aspect, the concept would be defined, but it would be too restricted to serve by itself as the object of a science, for this would be tantamount to reducing sociology to considering nothing but the substratum on which social life is based.
>
> (in Karady 1975: 17)

In essence, Durkheim's response to Simmel's position was to reappropriate for sociology the study of the 'content' of social activity. He did so by replacing Simmel's distinction between social form and the content of social life with the by now familiar classification of social morphology, to study the external and material forms of society, and of social physiology, to examine 'functional phenomena' and 'social ways of acting'. Durkheim's subsequent elaboration of social morphology is probably the most complete and unambiguous of all his statements on this topic. Many of the previous elements of social morphology are to be found in this discussion, but it also contains evidence that he had absorbed a good deal from his reading of Ratzel which he was ready to incorporate, and that he was also prepared to suggest a preliminary internal organization of social morphology, influenced in turn by the language if not the intention of Simmel's distinction between form and content (in Karady 1975: 19–22).

The internal division of social morphology proposed by Durkheim may be summarized briefly as follows:

1 The *external form* of the social substratum, defined principally by: (a) its territorial extent; (b) its relative geographic allocation vis-à-vis the continents and surrounding societies; (c) the nature of its frontiers.[11]
2 The *content* of the social substratum, comprising: (a) the total mass of population, measured by numerical volume and density; (b) secondary groupings of varying importance, each with a material base (such as villages, towns, districts and provinces). For each of these secondary groupings there were questions to be raised concerning the spatial extent and sizes of settlements, population density, water supply, and so on.
3 Land utilization and the human occupation and modification of the land, according to individual and social needs, including settlement fortification, house styles, routeways, roads, etc.[12]

Durkheim specifically denied that this definition was complete, and went on to discuss how the sociologist must attempt to explain the causes and functions of the various phenomena which comprise the social substratum just described: 'all these causes and all these effects consist necessarily in movements' – external/international migration, internal and urban rural–migration, birth and death rates.

A number of points might be made about this description of social morphology. Several of the morphological facts identified from the pre-*Année* writings are retained (population size, territorial extent, material artifacts, channels of communications, population movements, etc.). The list is distinguished, however, by the absence of any explicit mention of 'dynamic density' or social interaction, which was, after all, one of the most significant of the morphological factors in Durkheim's *Division* and earlier writings. Although 'density' is mentioned, the context suggests the reference is to simple 'material' density alone. Finally, the three-fold division of social morphology and the subsequent discussion of the explanatory tasks it faces is remarkable for its proximity to the broad definitions of human geography then in the process of emerging in France (George 1958: 255–74).

While Simmel was evidently at pains to define the field of sociology in such a way as to avoid its incursion upon the domains of existing disciplines (including 'political economy, history of civilization, statistics, demography'), Durkheim's perspective necessarily embraced all of these, and more. In part reiterating points he made the previous year in introducing social morphology in the *Année* (1899a), Durkheim went on to defend his larger vision of sociology by insisting that far more than a simple change in terminology was implied by assembling the various existing 'special sciences' under the rubric of sociology, and a profound change in the substance of each was involved:

> In reality, all these specialized sciences, political economy, the comparative history of law and religions, demography and political geography, have hitherto been conceived and applied as though each constituted an independent whole, whereas, on the contrary, the facts they are concerned with are no more than the various manifestations of one and the same collective activity. As a result, the bonds which united them have gone unnoticed. Until recently, who might have supposed that there were links between economic and religious phenomena, between demographic practices and moral ideas, between geographical conditions and collective manifestations, etc.?. . . Before Ratzel, who would have thought of regarding political geography as a social science, or, in more general terms, as an explanatory science in the proper sense of the term? Moreover this insight can be given a much broader application. Not only is there nothing sociological about many of these areas of research; many are barely scientific at all. By failing to link the social facts with the social milieu in which they are rooted, such areas of research hang suspended in the air, unrelated to the rest of the world, lacking all visible evidence of the links between them which constitute their unity. . . . There is no need to demonstrate at length how this drawback is removed by considering these different sciences as branches of one single science embracing them all and called sociology.
>
> (in Karady 1975: 32–3)

Ultimately, however, as Durkheim noted in concluding this important paper, the value of any synthesis achieved in sociology would depend on the value of the analyses carried out by these different disciplines.

It was, of course, precisely this task of monitoring and evaluating the analyses accomplished by these separate disciplines that formed the rationale for the *Année Sociologique*. Although Durkheim wrote a number of shorter accounts of social morphology after 1900, it is in the pages of Section VI of the *Année* that we must look for signs of its subsequent development (cf. Durkheim 1909: 259–85; Durkheim and Fauconnet 1903: 465–97; Durkheim and Mauss 1913: 46–50).

Figure 5.2 is an attempt to summarize the development of Durkheim's views on the internal composition of social morphology through an

EMILE DURKHEIM

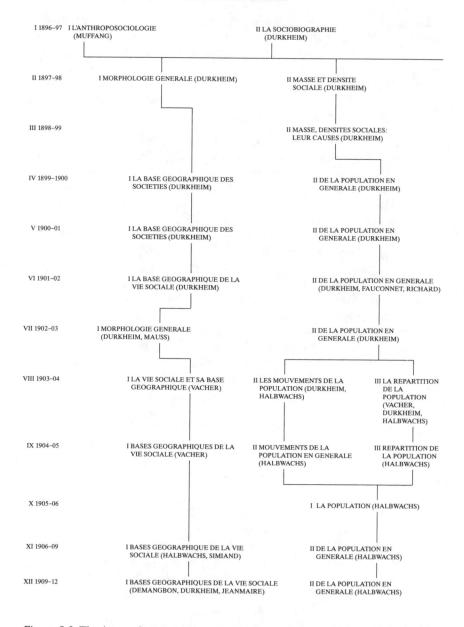

Figure 5.2 The internal organization of social morphology. (Subsection headings for Section VI, *Année sociologique*, 1898–1913).

DURKHEIM AND SOCIAL MORPHOLOGY

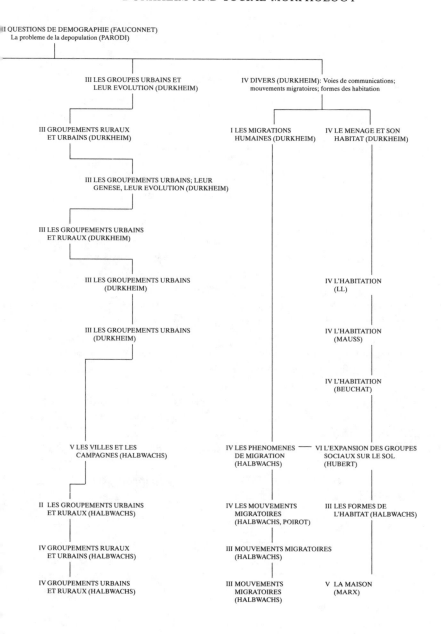

II QUESTIONS DE DEMOGRAPHIE (FAUCONNET)
La probleme de la depopulation (PARODI)

III LES GROUPES URBAINS ET
LEUR EVOLUTION (DURKHEIM)

IV DIVERS (DURKHEIM): Voies de communications;
mouvements migratoires; formes des habitation

III GROUPEMENTS RURAUX
ET URBAINS (DURKHEIM)

I LES MIGRATIONS
HUMAINES (DURKHEIM)

IV LE MENAGE ET SON
HABITAT (DURKHEIM)

III LES GROUPEMENTS URBAINS; LEUR
GENESE, LEUR EVOLUTION (DURKHEIM)

III LES GROUPEMENTS URBAINS
ET RURAUX (DURKHEIM)

III LES GROUPEMENTS URBAINS
(DURKHEIM)

IV L'HABITATION
(LL)

III LES GROUPEMENTS URBAINS
(DURKHEIM)

IV L'HABITATION
(MAUSS)

IV L'HABITATION
(BEUCHAT)

V LES VILLES ET LES
CAMPAGNES (HALBWACHS)

IV LES PHENOMENES
DE MIGRATION
(HALBWACHS)

VI L'EXPANSION DES GROUPES
SOCIAUX SUR LE SOL
(HUBERT)

II LES GROUPEMENTS URBAINS
ET RURAUX (HALBWACHS)

IV LES MOUVEMENTS
MIGRATOIRES
(HALBWACHS, POIROT)

III LES FORMES DE
L'HABITAT (HALBWACHS)

IV GROUPEMENTS RURAUX
ET URBAINS (HALBWACHS)

III MOUVEMENTS MIGRATOIRES
(HALBWACHS)

IV GROUPEMENTS URBAINS
ET RURAUX (HALBWACHS)

III MOUVEMENTS
MIGRATOIRES
(HALBWACHS)

V LA MAISON
(MARX)

129

examination of the subheadings which were employed in Section VI of the *Année* to group the various reviews, critiques and commentaries. Durkheim attached considerable importance to the internal classification of the materials of sociology, and there are frequent notes throughout the *Année* which attempt to clarify the rationale and terminology of section headings and subheadings.[13] Each row in the diagram represents a single volume of the *Année* and repeats the wording of the subheadings used in Section VI for that year: the names are of those who contributed reviews or notes to the subdivision, and the roman numerals identify the order in which each subdivision appeared in the given volume. Reading from left to right, the published sequence of subdivisions has been rearranged where necessary, in order to line up vertically those subdivisions carried over from one year to the next.

A variety of points might be made from an examination of the diagram but, given the focus of this chapter, three in particular may be highlighted. First, it is clear that Durkheim's personal involvement with social morphology, measured by his contributions of reviews and commentaries for this section of the *Année*, waned considerably after about 1902. Three phases may be seen in the composition of the contributors to the 11 volumes in which social morphology had its separate section. For Volumes 2–5 (published 1899–1902), Durkheim alone was responsible for the reviews and commentaries. The second phase marks a transition, in which Durkheim contributed to each volume, but several other co-workers were also involved (Volumes 6–8, published 1906–13). Note also that, with the minor exception of Vacher, Halbwachs is the only contributor other than Durkheim common to both the second and third phases identified here. In fact Halbwachs appears to have taken over a role for the final four volumes which was almost as dominating as that of Durkheim in the earlier period.

Secondly, both continuity and change in the organization of subheadings to group the materials of social morphology may be seen, suggesting that, given a broad framework for the internal structure of social morphology (see below), a certain amount of inductive 'fine tuning' of subheadings went on over the years, based in part at least on the nature of the material that became available for review each year. The particularly Durkheimian terms of 'social mass' and 'social density' gave way after 1900 to the more widely accepted notion of 'population', later subdivided, for two successive issues only, into 'population movements' and 'population distribution' (Volumes 8 and 9, published 1905 and 1906). Settlement form and house types received somewhat uneven treatment in this section, and were actually shifted from the social morphology rubric to that of 'technology' (Section VII) in 1901.[14]

Finally, although the different subsections of social morphology were given various and changing titles over time, its basic internal subdivision, described by Durkheim in 1900, is readily apparent over the span of the journal's publication. The subject matter of the first subdivision, concerning the *external form* of the social substratum, is recognizable in the first of the subheadings, variously titled 'general morphology' and the 'geographical bases of societies' or 'of social life'. Durkheim's second component of social morphology, the *content* of the substratum, was subdivided into the 'size and density of population' and 'secondary groupings'. These two topics are clearly represented in Section VI by the subsections dealing respectively with 'population' and 'urban and rural groups', this latter subsection experiencing frequent changes in title over time. Land utilization and the human occupation of land, the third constituent of social morphology described by Durkheim in 1900, did not receive as distinctive attention in the *Année* as other aspects of social morphology; it is seen in Section VI in the subsection dealing with 'l'habitation'. Finally, the idea of population movements, as both cause and effect of variations in the characteristics of the social substratum, was also recognized by a separate subsection dealing with 'migratory movements'.

SUMMARY AND CONCLUDING COMMENTS

This chapter has attempted to describe evidence showing the development of Durkheim's thinking on social morphology. A distinction has been drawn between, first, the focus of his attention to this topic in the years before and for a short period after the publication of his doctoral thesis in 1893, and, second, the direction of his thought during the publication of the first series of *Année Sociologique*, to 1913. The first period is marked by an increasing awareness of the importance of morphological factors for the explanation of patterns of social activity and collective beliefs. Indeed, by the time of the *Rules*, Durkheim appeared to be *stressing* the morphological characteristics of the social environment as the fundamental origin of the causes in sociological explanations. Shortly thereafter, he began to perceive that ideas and beliefs, although originally anchored to the characteristics of the social base, would over time develop and change in reaction to each other, so that later forms and variations appeared as largely independent and autonomous phenomena. This change of viewpoint accompanied Durkheim's initial efforts to come to grips with the sociological nature of religious phenomena, and it is religion and not social morphology that acquires more significant explanatory priority from the late 1890s on.

The direction of Durkheim's thinking about social morphology in the period of the *Année Sociologique* appears to have evolved primarily through his reaction to the works of others – notably Ratzel and Simmel – and is tied more clearly to his broader concerns for the clarification of his sociology and its sub-fields. The basic lines of social morphology, always reflecting earlier thinking from the 1880s and early 1890s, were laid down by 1900 and remained more or less constant for the rest of his involvement with the *Année Sociologique*, although he himself wrote fewer and fewer of the reviews and critiques published under its rubric. In this account of the development of social morphology, it has been certain aspects of selected works of Durkheim alone that have obviously received exclusive attention. No mention has been made of the work of other Durkheimians who wrote at length on social morphology or discussed the explanatory significance of morphological facts in their own studies. Works by Bouglé, Mauss, Hubert, Hertz, Simiand and especially Halbwachs, as well as others, would all have to be taken into account for a more complete rendering of the development of social morphology. As a related consideration, there obviously has been no attempt here to discuss the later developments of social morphology which took place during the interwar period, principally in France but elsewhere in Europe and in North America as well. Such a discussion would also be a necessary part of a more complete rendering of the development of social morphology, including as it must a detailed consideration of Halbwach's short sketch, *Morphologie Sociale* (1938), which remains the only attempt at a comprehensive statement of the topic.

Despite these limitations, it is hoped that enough *has* been said to indicate an aspect of Durkheim's sociology deserving far more attention than it has received to date. Although in the division of the material reviewed each year in the *Année*, social morphology attained only modest proportions relative to other sections, it seems most unlikely that this was a reflection of Durkheim's estimation of its importance within sociology, and had the *Année Sociologique* continued beyond 1913, it is quite possible the profile of social morphology might have been enhanced (Mauss 1924–5).

NOTES

1 This same distinction, of course, is made in various places before the *Règles*; see, for example, Durkheim's review of DeGreef's work (1886; 1888c).

2 De la somme de nos connaissances, de nos sentiments, de nos habitudes soustrayez tout ce qui nous vient de nos ascendants, de nos maîtres, du milieu où nous vivons, que nous restera-t-il?

(1885: 87)

3 Durkheim writes, in reviewing DeGreef's *Introduction a la Sociologie*, 'N'est-il pas évident en effet que l'évolution des sociétes dépend du milieu physique où elles sont placées?' (1886: 659).

4 Note also Durkheim's views at this stage on the importance of demography and statistical data for sociological studies (1888a: 271).

5 The explanatory significance of morphological structure in the theory of

integration-regulation which underlies Durkheim's *Suicide* has been discussed by W. Pope (1976: 57–60).

6   La densité dynmaique peut se définir en fonction du nombre des individus qui sont effectivement en relations non pas seulement commerciales, mais morales; c'est-à-dire, qui non seulement échangent des services ou se font concurrence, mais vivent d'une vie commune.

(1895: 112–13)

7 Elsewhere in the same work, Durkheim also insists that morphological facts are 'of the same' nature as other facts for example:

Sans doute, il peut y avoir intérét à réserver le nom de morphologiques aux faits sociaux qui concernent le substrat social, mais à condition de ne pas perdre de vu qu'ils sont de même nature que les autres.

(1950: 14)

8 That is during 1894–5: *Les Règles* was published in book form in 1895 and appeared in separate extracts in the *Revue Philosophique* during 1894.

9   Les états nouveaux peuvent être dus aussi aux changements qui se produis-ent dans le substrat social: étendue plus grande du territoire, population plus nombreuse, plus dense, etc.

(1898b: 70)

10 The review was unsigned, but is normally attributed to Durkheim.
11 Durkheim's reading of Ratzel is clearly discernable in the identification of points (b) and (c). See Durkheim's review of Ratzel's work (1899cc: 522–32; 1900b: 550–8; 1901: 565–83).

12   Le substrat social se differencie de mille manières sous la main de l'homme et ces différences ont une grande signification sociologique soit par les causes dont elles dépendent, soit par les effets qui en résultent.

(in Karady 1975: 21)

13 See, for example, his prefatory remarks to Volumes 1 and 2 of the *Année*; and the following comment from a letter to Bougle (July 6, 1900): 'Ces questions de classification sont importantes; car c'est la sociologie qui s'organ-ise anisi. Ce n'est pas rien que de mettre un peu d'ordre dans cette masse informe. Peut-être est-ce là une des choses qui resteront de l'*Année*. Peu à peu, nous nous rapprochons d'une classification rationnelle' (1976: 176).

14   Jusqu'à présent, nous avions fait figurer les études relatives à l'habitation dans la morphologie, parce que la formes des maisons contribue à déter-miner la forme matérielle des groupes qui y habitent. Mais il est peut-être plus rationnel de les classer ici [that is, under 'Technologie']. Il y a trop de rapports entre la maison et les instruments quotidiens de la vie.

(1901: 593–4)

REFERENCES

Andrews, H. (1984) 'The Durkheimians and human geography: some contextual problems in the sociology of knowledge', *Transactions, Institute of British Geographers* NS 9: 315–36.
Besnard, P. (ed.) (1983) *The Sociological Domain. The Durkheimians and the Founding of French Sociology*, Cambridge: Cambridge University Press.

EMILE DURKHEIM

Bouglé C. (1951) 'Préface', in E, Durkheim, *Sociologie et Philosophie*, Paris: Presses Universitaires de France.
Duncan, O. D. and Pfautz, H. W. (1960) 'Translators' Preface', in M. Halbwachs, *Population and Society: Introduction to Social Morphology*, New York: Free Press.
Durkheim, E. (1885) 'Schäffle, A., Bow and Leben des sozialen Körpers, Erster Band, *Revue Philosophique* 19: 84–101.
— (1886) Review of DeGreef, *Revue Philosophique* 22: 658–63.
— (1887) 'La Science positive de la morale en Allemagne', Revue Philosophique 24: 33–58, 113–42, 275–84.
— (1888a) 'Introduction à la sociologie e la mille', *Annales de la Faculté de Lettres de Bordeaux* 10: 257–81.
— (1888b) 'Suicide et natalité: étude de statistique morale', *Revue Philosophique* 26: 446–63.
— (1888c) 'Cours de science sociale; leçon d'ouverture', *Revue Internationale de l'Enseignment* 15: 44–5.
— (1889) 'Review of Tönnies' Gemeinschaft und Gesellschaft', *Revue Philosophique* 27: 416–22.
— (1893) *De la Division du Travail Social: Étude sur l'Organisation des Sociétes Supérieures*, Paris: Alcan.
— (1895) 'Lo stato attuali degle studi sociologici in Francia', *La riforma sociale* 3, 2: 705.
— (1897) 'Review of A. Labriola, *Essais sur la conception materialiste de l'histoire*', *Revue Philosophique* 44: 645–51.
— (1898a) 'Représentations individuelles et representations collectives', *Revue de Metaphysique et de Morale* 6: 273–303.
— (1898b) 'La prohibition de l'incest et ses origines', *Année Sociologique*, 1: 1–70.
— (1898c) Review of *Der Staat und sein Boden geographisch beobachtet*, *Année Sociologique* 1: 533–9.
— (1899a) 'Morphologie sociale', *Année Sociologique* 2: 520.
— (1899b) 'Preface', *Année Sociologique* 2: ii, v.
— (1899c) Review of Ratzel's work in *Année Sociologique* 2: 522–32.
— (1900a) 'La sociologia e il suo domino scientifico', *Revista italiana di sociologia* 4: 127–48. (French translation in V. Karady, [ed.] [1975], Paris: Minuit.)
— (1900b) Review of Ratzel's work in *Année Sociologique* 3: 550–8.
— (1901) Review of Ratzel's work in *Année Sociologique* 4: 565–83.
— (1907) 'Lettre au Directuer', *Revue Neo-scolastique* 14: 613.
— (1909) 'Sociologie et sciences sociales', in H. Bouasse *et al.*, *De la Méthode dans les Sciences*, Paris: Alcan.
— (1921) 'La famille conjugale: conclusion du cours sur la famille', *Revue Philosophique* 90: 1–14.
— (1930) *Le Suicide: Étude de Sociologie*, Paris: Alcan.
— (1950) *Les Règles de la Méthode Sociologique*, Paris: Alcan.
— (1969) *Journal Sociologique*, intro. and notes J. Duvignaud, Paris: Presses Universitaires de France.
— (1976) Letter to Bouglé, published in *Revue Française de Sociologie* 17, 2: 176.
Durkheim, E. and Fauconnet, P. (1903) 'Sociologie et sciences sociales', *Revue Philosophique* 55: 465–97.
Durkheim, E. and Mauss, M. (1913) 'Note sur la notion de civilisation', *Année Sociologique* 12 (1909–12): 46–50.

Duvignaud, J., Introductory Notes to Durkheim, E. *Journal Sociologique* (1969) Paris: Presses Universitaites de France.

George, P. (1958) 'Problèmes de morphologie sociale: sociologie geographique', in G. Gurvitch (ed.), *Traite de Sociologie*, Vol. I, Paris: Presses Universitaires de France.

Giddens, A. (1970) 'Durkheim as a review critic', *Sociological Review* 18, 2: 171–96.

Halbwachs, M. (1938) *Morphologie Sociale*, Paris: Colin.

Karady, V. (ed.) (1975) *Textes*, Paris: Minuit.

Lukes, S. (1973) *Emile Durkheim*, London: Allen Lane.

Mauss, M. (1924–5) 'Divisions et proportions des divisions de la sociologie', *Année Sociologique* NS 2: 98–176.

Poggi, G. (1972) *Images of Society*, Stanford: Stanford University Press.

Pope, W. (1976) *Durkheim's Suicide: A Classic Analyzed*, Chicago: University of Chicago Press.

Schnore, L. F. (1958) 'Social morphology and human ecology', *American Journal of Sociology* 63: 620–34.

Simmel, G. (1898) 'Comment les formes sociales se maintiennent', *Année Sociologique* 1: 71–109.

Wallwork, E. (1972) *Durkheim: Morality and Milieu*, Cambridge, MA: Harvard University Press.

Part II

MORAL AGENTS, SOCIAL BEINGS

6

DURKHEIM ON SOCIAL ACTION

Paolo Ceri

Every theoretical framework for the explanation of action is linked to a conception of social structure. Action and structure form the conceptual pair that, more than any other, is at the basis of theoretical questions in sociology. The alternative conceptions of the relationship between the two concepts range from theories that deny social action a place within the reproductive mechanisms of the structure, which is seen as a system governed by a unitary 'logic', to theories that dissolve the structure in the interaction that links the subjects, who are considered as independent players, in a mobile and variable way. The approaches conventionally classified as action theories are to be found in the second half of this continuum. Action theory is usually taken to mean a theory that aims to explain behavior by subjective causes and by the relationship that, depending on the motives, the actor sets up between means and ends. No action theory of this kind is to be found in Emile Durkheim's work.

Standard action theories are built, explicitly, on individualistic and subjectivistic premises. Durkheim, on the other hand, considers social action from collectivistic and objectivistic assumptions: to such an extent that, if we stick rigidly to the conventional taxonomy of action theories, we would have to acknowledge the absence of a framework of social action in Durkheim's sociology. This assessment would, however, be hasty and substantially incorrect. Only an *obéissance éclairée* is owed to the conventional categories of the scientific community. Before taking up a position on the presence or absence of an action theory, it is worth asking whether and how Durkheim explains social action. Talcott Parsons, of course, has shown that there are conceptual elements in Durkheim's work that can be incorporated within a theory of social action. In this chapter we would like to ascertain if, beyond this, a theoretical framework of explanation of the action can be found in Durkheim's own texts. The argument of this chapter is that such a theory is to be found in the most developed areas of Durkheimian thought: the theory of order and the theory of social change, where the two categories – structure and action – are most systematically related to each other.

Their relationship can be usefully investigated by asking the following questions:

1 How does social structure influence action?
2 How does action reproduce social structure?
3 How does social action change social structure?

ORDER AND ACTION: SOCIAL FORCES VERSUS INDIVIDUAL FORCES

When the phrase 'social action' appears in Durkheim's writings it does not refer to the action of subjects, individual or collective, but rather to the action of society toward them, that is, generally speaking, the moral influence exercised on the individual by the group ([1893a] 1902: 181–2; 1912: 299).[1] We should therefore reserve the expression 'social action' for behavior and processes that Durkheim denotes differently. However, Durkheim's use of the term is illuminating. Because it is the action of society, it cannot be moved by purposes and motives, but by forces that produce effects: the influence of forces – moral forces – that, penetrating the individual, propel him or her into action. So the action of individuals is a socialized action that is exercised by socialized subjects (1897: 226).[2] From this standpoint the construction of the social actor and the explanation of the action are two operations that shed reciprocal light on each other. In Durkheim the first operation has a logical priority and leads back to the problem of order.

For Durkheim there is social order when there is unity and duration among people living together in society, that is to say, unity and duration of association (1912: 609ff).[3] Let us for a moment leave to one side the question of unity, which Durkheim reformulates in terms of solidarity and collective conscience, and look at the question of duration – a question that is more directly related to the problem of action.

Duration of association is a function of the predictability of behavior, which to be predictable must not be casual. There is a direct link between order, duration and predictability. To have order, behavior must to a certain extent be predictable; to be predictable it needs to be characterized by some degree of determination and impersonality (cf. Durkheim 1925: 48ff). These two characteristics are absent when order is conceived on individualistic and utilitarianistic assumptions. Only a social condition having the characteristics of indetermination and personalization can be built on these assumptions. This condition is the negation of predictability and therefore of order. Only regulated action and behavior that conforms to common rules and ends can be predictable, and thus guarantee social order.

But why should the individual conform to rules that limit him or her?

For Durkheim, the need to guarantee security, the core of Hobbesian theory, is not a convincing explanation, since society comes before the individual. More generally, utilitarian grounds are not tenable: the return for the individual would be negative (1897: 227). The only possible solution is this: rules are upheld because upholding them is a duty. The sentiment of duty depends on the moral authority exercised by society on the individual. This way the reality of the interests does not disappear, but order comes to be a function of the social capacity to regulate interests.

From the point of view of a theory of social action, the general problem is thus the determination of the relationship between duty and interest, as an expression of the relationship between society and the individual. Durkheim set the moral constitution of the group against utilitarian motivation and instrumental orientation. In Durkheim the usual train of thought is inverted. He elaborates a systematic theory of morality, from which it is possible to extract a theory of social action, rather than attempting to explain morality from a theory of individual motivation.

Duty means the imposition of behavioral regularity, the adoption of impersonal codes of behavior: 'des moules dans lesquels nous sommes tenus de couler notre action'.[4] It follows that deviants do not do their duty: they set themselves outside morality (1925: 29–30). In Durkheim's perspective, action is fundamentally related to two conceptual polarities, (completely) moral action and (utterly) amoral action, between which there is a full range of intermediary shades, as a result of the different combinations of moral and utilitaristic causes. Moral action is an action according to the rules, action performed within socially established limits, subject to the spiritual force of the group – *la conscience commune*. This force, expressed as the authority 'carried by moral rules' (1925: 36), is a force that contrasts to and thus limits the individual spiritual forces, which, if left to themselves – to their own *penchant* – would never meet limits and, for this very reason, would 'disorganize' first the individual and then society (1925: 35–6). But if even morality is, 'a vast system of prohibitions', it is not merely a means of containing individual impulses. The restrictions are linked to the allocation of ends and tasks (roles). It is this limitation which makes it possible to finalize activities as well as behavior. The possibility of doing so depends on specialization and, more generally, on reducing the lack of determination.

Durkheim's position rests on a conception of society, and more generally of nature, as a field of forces: spiritual forces on the one hand, material forces on the other. Since the vital energies are limited, and given that every force left to its own devices tends to disappear into infinity, every form of activity, whether biological or social, needs to be contained by opposing forces in order to manifest itself (1925: 34–5).[5] To halt their own dissipation people can only, to a minimal degree, trust in the forces of instinct; so forces of another nature, that is of another origin, are required to perform this function of control. Indeed, individual forces manifest individual representations that direct behavior towards the affirmation of individual interests – that is, of particularism and egoism – which push in the opposite direction from individual integrity and social order. Only social forces can oppose individual forces effectively. Collective representations have this capacity. They possess a psychological energy, produced by the concentration of collective activity, far superior to that of the individual.[6] They are common – that is, shared – and have the authority of sacred things, and therefore can prevail over the individual conscience, establishing themselves in it and guiding behavior towards collective ends – that is, impersonal ones (1955: 173). As expressions of the collective conscience, values and norms, interiorized and subjectively experienced, remain no less external to the individual than to their source. Sacredness and exteriority confer on them the character of moral obligation (1912: 298–9). Social forces, therefore, are moral forces that, provided with imperative impersonality (1969: 91), spur the individual à dépasser soi-même, to oppose his or her own interests in favor of collective interests (1924b: 117).

There is a reciprocity present in Durkheim that has often been observed between a dualistic conception of people – affirming the 'dual constitution of human nature' (1970a: 314–32) – on the one hand, and a dualistic conception of society on the other: between organism and personality, and between economic life and moral life. What has not been demonstrated convincingly is the theoretical reasoning behind this position. The reciprocity has mostly been construed as philosophical or ideological: economics and morality are counterposed in the same way as egoism and altruism are (1912: 23). Durkheim does, however, give a sociological, that is a scientific, explanation for the distinction. In the market individuals exchange commodities. They are independent operators in this exchange. The exchange leads to – given the independence of the contracting parties and the consequent predominion of the contingency – a kind of relationship that cannot on its own produce a stable relationship. Only reference to common interests can produce a stable relationship in which the independence of the subjects is compatible with the pursuit of private ends. This leads to the dichotomy between economics and morals, to the 'irreducibility of moral ideals to utilitarian motive' (1912: 23).

The market exchange is therefore a centrifugal force which tends to stress particularistic interests, since they stem from the chance distribution of individual sensibilities. It follows that in order to guarantee the maintenance of social order – and of the market itself – the exchange needs to be regulated, to be submitted to disciplinary action, that is to the control of social rules: these are pre-contractual elements of the exchange.

The two empirical features of the action – impersonality and determination – thus acquire a sociological foundation. The action's degree of determination (in a certain kind of activity) depends on the degree of cooperation in a specific field of action, which in turn is determined by the content and the authority of social rules. These, where individuals are concerned, perform the specific role of 'assigning them certain ends which, for the same reason, limit their horizons' (1925: 41). It follows that the more the subject acts in a way that conforms to the rules, the more his or her behavior is determined, and vice versa. The action's degree of impersonality depends on the degree of nearness–farness from the group, which in turn depends on the attraction that the group exercises over the individual; so that the more closely a subject sticks to the group, the more he or she will tend to act in an impersonal – that is, a universalistic – way, and vice versa (1925: 49).

From this point of view individual action – whatever its specific content – is determined by the intensity of the spirit of discipline and by the strength of the attachment to the group: both of which are determined by the degree of regulation and by the degree of integration of the associated life.

Regulation and integration are the two basic structural variables of the Durkheimian framework for the explanation of social action. Therefore, far from being able to provide explanations of systematic – that is, generalizable – behavior, starting from individual preferences, the Durkheimian sociologist can only explain behavior by referring to the state of the social relationships – the moral composition of the group – and to the individual's position with regard to these. What must not be forgotten is that for Durkheim the task of sociology – like that of every science – is the production of laws, that is of causal explanations of the systematic variations in behavior. Yet, being casual, strictly individual elements cannot provide an adequate basis for systematic explanations. The decisive challenge to methodological individualism of every kind needs to be pointed out here: the strategy of reducing systematic variations in collective phenomena to purely statistical recurrences can only lead to *post factum* explanations. On the other hand, everything that is systematic comes from society and, coming from society, is in this sense external to the individual. This, incidentally, is the meaning that *social fact*, understood as an object, has in Durkheimian methodology.

So behavior must be explained by collective factors (structural and cultural) that, in the relationship between society and individual, operate as moral forces. They determine the moral constitution of society at a given moment. Durkheim examines two dimensions of the constitution of society: the state of (moral) regulation of the social relationships and

143

the state of integration of the individuals in the group. Regulation and integration are the outcome of corresponding *tendences collectives* that, as centripetal forces, oppose, and opposing contain, the centrifugal forces constituted by individual tendencies (1897: 360).

Moral forces, which Durkheim also calls collective passions or collective tendencies, which provide the external energy that determines from outside our actions (1897: 349), of course have a variable intensity. They are in fact made up of representations (especially of values and norms), which are associated with more or less intense collective sentiments, reflecting the force of the associative relations within the group.

Besides the different intensity with which they penetrate the individual, moral elements are characterized by the different degree of crystallization with which they are distributed in the social structure. This ranges from elements established over time and formally codified in the social conscience to momentary states in the collective mood. Analysis of various parts of Durkheim's work enables two dimensions to be distinguished within 'crystals': stability and concentration. Moral elements can be more or less stable and more or less mobile, that is more or less institutionalized – leaving aside the form that the institutionalization might take. The degree of stability reflects the scale and the rhythm of the changes to which the social system is subject. In the second dimension the moral elements are differentiated according to whether they are more or less concentrated or more or less diffuse, thus reflecting the degree of nearness or farness from a state of collective fusion.

If we represent the dimensions of the crystals of moral elements as two dichotomous variables, we can reconstruct the picture of the kinds of action that are considered and analyzed, in various ways and to various degrees, in Durkheim's work. See Table 6.1.

Table 6.1 Kinds of actions considered in Durkheim's work

Moral elements	Concentrated	Diffuse
Stable	Conformist collective actions	Conformist individual actions
Mobile	Non-conformist collective actions	Non-conformist individual actions

The attribute of conformity/non-conformity in behavior is determined by reference to the normative system in force in the social system where the action in question occurs.[7] Each of the table entries shows the most probable kind of action, given a certain degree of crystallization of the moral forces.

Table 6.1 enables us to specify Durkheim's contribution to the development of action theory. Three broad thematic areas can be distinguished. At the center of the first – in the 'Concentrated/stable' entry – are ritual actions: reproduced actions that are eminently collective. At the center of the second thematic area – in the 'Concentrated/mobile' entry – are actions in a state of fusion – collective enthusiasms – which are at the basis of the formation of collective identity. At the center of the third thematic area (in the two 'Diffuse' entries) there is, finally, all of the individual behavior typical of everyday life where the subject acts individually – in interaction with others, as in exchanges, or on their own, as in suicide – whether conforming to the norms and values of the social system or not. It needs to be remembered that conformity and non-conformity are objective facts, dependent on collective opinion. This leads to the warning that although so-called deviant behavior is classifiable among non-conformist individual actions, it does not, for example, follow that suicide is always classifiable among them. Even if suicide is generally execrated, there are types and cases of altruistic suicide that enjoy collective approval. This, therefore, is conformist behavior, whether or not it is standardized.

After making these distinctions it still needs to be borne in mind that for Durkheim there are no sudden changes or breaks in the continuity between social phenomena and between kinds of behavior, but only gradual changes. Those which might appear to be 'leaps from quantity to quality' are not, in actual fact, determined by dialectical changes, but rather by the acceleration of the rhythm of social change.

Given the highly systematic nature of Durkheim's thought, the analysis of three kinds of action – creative action, ritual action, and individual action (conformist or non-conformist) – is made on the basis of common principles, some of which have already been presented. Nevertheless, it is possible to extract a specific explanatory framework for each kind of action from Durkheim's work, as I have shown elsewhere with reference to individual action and creative action. Here I will limit myself to some general considerations.

The explanation of individual action

It is well known that sociology is not interested in explaining single specific actions: that is the task of historians and psychologists. Sociologists are interested in the action in as much as it has generalized features, and only from this perspective can the single specific course of action be considered. Two antithetical positions, however, stem from this point of general agreement.

The first position is that an action possesses generalized traits if these are found in other courses of action, that is if they are recurring. Individual action is considered social if it is general. If this is the case, the explanation of a single course of action, given that this explanation is in individualistic terms of the actor's motivations, can also be generalized for others. This position is in opposition to the second, which maintains that 'a phenomenon is not social because it is general, but it is general because it is social', that is, collective. If we find actions that have similar characteristics in a number of places in a certain social system, the explanation will be collectivistic, starting with the properties of the social system. This is because the *explanandum* is not individual action understood as a series of similar single individual actions, but rather a collective phenomenon made up of a series of separate similar individual actions. The theorists working from the first point of view look for the micro-analytical and subjective elements of the action, while those who work from the second point of view try to find the objective macro-analytical and molecular elements of the action, *in primis* the state of social relations within which the action is performed.[8]

Emile Durkheim is the author who has upheld this second position most consistently and conclusively. The phrase 'individual action' must be understood from this perspective, if the framework of the explanation of the action whose general features we are now going to illustrate is to be understood correctly.

By explaining voluntary death in *Suicide* on the basis of the moral constitution of the group, Durkheim gives a central role to representations and collective sentiments in the explanation of social action. Certainly both individual and collective representations are present, together with other factors, in every faction, but to explain the action as a specific social fact, reference needs to be made to collective representations and sentiments. Individual representations and sentiments vary from one person to another, not only in intensity but in nature too, and they cannot therefore explain the action as a social fact. The Durkheimian framework accounts for the way they operate, as it were, in the negative, since, despite their being ever present, the more active they are the weaker the hold of the collective States (representations and sentiments) on the individual. Social action is thus explained in the first instance by the State and by the variations in the morality present in a group or in society. The fact that this type of action is performed by given individuals rather than others is not extraneous to the problem. But in Durkheimian terms it arises in another way: not as a matter of establishing why a certain action takes place, but as a matter of explaining why it is performed by given individuals – how many individuals perform it, and who they are. The answer is that it is performed by those individuals who are most available, being most exposed to and receptive of the moral currents, that is, to the variations in collective morality. It is clear from this, incidentally, that in the explanation of social action, the action comes first, and the subjects are defined by the specific kind of actions they perform. For Durkheim, they are the subjects of a given action.

146

The explanation of collective action

Why do moral representations help explain action? Because they are not merely cognitive representations: they are also normative representations. While they provide the individual with an image, a way of conceiving and seeing reality, they are also linked to value and conduct parameters: they indicate how this reality must be evaluated and, consequently, how we must behave. In the vast world of collective representations, moral representations are both, and inextricably, images and value and regulatory parameters, that is to say criteria for judging and orienting action. But can representations on their own *cause* a person to will, cause a subject to act? No, they cannot. For Durkheim they are key factors, but they are not enough. They need to be associated with sentiments. The intensity of collective sentiments gives life to moral representations and makes them effective. Collective sentiments make representations into moral forces: 'sous la maxime, il y a les sentiments collectifs, les états de l'opinion dont elle n'est que l'expression, et qui font son efficacité. Car le sentiment collectif est une force' (1925: 78).

Apart from the specific content and form they have in single cases, representations are differentiated by their degree of diffusion and collective sentiments by their degree of intensity. It is these variations – in extent, clarity and intensity – that explain the disposition towards (and therefore the rate of) specific behavior. The intrinsic nature of behavior is instead explained by the meaning that the content of the representations and the sentiments have for social integration and regulation.

To analyze variations in morality, morals need to be studied first. In other words, it is necessary to determine the character of the moral rules, since diffuse morality and individual morality are degrees of distance – through absence or even through excess – from the morality of the group. In this sense 'la morale étudiée par la sociologie est idéale. C'est une morale que les hommes violent à chaque instant, que l'individu moyen se représente imparfaitement. Ni morale de la moyenne, ni morale de l'élite; morale du groupe entier' (1975a: 15–16; 1897: 359; 1975b: 311).

Once the difference between average conscience and common conscience has been established (1975a: 14), it becomes indispensable and a logical priority to determine the content and the formation processes of the latter. Now, the moral conscience is formed in the moments of collective fusion, when the group acts as a group at the highest level. In this way the study of morals, the analysis of the production of moral ideals, far from being a study of abstract categories, is equivalent to the analysis of collective action or, better yet, of action of the collective in *statu nascenti*, that is of the action in the formation phase of collective identity. This Durkheimian topic is also part of the sociology of social change, because the production of morals always means change in the moral order, the setting up of a new moral order.

Creative social action is a course of action where the group reveals the maximum level of its cohesion; it is an expression of the collective life in its original form. It is creative in two senses. It is the creative action of the group: the means through which the participants bring a new collective entity to life. It is the creative action of ideals: the means through which the group produces new values, aims, and moral rules. Representations produced by the group have the highest level of impersonality, so that while they are taking shape and asserting themselves they silence individual representations and interests. In atomistic exchange, individual action, even though permitted and regulated by social norms, is orientated at the highest level by individual representations and sentiments. In creative action, on the contrary, these have virtually no possibility at all of being expressed. The difference between the two cases is in the nature of the relationship between the individuals: in one case there is separation of consciences, in the other fusion into a unitary conscience (1975c: 40–1). Only in the state of fusion are the individual consciences in communion, caught up in the collective participation and communicating fully.

For Durkheim this communion is the self-consciousness of society: in creative social action, when society is taking shape as associative ties, the individuals recognize themselves in the *we* that they are forming (1912: 598). For this to take place, pre-existing social and individual differences need to be kept in the background until they are invalidated morally, so that those taking part in collective action – in the social movement – may participate as equals since they see themselves as such. Similarity generates communion and communion generates the sharing of ideals.

If the fusion of consciences is intense, it produces – like a chemical synthesis – the sacred; that is, ideals with sacred features. The sacred stems from the communion as well as from the need for the identification that this communion produces. So a collective identity – that is, a corpus of moral criteria to assess the interests and actions of the group and of the individuals belonging to it – is formed or reconstituted. These representations are binding because of the authority given them by the fact of being common and by the sacredness with which they are invested (1897: 173). This process gives birth to two typical outcomes: the creation of symbols and the creation of institutions. Collective identity is the result of the common experience – that is, of the specificity of the associative experience in a state of fusion. It is expressed in symbols, having the function of enabling individuals to identify themselves, to be connected with a common source, and to recognize themselves in a continuity (Fontana 1975d: 100).

148

For Durkheim, collective action is important to the extent that it affects the social order positively – that is, the state of institutions as systems of social rules. Revolutionary action in particular – considered in the genetic phase of fusion – creates new institutions (1938: 349). For collective action to have results of this kind is, obviously, neither easy nor frequent. Such *périodes créatrices* are exceedingly rare, due to the fact that they correspond to a state of maximum intensity in associated life and therefore to very unusual circumstances. According to Durkheim, we must therefore establish under what conditions creative action is produced and in which others it does not appear or, once triggered off, deteriorates to the point of jeopardizing its specific outcome. Finally, we must determine its internal process.

At the origin of creative actions are situations of crisis in the social order and in solidarity:

> il y a moments où l'idée de devoir faiblit et où on vient à se demander si l'idée d'obligation a un sens. Mais ce n'est que passager, que dans des périodes de crise, de changement où l'ordre moral ancien ne convient plus aux devoirs présents.
>
> (1975b: 307)

The analysis in *Suicide* is essentially based on economic crises, of depression or of growth, that have the moral effects of deregulating the social body. In *Elementary Forms*, instead, they are political–moral crises (the Dreyfus Affair, war, revolution, etc.) which menace moral unity and national cohesion. Crises of the first kind concern social regulation, those of the second kind concern social integration. In Durkheim's eyes, the effects of the former are pathological, and he gives them a negative interpretation. But in the overcoming of crises of the second kind he sees – from his typical evolutionistic point of view – the process of change and moral regeneration, which he gives a positive interpretation. Of course, not all political–moral crises are creative crises, but to the extent that they are, they constitute the main process of civilization.

The *subject* of action as conceived by Durkheim distinguishes his approach from standard action theories. In standard theories, the subjects possess consistent features, on the basis of which they adapt themselves more or less strategically to different situations. The social relations are 'around' the actors. In the Durkheimian framework of action the subjects are defined with reference to the relationships they are part of – 'inside' social relations. So the sociological features of the subject change with changes in the subjects' associative ties. From the moral point of view, all the concrete transformations of the subject are subsumed under the possibilities of variation and combination inherent in the distinction between the two states of society, characterized by the prevalence of individual or collective forces: the individual is transformed by collective effervescence, transported by collective enthusiasm towards an unaccustomed altruism. This happens because 'c'est l'âme du groupe qui vit en lui même', while far from the moments of fusion 'la société existe en nous . . . à l'état de représentation abstraite tandis que les forces individuelles sont senties' (1975a: 15–16). In 'revolutionary or creative periods' the subject 'vit plus et autrement qu'en temps normal. Les changements ne sont pas seulement de nuances et de degrés; l'homme devient autre' (1912: 301). In other words, in creative action the individual *abandons* his or her own criteria of utility or subordinates them to those of the collective, which the individual has helped create and takes on as his or her own. And the individual does this in the grip of a mixture of submission and voluntarism which reflects the authority of the common ideal, as much as the force that this transmits and gives.

Intermezzo on the typology of social action

Elementary Forms contains the conceptual elements of a theory of collective action, while *Suicide* presents those of a theory of individual action. We must now try and answer some questions about, on the one hand, their specificity and, on the other, the relationships between the two theories.

The first question is this: is the list of the kinds of action considered in *The Elementary Forms* coextensive with the full list of kinds of collective action? The answer is that it is not. In this book Durkheim makes a contribution towards the explanation of creative action and of *ritual* action as collective processes for producing and reproducing ideals. The interest in these two kinds of action is connected to the nature of the author's theoretical questions. As we have seen, he does not see action in the terms that are customary today, that is to say action as a manifestation of the subjects' autonomy; he sees in behavior an expression of the action of society on itself. So he privileges the actions of the collective in fusion (movements) and of the collective in a state of strong sharing of *ethos* (rites). In Durkheim's view these are the two pure kinds of communal action, that is action in a state of intense affective communion. But there are many other kinds of collective action, in which this communion appears only in a diminished way or not at all, as in those cases where the sharing of interests does not correspond to a common *ethos*. These range from movements of opinion, to movements of grievance, to the action of interest groups. These and other forms of collective action do not receive comparable coverage in Durkheim's works.

As regards individual action, Durkheim does explore exchange behavior and role behavior, conformist action and deviant action, and other forms of action. Yet some important kinds of action, such as rebellious behavior and the exercise of power, are not dealt with. In these cases it needs to be remembered that Durkheim's overwhelming interest in analyzing society's action on itself and on its own members leads him to overlook kinds of action that do not fall under its influence. The difference between the two explanatory frameworks is this: the kinds of collective action are selected and explained by exclusive reference to the dimension of integration, while the kinds of individual action are selected and explained with regard to the dimension of regulation.

Having made these observations about the limited domain of Durkheimian action theory, what can be said about its internal integration? More precisely: what relationships exist between the framework of explanation of collective action and the framework of explanation of individual action? In addition to some well known theoretical–methodological principles common to both frameworks, which give all Durkheim's work an extraordinary coherence and compactness, and despite the different phases in their formulation, there is one feature common to both kinds of action. Individual action as much as collective action is *social* action: not only in the general sense of being socially conditioned, or in the more rigorous sense of being socially oriented; but in the sense of both of them being collective phenomena, that is phenomena that directly reflect the moral constitution of the group. Every single case of individual behavior is analyzable sociologically only as a specific case in a constellation of acts, and it is only possible to consider those aspects that reflect the state of associative ties.

Given these premises, it is easy to identify the relationship between the explanatory frameworks. The representations which are elaborated in creative action (although modified by various factors, in the first place by the interdependence between representations, more or less crystallized and more or less individualized) penetrate the individual conscience, which interiorizes them to an extent that is proportional to the authority with which they are vested. Representations of rules and aims come in this way to constitute the main elements in the explanation of individual action, guaranteeing a strong integration between the two levels and frameworks of explanation.

The role played by collective representations in specific cases is determined by the nature of the social relations and the kind of moral influence they have over the individual. Durkheim's position is in marked contrast to other kinds of approaches – especially to neo-utilitarian approaches and those based on the framework of rational choice. In these approaches the social actor is always constructed from the same individual characteristics, so that the different kinds of action, distinguished on the basis of their more or less conventional external features, are explained in terms of a single formal framework of explanation (such as, for example, the rational choice framework explains on the basis of cost-benefit calculation). The difference in approach is reflected in the different grip that the action theories have on a variety of social phenomena. The more that individualistic theories are used, reductively, to explain the most varied kinds of action, the less they are able to differentiate these kinds of action in ways that are theoretically well grounded and fruitful. On the other hand, the Durkheimian collectivistic approach, while enabling diverse kinds of action to be distinguished theoretically, has a more limited explanatory range. Some kinds of action are not considered by Durkheim. Does this reduced range of application reflect a basic weakness of principle or is it an accidental fact?

DETERMINISM AND VOLUNTARISM: THE ACTOR'S AUTONOMY

To answer this question two issues in the foundations of action theory need to be considered first: voluntarism and subjectivism.

Durkheimian sociology has long been criticized for its determinism. Given the influence wielded by the group to determine behavior, the actor is in principle without autonomy. It follows that an action theory which rests on these anti-voluntaristic assumptions might not be able to explain those actions which enjoy a degree, even a minimal one, of freedom. Although it is a commonplace, this criticism is for the most part based on a seriously insufficient, and thus distorted, knowledge of Durkheim's work.

Collective influence is a variable: it ranges from a minimum to a maximum. The degree of influence is a structural and historical property and therefore variable. The group's (or society's) degree of influence on the individual might be high or low. This helps explain the apparent contradiction. In outlining, defining and classifying suicides as voluntary deaths, Durkheim emphasizes will as an essential feature of the act of suicide. At the same time he remains faithful to the empirical principle of the heterogeneity between ends and causes (1975d: 326). But by denying the existence of a direct and generalized link between ends and causes of action, the Durkheimian position distances itself from that shared by the standard action theories, so much so that from their point of view it appears anti-voluntaristic. The dispute is over concepts, and over what 'will' means. In Durkheimian empirical analysis the subject's will is not only not excluded, but recognized and postulated. But for Durkheim the topic of 'will' concerns the awareness of the consequences of action, but not the matter of causation. The element of will is denied any sense of self-causation, so that it is not possible to recognize any role of autonomous causality in subjective intentionality. The causes of the action should not be sought inside the subject, but rather outside him or her, that is in the special relations within which it is placed and in the corresponding moral currents (1897: 3). From this point of view Durkheim's approach, in that it postulates a necessary causality positivistically, is undoubtedly deterministic. But, it is at the same time volunta-ristic in a limited sense. This contradictory outcome, which at first sight seems a kind of 'compulsory voluntarism' – where 'la volonté individuelle apparaît comme régie par une loi qui n'est pas son oeuvre' (1925: 90) – leads us to consider the question of the freedom of the subject and the autonomy of action.

In situations of equilibrium between moral forces, the subject acts in complete conformity with group norms. The moral context establishes the nature of the action. The next logical step is made by relating liberty and morality. Action is always voluntary action – otherwise it is coercion and not action – but the degree of liberty with which it is accomplished is variable. When the subject is insufficiently bound to or controlled by the group, he falls under the influence of his own individuality and passions; when he is excessively bound to or controlled by the group, he is at the mercy of the group and its rules. In all these cases, the subjects' liberty diminishes to the point of vanishing. However, to under-stand the exact meaning Durkheim attributes to liberty, it is necessary to understand from whom and how the subject can be more or less free.

There is no doubt that Durkheim is concerned with the development of egoism, which he considered one of the greatest obstacles to the moral well-being of society. His position is in conflict with classical liberal conceptions, in which individual liberty is understood in a negative sense as the lack of impediments, so that the public sector and in particular the State are simply impediments to freedom. Durkheim sees the main obstacle to liberty as the deprivation of social bonds and duties and thus as being in the very nature of individuals. For Durkheim, being free means, in the first instance, being autonomous from oneself. On the basis of a rigidly dualistic conception of human nature, he upholds a fundamental principle: if the efficient causes of behavior were located entirely within the individual, his or her autonomy would be merely apparent, while in reality there would be the maximum determinism in his or her action. This occurs because, if no other independent force is able to counter the individual forces, the individual would become subject to natural determinisms and his or her own impulses (1897: 368).

Up to this point, Durkheim's view is a version of the negative concep-tion of liberty: man is free to the extent that he is free from himself. As early as *The Division of Labor in Society*, he had drawn attention to forms of limitation of liberty deriving from external restrictions, such as the 'forced' division of labor. But he became less convinced that the moral development of society, which is threatened periodically by anomy, and chronically by selfish individualism, can be grounded in the strength-ening of regulatory components. In later writings he entrusts this function increasingly to integrative components. Already in *Suicide* he refocusses attention away from the control and limitation of individual ends. In *The*

Elementary Forms, he concentrates on the processes of sacralization and identification which are the origin and foundation of individual ends. Because of the growing predominance that the integrative dimension assumes over the regulatory one, the analysis of fatalism in *Suicide* also receives only marginal attention.

A fuller development of the analysis of the forced division of labor and fatalism – which is merely mentioned – should have led Durkheim to examine liberty in relation to the breadth of choice, which varies according to the social relations in which the subject is set. But it did not. And not having explored this side of the question, he did not give sufficient space to power within the framework of explanation of the action and theory of social order. What most influenced the direction of Durkheim's thought was the effort he devoted to identifying the conditions of social order empirically and establishing them theoretically. Once he established that these are moral in nature, he was induced to neglect the role that asymmetrical, imperative and unequal relations can play in determining the autonomy of individuals, in favor of stressing the moral dimension of these relations.

The moral content of liberty is the product of consensus on the rules which are the foundation of moral obligation. Again on this issue, Durkheim diverges from individualistic and contractualistic models. For Durkheim, an individual is not sovereign of himself, but subject to his own biological determinism. One cannot escape from absolute determinism by slackening or cutting off social ties, but only by binding oneself to society and taking on a moral obligation towards it. The very humanity of an individual is a moral fact: a person is richer and more complex, and therefore more differentiated, by virtue of how much society (or how many societies) he or she has 'within himself or herself' – by virtue of the extent to which he or she accepts impersonal rules and ends.

The issue of the compatibility of determinism and voluntarism is less obscure once the distinction between liberty and independence has been appreciated. Those who, from an individualistic standpoint, accuse Durkheim of determinism have always started out from a conception of liberty as independence, whereas for him the problem of liberty is not posed while subjects remain independent as long as, strictly speaking, they have no social relations. Durkheim contrasts liberty *as autonomy* to liberty *as independence*. Liberty, which is the fruit of 'submission' to group rules and ends,[9] is only real if the norm is accepted. If the individual conforms only out of fear of sanction or interest, his behavior would be lacking in moral content (and order would not last).[10] Durkheim says two things on this question: that the bases of consensus are variable, and that they are determined through historical development. Moral obligation and consensus are thus not metaphysical categories of reason but historical

DURKHEIM ON SOCIAL ACTION

variables. On this important point, he differs quite clearly from Kant, whose thought on morals he historicizes.

The autonomy of the will is a third dimension of morals, which is developed only after a certain stage in social evolution. It is only with a certain degree of extension and complexity of society that a 'contradiction' emerges between the universal fact that we 'obey a law which we did not make' and the sentiment (very much alive in the contemporary moral conscience) which leads to 'connecting the morality of the act to the autonomy of the agent' (1925: 94–5). This moral imperative – *représentation* and sentiment – takes shape, acquires strength, and grows with the progress of the process of individualization, which together with secularization and the development of modern rationalism is the result of the growing differentiation and intensification of social life. The differentiation of functions and the specialization of roles are the source of the phenomena of belonging to 'multiple societies', and of the consequent extension of space for individual action, corresponding to the multiplication and autonomization of spheres of action.

The same process is the basis of the progressive restriction of the collective conscience, corresponding to the increase in the variety of life experiences. Individualization is thus the direct consequence of the structural process of the extension of space for action and the cultural process of the contraction of the collective conscience.

Growing individualization is in itself a disintegrative tendency, as it gives a place to forms of hedonistic individualism. However, the same process secretes, so to speak, the antibodies functionally necessary for social order: universalism and the sacralization of the person. Universalism is the effect of the weakening of monolithic and localistic ties. The sacralization of the person (*la religion de l'humanité*) follows from the restriction and concentration of the collective conscience to the (unique) value of the person as the only possible foundation for normative consensus. All social duties tend to be oriented and justified as a function of the acknowledgement and defense of the rights of the individual as a person (in a universal, Kantian sense) which thus acquires the features typical of sacred things – sacred because they are the expression of the common conscience. The value of the subject's dignity becomes the element of legitimization of the rules and the foundation of the bond with the group, which tends to become extended to the whole of humanity.

While Durkheim is convinced of the centrality of individualistic values for normative consensus, he is also convinced that to *share* them is not enough to ensure social order.[11] There is too great a distance between the emancipated individual and society, and individualistic morals on their own are not sufficient to regulate private interests and to contain the selfish tendencies inevitably associated with it. Because individualization means the growing distancing of moral pressure from the relations of submission–protection, there must be other, novel sources of moral pressure.[12] The search for a solution to this problem leads Durkheim to highlight – with emphases that vary over time – intermediate functional groups (the corporations), education (lay schooling) and processes of collective fusion (social movements and *rassemblements rituels*). He assigns these the function of making the individual who lives in an individualistic society feel his dependence on the collective body: of making him still feel 'une partie du tout dont il est fonction'.

The process of individualization involves an objective development – in behavior as in common opinion – of the autonomy of will. Why should this be so? On the one hand, autonomy, as we have seen, is the causal effect of less pervasive collective control. But it is also the functional reply to the individual and social need to deal with the uncertainty that derives from the contraction of the area of shared representations. The intensification of collective life, the multiplicity of ties, and the great variety of experiences enrich the personality, making it more complex and therefore more fragile (exposed to a greater number of interdependencies). The increased fragility and lesser moral pressure expose behavior to less determination and make it subject to greater uncertainty. The functional reply to this problem is the sacralization of the person and thus the development of the autonomy of the subject.

But what does Durkheim mean by 'autonomy' of the will? He does not simply mean the faculty of choice between behavioral alternatives. *Awareness* of one's own action – *la conscience de soi* – comes to be the content of autonomy. In an individualistic society, the subject acts autonomously when, thanks to an adequate development of science – of sociology, in particular – and its correct use, he consciously chooses 'to act according to the nature of things'. The individual is free – and his capacity for action extended – to the extent that he is (scientifically) conscious of his bonds of dependence on society and nature (1938: 387). Autonomy is therefore still obedience, but no longer passive obedience, rather enlightened adherence to norms (1925: 96ff).[13] Durkheim arrives at the point of associating determinism and voluntarism, the hold of society on the individual and the autonomy of the subject, causality and liberty.

In short, Durkheim analyzes the autonomy of the will as a function of the moral order, and as moral order means duty and duty means obedience to norms, autonomy cannot negate duty, otherwise it is purely arbitrary, a 'false liberty': liberty must therefore be a voluntary and self-conscious acceptance of duty. The reasoning is this: when collective consciousness is narrowed and group control is no longer extended, (voluntary) acceptance of norms can only be the result of the relation which the subject establishes rationally between himself and society (in its different spheres and institutions). If, in contrast, he decides to conform or not on the basis of his own personal preferences, he would be acting as a selfish individual and his behaviour would be neither free nor moral. He is free and his actions are moral to the extent to which conformity to (or rejection of) that norm expresses the rational acknowledgement of its validity with respect to the needs of society. Duty and liberty are thus reconciled.

We posed the question of the deterministic character of Durkheim's framework of social action. We can conclude our analysis with a four-point answer:

1 To explain action, Durkheim systematically introduces voluntaristic elements. But as the structural data are not considered simply as elements of a situation in which the actor chooses according to his or her own preferences, but in relation to social norms which are part of the very construction of the actor, the voluntaristic elements are always examined considering their tense relationship with deterministic ones.
2 The 'autonomy' of the will is not a property which can be presupposed theoretically, but is a variable empirical fact, to be ascertained in each specific case. It appears gradually and develops from a certain stage of civilization onward, a stage which sees the affirmation of individualistic values leading to the cult of the person. Much of the dogmatism and aversion to Durkheim on the part of methodological individualists originates in the lack of distinction between ethical individualism and methodological individualism. This distinction can only be made if individualistic values are adequately historicized, and thus rendered relative. The ethical plane is independent of the methodological one: one can be individualistic in ethics and collectivistic in the explanation of social phenomena, or vice versa. Durkheim had this distinction very clearly in mind.
3 In sociology it is necessary to have a general framework of social action, but this framework must be coherently associated with a theory of the actor focussed on the historical and social construction of the actor and not on a formal dehistoricized framework, as is the case with standard theories of action.
4 The connection between the framework of action and the theory of the actor enables us to move on, from analysis of the *structure of social action* to the analysis of the *social structure of action*.

Autonomy, consensus and the pluralism of values

Having established these elements of Durkheim's position, we can turn to some criticisms. Many important sociological topics do not receive an adequate treatment from Durkheim, for reasons intrinsically connected to his approach to action. Durkheim's conception of *autonomy* for example, restricts sociological analysis in several ways. Because he makes autonomy the foundation of consensus, Durkheim does not define autonomy as a variable state of social relations. For him, it is a matter of consensus on rules and of conscious obedience, and not of liberty of decision – 'c'est la science qui est la source de notre autonomie' (1925: 98). But one can be autonomous even by acting according to rules without any scientific basis or that are functionally inadequate to the structure of society. Why does Durkheim ignore this possibility?

The fact is that Durkheim only considers a single dimension of autonomy, *moral autonomy*, and does not see the other dimension, which we could distinguish by calling it *structural autonomy*. He circumscribes his analysis to autonomy *with respect to* rules and neglects – increasingly, the more he moves away from the type of problems examined in *The Division of Labour in Society* – autonomy *within* the rules; that is within social relations regulated by norms. Thus he can claim that one is (morally) autonomous when one accepts rules and acts in conformity with them: 'un conformisme ainsi consenti n'a plus rien de contraint' (1925: 99). But it is evident that the rules one consents to can allow varying degrees of autonomy. One can agree to one's own subordination or to one's own segregation, but one is not autonomous because of this: one consents autonomously, in fact, to one's loss of autonomy. Of course, one may think that, in a relationship which persists in time, the *ego* reconfirms (rationally) its assent to the norms which regulate the relation each time, prescribing that it must in any case obey *alter*; this does not deny, however, that it is *alter* who decides and not *ego*.

Durkheim therefore gets to the point of establishing an equation between morality and autonomy (or more precisely, normality, morality and autonomy). But if it is true that (in the case of civilized man), moral behaviour is also autonomous behavior, it is equally true that not all autonomous behavior is in itself moral, in the sense understood by Durkheim. For the construction of a theoretical framework of action, a concept of consensus as the acknowledgement of the functional necessity of the norms is limiting; a generalized concept of consensus is required, understood as acknowledgement of the validity of norms in reference to their subjective representation.[14]

According to Durkheim, morals help to create order in the social body, and order means obedience to norms. There is, therefore, only one class of actions in which the (collective) refusal of rules is moral: this is a refusal which, in a state of turbulence, leads to the creation of a new system of norms and which could be called, to use an expression of Guglielmo Ferrero's, a *révolution constructrice*. This occurs when the norms have already lost their authority, and they have lost authority because they have shown themselves to be inadequate with respect to the needs of society. In a similar evolutionistic perspective, all the other cases of dissent or of refusal are considered cases of deviance, even if sociologically normal and not necessarily pathological. So, in Durkheim's work, conflict and power, understood both as actions and as social relations, are not given sufficient space. Power appears, in fact, in only a few marginal passages (1893a: 66; 1969: 246). On the other hand, the theory of social control and its exercise and the theory of collective authority and its production are developed extensively. They intersect in his discussion of the socialization of the individual. There are, then, significant elements – which are, however, undeveloped – of a theory of imperative relations, particularly in his account of the forced division of labor and where fatalistic suicide is mentioned.

Even Durkheim's analysis of the State, which was original and before its time, above all in its conception of democracy, does not take imperative relations into account. It proceeds by analyzing the authoritative control conferred on the state as the institutional organ of the collective conscience (1950: 118ff; 1893a: 51–3). Because of this, a theory of legitimization is missing.

The inadequate treatment of social conflict may be attributed to the fact that his account of the State is formulated mainly in terms of war and, above all, of competition. When, for example, referring to the distribution of roles and to vertical mobility, Durkheim talks of struggles with winners and losers, he does not mean conflict, but exclusively competition for access to functions and rewards (1893a: 371). To develop the analysis of social conflict he would have had to consider power and culture in other terms: power not only as pressure on the individual, but as action which modifies social relations, and culture not only as a system of representations and moral currents, but also as a pattern of orientation of action which functions in a pluralistic normative context. This is not to suggest that Durkheim does not see the pluralism of values; on the contrary, he often focusses on this in his analysis of social change. But he considers it in a strictly evolutionistic perspective (even if it is a multilinear evolutionism). Consequently, we have an analysis of conflict which, because it generalizes the dialectic between conservation and progress and the struggle between conservatives and progressives, does not constitute a sufficient basis for a generalized theory of social conflict.[15]

An indication of the reductive perspective from which Durkheim views the question of the pluralism of values is given by the inadequate acknowledgement of the phenomenon of multi-membership. If there is a phenomenon which Durkheim, the theorist of social differentiation, considers, it is precisely that of the *sociétés multiples*. But he does not consider the social and sociological problems caused by multiple membership; that is by the fact that individual membership in a number of groups or institutions gives rise to – according to the degree of normative compatibility or incompatibility – intra-individual and social synergies, tensions or conflicts. This failure occurs because, once the function of forming and articulating the common conscience has been assigned to the various groups so as to ensure the moral integration of their members into society at large, Durkheim considers membership in a unifying and hierarchizing perspective: unifying because 'l'homme n'est pas complet que s'il appartient à des sociétés multiples', and hierarchical because 'toutes les sociétés dont l'homme fait ou peut faire partie n'ont pas une égale valeur morale' (1925: 67–8). Hierarchies in society, between the family, the corporation, political association, the nation, humanity, result from the varying degree of impersonality; that is of the universalism of the normative system. The varying degree of moral universalism reflects, in turn, the different stage of evolution of their functional centrality: 'Famille, patrie, humanité représentent des phases différentes de notre évolution sociale et morale . . . il existe entre elles une hiérarchie' (1925: 63).

It seems strange that Durkheim should have attributed so little importance to the phenomenon of voluntary association typical of mass democratic societies, and that he largely limited himself to examining functional groups. It is certain that if he had given them the importance they deserve, he would have had to rethink his conception and face the question of normative pluralism and, as a consequence, of social conflict on a different basis, without reducing it to the tensions between conservation and progress, and between egoism and individualism.

Durkheim does recognize that the normative systems of different groups can be in conflict, at least for a certain period. But the implications he draws from this for the explanation of action do not lead him to conceptualize either multi-membership as such, or normative conflict. His explanation of the suicide of soldiers in a situation of normative conflict between the military system and outside society is exemplary: the diversity of normative systems, just as that of moral currents, weakens moral control of the individual, just as similarity strengthens it, with direct consequences for the number of voluntary deaths (1897: 257ff). If, for example, he had explained the suicide rate as a function of the degree of difficulty of the moral adaptation of soldiers to discipline which is more or less in conflict with the values, the rules and the legitimate expectations of their society or group of origin, he would have been able to put forward alternative hypotheses to those given in *Suicide*. This alternative would have required a more complex construction of the individual actor, but a more realistic one. But it would not have required reverting to methodological individualism.

ACTION AND PARTICIPATION: STRENGTH AND WEAKNESS OF DURKHEIM'S FRAMEWORK

In order to understand fully the reasons for these limitations of Durkheim's approach, it is necessary to consider a central aspect of Durkheimian sociology which has remained implicit up to now. It has often been said that the causal role assigned to social relations in the explanation of action constitutes a fundamental principle. It is a principle which is increasingly ignored in contemporary sociology. What aspects of social relations, and what dimensions, does Durkheim examine?

Whether they are exchange relations, imperative relations, ritual relations, competitive relations or relations of any other kind, Durkheim always attempts to determine whether associative bonds are strong or weak. Moral bonds are forces which tie the individual to the group; and they tie him through a double dynamic of attraction–distancing, which for Durkheim constitutes the most typical property of relations in society, and whose original matrix is the experience of the sacred. Given the absolute pre-eminence which the individual–society relation always maintains in Durkheim's thought, social relations, as associative bonds made up of forces capable of attracting an individual or keeping him at a distance, are examined according to the dimension of participation in collective life. Social relations are thus first understood as the bases of (variable) participation in society. Participation – the outcome of the play between the moral forces present in the relations – is conceptualized as the degree of the subject's active adhesion to collective life, so that, over and beyond the variety of forms, what counts at the end is the *intensity of participation*. Participation is at its greatest in the state of fusion, when attraction is at its peak and distancing at its minimum, and it is lowest in the total institution where, because of the 'excess of regulation', attraction is nil and distancing is total.

The intensity of participation is linked in a virtuous circle – through the dynamogenic influence it exerts (1970b: 309) – to the impersonality of ends. And it is because of this interdependence that participation, as a dimension of social relations, comes to be a central analytical element in the framework of explanation of social action. So Durkheim's approach consists in the subordination, if not actual reduction, of the other dimensions of social relations to the dimension of (the intensity of) participation. Durkheim subordinates the dimension of the field of action intrinsic to the social relation, just as he does with the questions of structuration and of the choice between alternatives. This specific kind of subordination can be explained by the theoretical prominence given to the problem of order, of which it is a clear expressive indicator. Together with the evolutionistic perspective, this is the element which best explains the limitations of Durkheim's contribution to the explanation

161

of social action discussed in the last section. In approaches in which the dimension of participation is subordinated to that of the field of action, the limits to the explanation of action mirror Durkheim's.

What does the intensity of participation depend on? Certainly not on individual preference, but on the strength of moral relations, which bind the individual more or less closely to the group. These bonds are composed of representations and collective sentiments, whose strength is the main factor of explanation of the type and degree of participation in social life and thus of explanation of action, understood in a Durkheimian sense.

This brings us back to the question of the specific role that the two elements of moral relations play in the explanation of action; that is to say, to determine the relations that exist between them.

Representations and sentiments

Durkheim elaborates a notion of collective representation as an element which, by being interiorized by the subject, is located in an intermediate position between social structure and behavior (1912: 376).[16] Because of the importance given to processes of interiorization of beliefs, Durkheim's position is distinguished from deterministic positions of a materialistic kind based on external constraint. His definition of the symbolic and normative elements in terms of duration stops him falling into a 'contingency' perspective.

Collective representations are images and symbols which express collective life and which act on the individual to the extent that they express it. This does not mean, however, that the explicit content and the formula of representation have influence over behavior. On the contrary, for Durkheim, they exert *no* specific influence, a point illustrated by penal norms. The principle of the irrelevance of content in beliefs is reiterated effectively with reference to the precepts of religion (1970b: 310). What counts is *not* what the norm says, but how much it is an integral part of the group's nature. The influence lies in the group's moral state, which is transmitted to the individual by representations. Nevertheless, representations on their own – as we have already noted – do not cause the will. They only become effective in association with collective sentiments capable of arousing emotions in the individual. From this it can be deduced to what extent the cognitivistic perspectives should be considered inadequate – and inadequate because they are reductive – to explain action.

Emotions constitute, if we can put it this way, the energy component of action. They are stimulated by the sentiments, which may be more or less intense and may be combined to a greater or lesser extent with the attraction and reverential fear associated with representations. What drives one to act is the intensity of collective sentiments experienced individually, proportionally to the degree of sacredness with which the social object is represented. In Durkheim's later works – in *The Forms* in particular – there is an accentuation of the role attributed to collective sentiments, deriving from the greater significance assigned to the dimension of integration and the experience of the sacred. It would, however, be wrong to think that this marks a radical break with Durkheim's previous positions. The essential lines of his viewpoint are clearly present from the time of his first systematic works (1893a: 68). What is developed further in *The Forms* is the determination of the relation between sentiments and representations. In previous works, this relation was defined with reference to social order or, in other words, to the level of the reproduction of everyday life. On the analytical level, representations are given causal priority over emotions: sentiments vary with representations and are aroused by them – in this, Durkheim follows the lesson of Wilhelm Wundt (1975d: 320).[17] Emotions are associated with representations and drive one to act to the extent that representations are in play (1893a: 65).[18]

The force of representations exists therefore in the emotions they are capable of arousing. Already in the early Durkheim we can see the idea that values and beliefs are rooted in the consciousness to the extent that an affective state is associated with them. In passing from the level of order to that of social change, this idea was to lead Durkheim to invert the relation between representations and sentiments. Just as, on the level of structure, representations arouse sentiments, so on the level of genesis it is sentiments which give form and substance to representations. The fact that the relation between representations and sentiments appears in two opposing ways is explained on the basis of the same theoretical principles. The explanatory variable is the strength of associative bonds. When communion is intense, as in the state of fusion, collective sentiments are a direct and immediate emanation of common life and therefore constitute the matter and energy with which representations are produced. Far from being cold cognitive constructions, they are ideals capable of bonding the individual to the group and directing his or her actions in a process of identification (1912: 603).

When one passes from the formation of identity to the functioning of social organization, when one is, in other words, in everyday life, associative bonds are felt less, and they are felt less both because they have been worn down by routine and because they are in conflict with individual interests. In this situation it is up to the representations – the ideals created in the process described earlier – to arouse the sentiments necessary to make the individual participate actively in social life.

It is wrong to assert that Durkheim ends up as an 'idealist' legitimating the development of a sociology on emotional and purely symbolic bases.

This interpretation, which depends on the distinction between an early and a later Durkheim, reflects a misunderstanding of the distinction between genesis and structure, indicated above, and a separation of the symbolic and emotional dimension from social structure.

It is true that, in going from a quasi-materialistic image of civilization to a spiritualized one, Durkheim ends up formulating the principle of the relative autonomy of symbolic structure from social organization vigorously. But this is not the same as postulating the independence of the two levels, nor does it mean overturning the relation to the point of making the social structure a mere externalization of emotions (1969: 585; 1975e: 431).[19]

The link between the intensity of sentiments and the intensity of participation

Having clarified the relation between representations and sentiments, it is now possible to go back and consider the role assigned to them in the explanation of action. We have seen how Durkheim upholds the principle of the irrelevance of the content of beliefs. An analogous principle holds for sentiments, whose specific characteristics, which derive from their reference to certain social objects or groups, he does not consider relevant. It is not the specific content or reference of sentiments – whether they be maternal, conjugal, patriotic or any other – that explains behavior, but their *intensity*, as an expression of the moral state of the group (1897: 434–5). For Durkheim the intensity with which collective sentiments are felt is the measure of the strength of associative bonds. There is, therefore, a perfect correspondence between the intensity of sentiments and the intensity of participation. Just as social relations are considered from the aspect of the intensity of participation, representations and sentiments are assessed for their intrinsic intensity.

Durkheim can assert the principle of the irrelevance of the content of representations and sentiments, however, only because the behavior which he considers falls into only two types: loyalty and exit. In expressing the means and the degree of adhesion to the group, the various forms of loyalty and exit are forms of behavior which correspond to different degrees of participation in collective life. But as we saw earlier, certain fundamental types of action and social relations do not fit this schema.

Although it unduly restricts the field of sociological analysis, Durkheim's manner of defining social relations and the role of representations and sentiments, at least for the relations and social actions which fall within its domain, enables us to analyze and explain the intensity of participation; that is how much action there is, though not what action takes place, and only partially how it does.

With respect to the 'what' of action – that is, the content of behavioral choices – Durkheim's 'participationistic' approach can give a full answer only in the socially extreme cases of fusion and total alienation, in which the intensity and content of action virtually coincide. In all other cases, Durkheim's framework of explanation is less effective, for once the question of 'how' the subject acts (for example, in conformity or not with the norms) has been included in (and virtually identified with) the problem of how much he or she participates in social life, the explanation of 'how' cannot help losing all its specific connotations, or becoming pure tautology.

Durkheim's approach nevertheless offers a fundamental contribution to the explanation of the causes of individual or collective behavior. The determination of the specific relation between the individual and the group (and its transformation) through the analysis of the *milieu*, of collective conscience, of the moral structure of the group and its moral currents, enables the identification of the causes endogenous to the system of action, and thus to the main explanatory variables of action understood as intentional and voluntary action, as matters of choice and decision. It is peculiar, but completely understandable, that the merits and the limits of Durkheim's framework of social action are perfectly reciprocal to those of standard action theories, in particular those deriving from Weber. These theories are strong in the explanation of the 'how' of action, such as 'how' the actor chooses to relate means to ends. Durkheim's framework is strong, in contrast, in explaining 'how much' and 'why' (in the sense of objective causes rather than subjective motivations). A revision and strengthening of Durkheim's framework, carried out on the basis of his own theoretical and methodological principles, is quite possible. To give an effective answer to the question of 'how', it is necessary to find room in the framework for the elements of structuration and the choice of alternatives. But in order to do this, there must be a reassessment of the dimension of social regulation: a dimension present more in *Division of Labour* than in *The Elementary Forms*.

For an explanation of the content of action (the 'what') we need to undertake a more complex and problematic operation: to conceptualize action orientations themselves in a collectivistic perspective, as a voluntaristic translation of the states of collective conscience and moral currents. To accomplish both operations it is necessary to relativize the dimension of participation, so that this, although retaining a central role, is not exclusive, so that social relations can be redefined in a multi-dimensional perspective. This is such a problematic undertaking that it risks sidetracking us from the principles of Durkheimian sociology. But it is a risk which is worth taking if, having surveyed the horizon from the shoulders of giants, one wishes to take the next steps on one's own two feet.

NOTES

1 The meaning of social action as society's influence over the individual is present and explicit in all Durkheim's work, from the first to the last of his writings ([1893a] 1902: 181–2; 1912: 299).

2 Sociability itself, present in varying degrees in all individuals, is produced by society, more than it is the expression of an original sociality: 'C'est l'action de la société qui a suscité en nous ces sentiments de sympathie et de solidarité qui nous inclinent vers autrui' (Durkheim 1897: 226).

3 The meaning assumed by the dimension of duration is rendered explicit in particular in the case of religious symbolism.

4 The 'Introduction' to the first edition (1893) of *De la Division du Travail Social*, omitted in the second edition (1902), was later republished (Karady 1975, II: 268–9).

5 Durkheim's position on this key point remains unchanged, as is revealed, among other things, by the notes taken by Armand Cuvillier, in the 1908–9 academic year, successively transcribed by Steven Lukes in 1968, and then published, with the title 'Leçons sur la morale', in Karady (1975, II: especially the notes on 309).

6 Collective representations are moral ideals capable of orienting the actions that 'visent une fin supérieure à l'individu que je suis, ou aux individus que sont les autres hommes' (1924a: 70).

7 An important criticism of this aspect which needs to be pointed out will be developed later. To explain action, reference to a social system is often not enough: the action which is non-conformist with regard to a normative order might be so because it conforms to the norms of another social system. In these cases it is the individual's positive reference to this other system which enables the action to be explained – as reference groups theory (a significant part of which rests on Durkheimian foundations) establishes well.

8 In this sense sociology must

> expliquer les phénomènes qui se produisent dans le tout par les propriétés caractéristiques du tout, le complexe pour le complexe, les faits sociaux par la société, les faits vitaux et mentaux par les combinaisons *sui generis* d'où ils résultent. C'est la seule marche que puisse suivre la science.
>
> (1924c: 44)

9 > C'est sous l'action, c'est par la pratique des règles morales que nous acquérons le pouvoir de nous maitriser et de nous régler, qui est tout le réel de la liberté.
>
> (1925: 47)

10 The parallel with the Weberian analysis of the bases of the legitimacy of domination can be made in effect, on condition that due account is taken of the evolutionistic character of the Durkheimian perspective, absent in Weber.

11 The question is posed clearly at the end of the 'Préface' to the first edition of *De la Division du Travail Social* (1893b): 'Comment se fait-il que, tout en devenant plus autonome, l'individu dépende plus étroitement de la société? Comment peut-il être à la fois plus personel et plus solidaire?' ([1893a] 1902: XLIII). The question and the empirical observation which it generates do not change; what change slightly are the answers which Durkheim gives in the course of his reflection.

12 The empirical acknowledgement of autonomization, relative but growing historically, of moral and cultural elements from the morphological base and

from the social structure is at the origin of the role, more and more central and generalized, which collective representations assume in Durkheim's explanatory framework.

13 Durkheim the philosopher takes over from Durkheim the sociologist at this point. His position is debatable: what happens if the order has as its specific content that of producing effects contrary to other values autonomously accepted by the passive subject?

14 The reference to subjective representation does not necessarily imply the adoption of an individualistic methodological perspective. It is something quite different from the subjectivism of representation.

15 The evolutionistic presuppositions are fully explicit in the part of *Formes* dealing with movements towards a state of fusion.

16 La société . . . ne se borne pas à nous mouvoir du dehors et à nous affecter passagèrement; elle s'organise en nous d'une manière durable. Elle y suscite un monde d'idées et de sentiments qui l'expriment, mais qui, en même temps, font partie intégrante et permanente de nous mêmes.

17 Tout motif est un sentiment; mais tout sentiment est déterminé par une représentation et varie avec le genre de représentation qui le détermine.

18 Quand il s'agit d'une croyance qui nous est chère, nous ne permettons pas et ne pouvons pas permettre qu'on y porte impunément la main. Toute offense dirigée contre elle suscite une réaction émotionnelle, plus ou moins violente, qui se tourne contre l'offenseur.

19 The relations are governed by two empirical generalizations made by Durkheim. The first is the functional and historical–evolutionary correspondence between moral systems and *milieux sociaux*: 'pour expliquer ces variations par lesquelles a passé une règle morale, il faut, de tout nécessité, mettre ces variations en rapport avec les milieux sociaux où elle s'est élaborée et transformée'. The second generalization, which is also an anti-idealistic methodological principle, holds that social relations do not derive from the symbolic sphere: 'si les idées viennent de la réalité sociale, elles peuvent bien réagir sur cette réalité, assurément, mais non leur faire la loi'. Durkheim's point is that social reality is not made up simply of the morphological base and the economic structure, but also and above all by the moral structure of the associative relations. On the limited role given to economic factors see, among others, Durkheim's contribution in 'Débat sur le patriotisme et l'internationalisme des classes sociales' (1975f: 186).

REFERENCES

Durkheim, E. ([1893a] 1902) *De la Division du Travail Social*, 2nd edn. revised, Paris: Alcan.
—— (1893b) 'Introduction' to first edition of Durkheim, *De la Division du Travail Social*, Paris: Alcan.
—— (1897) *Le Suicide: Etude de Sociologie*, Paris: Alcan.
—— (1912) *Les Formes Elémentaires de la Vie Religieuse: Le Système Totémique en Australie*, Paris: Alcan.
—— (1924a) 'La détermination du fait moral' in Durkheim, *Sociologie et Philosophie*, Paris: Alcan.
—— (1924b) 'Jugements de valeur et jugements de réalité', in Durkheim, *Sociologie et Philosophie*, Paris: Alcan.

— (1924c) 'Représentations individuelles et représentations collectives', in Durkheim, *Sociologie et Philosophie*, Paris: Alcan.

— (1925) *L'Education Morale*, Paris: Alcan.

— (1938) *L'Evolution Pédagogique en France*, Paris: Alcan.

— (1950) *Leçons de Sociologie*, Paris: Presses Universitaires de France.

— (1955) *Pragmatisme et Sociologie*, Paris: Vrin.

— (1969) 'Deux Lois de l'évolution pénale,' in Durkheim, *Journal Sociologique*, Paris: Presses Universitaires de France.

— (1970a) 'Le dualisme de la nature humaine et ses conditions sociales', in Durkheim, *La Science Sociale et l'Action*, Paris: Presses Universitaires de France.

— (1970b) 'Le sentiment religieux à l'heure actuelle, troisième entretien: la conception sociale de la religion', in Durkheim, *La Science Sociale et l'Action*, Paris: Presses Universitaires de France.

— (1975a) 'Idéal moral, conscience collective et forces religieuses', in V. Karady (ed.), *Textes*, Vol. II, Paris: Minuit.

— (1975b) 'Leçons sur la morale', in V. Karady (ed.), *Textes*, Vol. II, Paris: Minuit.

— (1975c) 'Le problème religieux et la dualité de la nature humaine', in V. Karady (ed.), *Textes*, Vol. II, Paris: Minuit.

— (1975d) 'La science positive de la morale en Allemagne', in V. Karady (ed.), *Textes*, Vol. I, Paris: Minuit.

— (1975e) 'Lettres à Célestin Bouglé', in V. Karady (ed.), *Textes*, Vol. II, Paris: Minuit.

— (1975f) 'Libres entretiens', in V. Karady (ed.), *Textes*, Vol. III, Paris: Minuit.

Fontana, P. (1975) Arguments gathered at a course held at the Sorbonne in 1907, in V. Karady (ed.), *Textes*, Vol. II, Paris: Minuit.

Karady, V. (ed.) (1975) *Textes*, Paris: Minuit.

7

ANOMIE AND FATALISM IN DURKHEIM'S THEORY OF REGULATION

Philippe Besnard

The word 'anomie' has had a strange journey. Coined by Jean-Marie Guyau (1885) as a pun on the Kantian term 'autonomy', it was then incorporated by Durkheim into the vocabulary of the infant discipline of sociology. Durkheim's usage was rediscovered in the thirties at Harvard University. In the sixties it became the name for a 'measure' that exemplified prevailing research procedures in American sociology (Besnard 1987). Its career ended in the greatest confusion. In its predominant usage, the word anomie has undergone a complete semantic revolution: its eventual meaning was antithetical to Durkheim's. Yet the vast majority of those who used the term had simply presumed that the concept had not changed since Durkheim's day.

Conceptual confusion has surrounded the word anomie since its origins. The semantic metamorphosis it underwent, it shall be argued here, is rooted in the relative obscurity of the concept in Durkheim's own writings. The notion of anomie is surprisingly poorly elaborated in his work. Thus, if one wishes to establish the specifically Durkheimian content of the concept, it must be purified of the parasitic, secondary connotations with which it has been encumbered and extricated from the network of concepts in which it has become entangled. But this is not sufficient to produce a clear concept, for Durkheim's own presentation contributes to the confusion. For example, in *The Division of Labor in Society* (1893), the 'anomic division of labor' is neither situated nor defined in relation to the other pathological forms of the division of labor. Anomie is conceived as the absence or defectiveness of the social regulation needed to bring about cooperation between specialized functions. But at the end of the chapter which Durkheim devotes to this anomic form, he discusses a different pathology of industrial societies: the alienation of the worker who performs fragmented tasks. Many readers of Durkheim have understandably concluded that the meaninglessness of fragmented work *is* anomie. Such an interpretation is erroneous. The alienation of the highly specialized worker as Durkheim conceived of it is a situation which is not only different from anomie but actually contrary to it.

The theme of anomie as a permanent malady of industrial societies is further developed in *Suicide* (1897). If one is to define as strictly as possible what the notion of anomic suicide entails, careful distinctions need to be made. To begin with, one has to accept the etiological distinction Durkheim makes between egoistic suicide and anomic suicide, and accept the independence of the two variables, namely integration and regulation, which he uses to explain variations in suicide. The suitability of this distinction has been questioned by most of those who have written about *Suicide*. Yet it has both a conceptual and an empirical foundation (Besnard 1987: 62–81). The stress on these two aspects of the relation between the individual and society is not unique to *Suicide*. It is also found in *Moral Education* (1925), where Durkheim differentiates between 'the spirit of discipline' and 'the attachment to social groups'. The confusion between anomie and egoism is a consequence of this frequent pairing. It also explains why Durkheim has so often been presented as 'the sociologist of anomie'. What I will show here is that this is an error: anomie is no more than a minor, passing theme in Durkheim's work and, moreover, a theme which is scarcely elaborated.

One of the peculiarities of *Suicide* is the contrast between Durkheim's treatment of his two independent variables, integration and regulation. The theory of integration is much more coherent and complete than the theory of regulation. A social group is said to be integrated to the extent that its members: (1) possess a common conscience and share the same feelings, beliefs and practices; (2) interact with one another; and (3) feel that they are pursuing common goals. Each of his three examples, namely religious society, domestic society and political society, provides an illustration of one of the three components. The theory of integration links collective feelings to the degree of social interaction and, in so doing, to the morphological structure of society, just as in *The Division of Labor in Society*, but of course the discussion is wholly devoted to the two situations, egoism and altruism, defined by the extreme values of the variables.

The theory of regulation is far less systematically developed. Reconstructing Durkheim's theory of regulation is the most difficult aspect of interpreting *Suicide*. Anomie must be situated in the context of regulation, and its relations with its presumed counterpart, fatalism, elucidated. But Durkheim made every effort to minimize the importance of fatalistic suicide and provided somewhat unconvincing empirical illustrations of it. Yet where regulation was concerned, he actually possessed the requisite empirical data – which he did not have in the case of integration – needed to construct a coherent and complete theory. Indeed the greatest peculiarity of *Suicide* is that he did not do so.

THE OCCULTATION OF FATALISM

Durkheim's effort to relegate fatalistic suicide to the background succeeded: many commentators have neglected this fourth type of suicide. Durkheim deals with it directly only in a footnote at the end of the chapter on anomic suicide, and some of the examples he gives he has already considered. He says that:

> The above considerations show that there is a type of suicide that is the opposite of anomic suicide, just as egoistic and altruistic suicides are opposites. It is the suicide deriving from excessive regulation, that of persons with futures pitilessly blocked and passions violently choked by oppressive discipline. It is the suicide of very young husbands, of the married woman who is childless. So, for the sake of completeness, we should set up a fourth type of suicide. But it has so little contemporary importance and examples are so hard to find, aside from the cases just mentioned, that it seems useless to dwell upon it. However, it might be said to have historical interest. Do not the suicides of slaves, said to be frequent under certain conditions . . . or indeed all suicides attributable to excessive physical or moral despotism, belong to this type? To bring out the ineluctable and inflexible nature of a rule against which there is no appeal, and in contrast with the expression 'anomie' which we have just used, we might call it *fatalistic suicide*
>
> (1897: 311).

At first glance it seems strange that Durkheim should grant so little importance to this fourth type of suicide. His lack of interest is easier to understand when one recalls that the text to which this footnote is appended is concerned with conjugal anomie. Durkheim doubtless uncovered the possibility that excessive social regulation could be pathogenic through studying this form of regulation. But his prime concern was the implications for suicide of the weakening of marital discipline, which he himself had observed. The law instituting divorce in France dates from 1884 (three years before Durkheim's own marriage). Even if this law merely sanctioned an 'enervation of regulation', the legal establishment of divorce seemed to him to have had clear effects on matrimonial instability (1897: 307).

This was a subject he was particularly fond of and to which he frequently returned, using the empirical results of *Suicide*. One example of this is an article (which is virtually a postscript to *Suicide* in some respects) published in the *Revue Bleue* (1906), in which Durkheim takes a public stand in the debate set in motion by Paul and Victor Margueritte on divorce by mutual consent. In this article (analyzed elsewhere in greater detail: cf. Besnard 1973: 57–60), Durkheim claimed to show, though it required misinterpreting the figures, that the fragility of the matrimonial bond is just as harmful to married women as it is to married men. Consequently, he maintained, if the possibility of divorce has scarcely any effect on female suicide, it is because of a 'more general law': that 'the state of marriage has only a weak effect on the moral constitution of women' (1906: 551). This bold assertion is contradicted by the statistical evidence in *Suicide*. But it enabled Durkheim to state that divorce is harmless to women only 'because the marriage is inoperative' (1906: 552). This claim enabled him to state his opposition to divorce by mutual consent on the grounds that it would destroy the 'matrimonial regulation' necessary to 'this peace of mind, this inner balance, which are the essential conditions of moral health and happiness' (1906: 552). Durkheim uses the 'happiness of the spouses', including here the happiness of the wives, as the basis of his argument against the legalization of this 'type of *sui generis* divorce, which is separated from the other types by an abyss' (1906: 552). He explicitly denies the distinctiveness of female suicide and implicitly denies the very existence of fatalistic suicide. Thus the importance of the historical context in which Durkheim encountered the problem of excessive social regulation cannot be overstated. The fact that he discussed it in connection with divorce probably led him to miminize the significance of fatalism and, subsequently, to reduce it to nil.

The many reviews he published in *L'Année Sociologique* of books or parts of books concerned with divorce indicate his special interest in this question and his desire to deduce practical lessons from these studies. Indeed, of all the 'social problems' of Durkheim's age, divorce is perhaps the one he returned to most often and upon which he took the clearest public stand. He knew that this stand carried with it the risk of his falsely 'being regarded as a retrograde spirit', and he did not feel he had 'a reactionary soul' (1906: 549). It is therefore no exaggeration to say that this particular social problem was largely instrumental in determining his sociological treatment of social constraint. Obsessed by the relaxation of conjugal discipline, he scarcely even questioned 'the enervation of regulation' in other areas of social life, and seems insensitive to the 'constraining' character of the rationalizing trends of modern societies. These societies appear to him simply to be moving towards increasingly lax regulation. Thus he concludes that fatalistic suicide can be of no more than 'historical interest'.

Durkheim's convictions about the future do not, however, justify the striking disproportion between this footnote and the entire chapter devoted to altruistic suicide. After all, the only 'modern' example provided

172

in this chapter is military suicide, which in any case might just as well be interpreted – up to a point – in terms of excessive regulation: Durkheim himself refers in this chapter to 'rigid' discipline, which 'represses the individual' (1897: 260). He immediately makes clear in a footnote that it is not 'repression' itself but rather the lack of individualization which encourages suicide. Yet nothing is said to support this assertion. In a subsequent chapter of the book, when Durkheim considers another modern example of altruistic suicide, the suicide of prisoners, he seems to be introducing two factors in parallel: the coherence of the society of evil-doers and prisoners, in which 'the individual is completely submerged', and 'prison discipline' (1897: 391, n. 1).

The handling of fatalism is connected to another important feature of *Suicide*, the modification of Durkheim's frame of reference. The conception of social and individual happiness which emerges from Durkheim's early writings can be described as a philosophy of the happy medium: nothing that is extreme or excessive can produce anything useful or pleasant. More precisely, this conception can be said to derive from the model of the U-shaped curve (whose influence and importance in *The Division of Labor in Society* has been shown in Besnard 1973: 33–4), which was visible in Durkheim's first foray into the subject of suicide in 1888. So it is surprising that, when dealing with social regulation in *Suicide*, Durkheim considered only one of the two sources of social pathology, and did his utmost to minimize the importance of fatalistic suicide, which, at first sight, is to anomic suicide what the forced division of labor is to the anomic division of labor. What this lack of interest in fatalism reveals is a gradual relinquishment of the U-curve model as a frame of reference: the philosophy of moderation between extremes is replaced by a philosophy of equilibrium between conflicting forces.

We will not examine in detail here this transformation of the intellectual frame of reference, which, moreover, is bound up with other changes in Durkheim's approach and even in his favorite metaphors (cf. Besnard 1973: 36–40). Suffice it to say that the work as a whole hinges on the chapter on anomic suicide (Chapter 5 of Book II), the point where the theory of the happy medium is in the process of being supplanted by the theory of equilibrium and references to variables by references to trends. It is in keeping with this ambiguous situation that the U-curve model was hardly applied to the relation between social regulation and suicide. Fatalistic suicide was given only a footnote and the note itself reveals the abandonment of the older framework. The example Durkheim gives, of the childless married women, obscures the curvilinear relation which actually exists between social regulation and the suicide rate. In reality, not merely childless married women but married women generally feel the consequences of excessive constraint, even if the presence of children partly offsets the harmful effect of matrimonial discipline.

This makes it easier to understand the logical process which led Durkheim to claim that fatalistic suicide was 'of so little importance today' and that it was 'so hard to find examples of it' that it seemed 'useless to dwell upon it'. The place occupied in this work by his exposition of social regulation, and the particular question he was dealing with, divorce, conspired to make him adopt a position somewhat out of line with his previous approach and even less in line with his own empirical data. There was nothing, in the original data Durkheim had used, to warrant his so clearly favoring one of the factors in the variation of suicide levels to the detriment of another.

The fact that the existence of this bi-polar variable, over- and under-regulation, is implied by his empirical analysis of conjugal anomie renders the reduction of the variable of social regulation to just one of its poles, under-regulation, all the more unjustifiable. Let us briefly recall the major lines of his analysis. After noting that the number of suicides and divorces vary in parallel from country to country, Durkheim, by a brilliant intuition, turns his attention to the likely effect of the possibility of divorce on the 'matrimonial constitution'. He therefore relates the divorce rate to the *effect of marriage*, that is, not the suicide rate of married people but their immunity relative to unmarried persons of the same sex. This leads him to the discovery that the more frequent divorce is, the more the immunity of husbands decreases relative to bachelors and the more the immunity of wives increases relative to single women. Incidentally, this result in no way implies that married women commit suicide less in places where divorce is frequent than where it is scarce, though Durkheim himself was to fall into this trap several times.

Durkheim uses a variety of comparative data in support of his case, among them the results of a comparison between the Seine Department and the provinces, based on original data on suicide in France from 1889 to 1891. At that time, divorce was four times more common in the Seine Department than in the other Departments. We are thus on solid ground when assessing the effect of divorce on the ratio defined by the suicide rates for single persons over the rate for married persons, especially if the influence of age is taken into account. (See Table 7.1, which quotes the figures from Table XXI drawn up by Durkheim (1897: 183)).

The introduction of this ecological test variable confirms the result already indicated by Durkheim: marriage provides greater protection for the man where divorce is rare (in the provinces) than where it is frequent (Seine). Conversely, it protects the woman more in Paris than in the provinces. The effect of the ecological context on the influence of marriage on suicide is therefore not the same for each of the sexes. This interaction effect may be formulated as follows: the effect of sex on the

Table 7.1 Ratio of single persons suicide rate/married persons suicide rate by sex and age, in the provinces and in the Seine Department

Age	Men		Women	
	Provinces	*Seine*	*Provinces*	*Seine*
20–25	2.25	3.80	1.82	3.06
25–30	3.53	2.01	1.90	3.18
30–40	2.92	1.99	1.36	1.80
40–50	3.30	1.21	1.54	1.64
50–60	3.07	1.18	1.30	1.29
60–70	3.07	0.96	1.14	1.09
70–80	3.01	1.02	1.04	0.48
80+	1.91	1.73	1.48	1.83

influence of marriage on suicide is not the same in Paris as it is in the provinces. Indeed, in the Seine, unlike France as a whole and the provinces, the gap between the married and the unmarried is no greater in men than in women; in most age groups it is even smaller. The urban environment nullifies – and even tends to reverse – the difference between men and women with respect to the immunity conferred by marriage, while in the provinces this difference is accentuated. This implies the existence and action of a 'conjugal regulation' variable which has a curvilinear relation to suicide. Since the marital tie is weaker in Paris than in the provinces, the fact that, in the provinces, the married woman is less protected when compared with the single woman than in the Seine (that is, greater fatalism) and the fact that the husband is more protected compared to the single man (more effectively contained anomie), fits with this curvilinear model. This relation of the effect of marriage with sex, sub-culture and suicide is expressed in Figure 7.1.

ANOMIE   FATALISME

Hommes —   Femmes —
Seine   province

Hommes — province   Femmes — Seine

Figure 7.1 The effect of marriage related to sex, sub-culture and suicide

THE CONTRADICTIONS OF FATALISM: DESIRE AND REGULATION

By emphasizing anomie and de-emphasizing fatalism, Durkheim was not only misrepresenting the data in his possession; he also gave interpretations which were unconvincing and which, above all, did not square with his own principle of seeking social explanations for social differences. This is evident in relation to matrimonial regulation, in the explanation he gives of the differential effect of marital constraint on the two sexes, as well. To account for this 'antagonism between the sexes', one of which 'needs constraint and the other freedom' (1897: 309), Durkheim constructs a theory of sexual desire. The unlimited nature of this sexual desire in man stems from the fact that it goes beyond the organism, and that it 'has partly liberated itself from the body and seems almost to have become intellectualized'. The benefit, for the male, of monogamous marriage is that it alone is able to provide the social regulation indispensable to control 'inclinations' which are no longer a function of 'organic necessities'. 'By forcing the man to attach himself forever to the same woman, it assigns a strictly defined object to the need for love and closes the horizon'. The married man thus is prevented from suffering from the 'morbid desire for the infinite which always accompanies anomie' (1897: 303–4; 1951: 220–1). In contrast, a woman's 'sexual needs have less of a mental character, because, in general, her mental life is less developed'. Because she is 'a more instinctive creature than man, she has only to follow her instincts to find calmness and peace' (1897: 306; 1951: 222). Monogamous marriage is therefore of no help to a woman in 'limiting her desires', because, unlike men's, they 'are naturally limited'. Since this restraint serves no purpose, it is excessive. Durkheim is forced to recognize here that social regulation does not invariably have happy results. Discipline such as that provided by monogamous marriage 'even when useful, has its inconveniences. . . . By limiting the horizon, it closes all exits and forbids all hopes, even legitimate ones' (1897: 306).[1]

Durkheim therefore ultimately excludes women from the field of application of the theory of anomie and expresses the opposition between the two sexes by the dichotomy between nature and culture or animality and humanity. Sexual anomie is but one form of the yearning for the infinite, which stems from the fact that, unlike animals, the power to regulate man's needs is not part of his organic makeup. Women are therefore excluded from the paradise – or the inferno – of desire and consigned to the limbo of the sub-social and the sub-human, where they join the company of children and old people: 'in both these cases, physical man tends to become the whole of man' (1897: 230; 1951: 215). Moreover, because society is a less vivid notion to them, children, old men and women are less inclined to suicide. Durkheim does not forget to make it clear that 'the immunity of the animal has the same causes' (1897: 231).

Many other instances from Durkheim's writings could be cited to show that, in his view, man and woman are not, as things then stood, 'creatures of the same nature' (1897: 444; 1951: 386; cf. Besnard 1973: 30–3).

176

Durkheim therefore does indeed resort to the 'natural' difference between the sexes to explain the antagonism between their interests in the institution of marriage. This is a surprising explanation coming from someone who has sought to reduce all the extra-social variation factors of suicide to social causes. After endeavoring, where the influence of sex is concerned, to reduce biological difference to social difference, he ends up accounting for social variations by resorting to biology. In Durkheim's view, social difference can no doubt not be reduced to organic difference, but the organism is one of the pre-conditions of social difference.

However, the seeds of another, simpler, more sociological interpretation of the situation of the two sexes in relation to marriage can be detected in *Suicide*. Durkheim comments in passing that morals grant certain privileges to men, whereas 'monogamy is a strict obligation, without qualifications of any kind' for women (1897: 306).[2] But the fact that Durkheim makes nothing of this point reveals, yet again, his neglect of fatalism and his abandonment of the curvilinear model in studying the relation between social regulation and suicide. By preferring to resort to variations in sexual desire rather than to variations in social constraint in accounting for the antagonistic situation of the sexes in marriage, Durkheim not only becomes a traitor to his own ambition of explaining social phenomena by social phenomena; he also assures the incompleteness of his theory of suicide.

The contrast between the two contemporary examples Durkheim gives of fatalistic suicide, married women and young husbands, shows why any explanation based on the intensity of desire is doomed. Durkheim observes (in the chapter on egoistic suicide) that early marriages have an exacerbating influence on the suicide rate of men. At the end of the chapter on anomic suicide he explains this as a consequence of the excessively rigid regulation of monogamous marriage: 'Their passions are too tumultuous and too self-confident to be subjected to such a strict rule; this rule seems to them to be an intolerable obstacle which their desires come up against and are dashed' (1897: 309; 1951: 275). Durkheim had informed us a few lines before that if 'man, at a certain moment in his life, [is] affected by marriage in the same way as woman', this is 'for different reasons'. It is indeed for completely different reasons and even, though Durkheim is careful not to point this out, for contradictory reasons. Marriage seems to be an excessive constraint for women because sexual desires are limited and for the young man because they are too intense. The fact that Durkheim amalgamates, under the concept of fatalistic suicide, these two conflicting situations demonstrates the lack of importance Durkheim ascribes to this fourth type of suicide. But this is not all: it is evident that, on this central point of the theory of regulation – that is the relations between desires and rules – it is not the rules which vary and which appear to be an independent variable, but the desires.

The incompleteness of the theory of social regulation is therefore patent and it is extremely difficult, on the basis of the disparate elements and the apparently contradictory examples provided by Durkheim, to reconstruct a concept of fatalism which fits in with his general theoretical framework. The concept which appears at the outset in the note on fatalistic suicide quoted above is that of 'excessive regulation'. In this respect, this fourth type of suicide 'is the opposite of anomic suicide just as egoistic suicide and altruistic suicide are opposites'. But the notes which follow do not fit this very well, and moreover describe such extreme situations that it is difficult to think of examples: 'persons whose future is pitilessly blocked', 'passions violently held in check by oppressive discipline' (which preceded the example of 'husbands who are too young'), 'excessive physical or moral despotism' and 'the ineluctable and inflexible nature of the rule' (1897: 311).

Durkheim attempted to illustrate the concept by three examples: husbands who are too young, the childless married woman, and 'the suicides of slaves, which are said to be frequent in certain conditions'. The rules are no doubt excessively rigid in all these cases; but is it in fact this excessive rigidity which is decisive, when it is only felt relative to the intensity of passion, as one sees in conjugal regulation? Should one not look elsewhere for the principle of fatalism? Later writers, such as Dohrenwend, found the cause in the externality of the regulatory power in relation to the group and the individuals composing it (Dohrenwend 1959). This interpretation might be applied to the case of suicides of slaves, or to other cases which Durkheim refers to elsewhere, suicides of prisoners (1897: 394) and the mass suicide of the Jews upon the capture of Jerusalem, which made them into 'subjects and tributaries of Rome' (1897: 326). But the cases better fit the more general principle of the impossibility of interiorizing rules which are unjust and illegitimate because they are imposed from the outside (slaves), pointless (married women) or excessive (young husbands). Apart from the fact that this principle has the advantage of reconciling the contradictory elements of the concept of fatalism, its application is supported by a remark Durkheim made in connection with young husbands: 'marriage probably produces all its beneficial effects only when age has tempered the man and made him feel the necessity for discipline' (1897: 309–10).[3]

If the core of the principle of fatalism is the impossibility of interiorizing an unacceptable regulation, the conception is very close to the contrast between the anomic division of labor and the *forced* anomic division of labor. 'Rules alone are not enough, they must also be just,' Durkheim wrote in summing up the contrary nature of these two morbid forms of the division of labor in the final pages of his thesis (1893: 403). This second pathological form of the division of labor 'is maintained only by force' and 'external constraint'. Constraint prevents individuals 'from occupying a place in the social hierarchy commensurate with their abilities' (1893: 369–71).

If we accept this interpretation of fatalism we are still left with ambiguities which prevent us from arriving at a clear and coherent theory of social regulation. The first difficulty is visible in connection with Durkheim's remark on the various effects of marriage depending on age. Should the mature, 'tempered' man benefit from conjugal discipline – or conversely suffer when it is weaker – if he has genuinely interiorized the necessity for conjugal constraint? Is the diminution of desire the necessary condition of the interiorization of the norm? As the situation is quite different for women, this interpretation of fatalism comes up against a further problem: unless one supposes that there is a happy medium of desire favorable to acceptance of the rule of monogamy, one is obliged either to formulate a new postulate, less economical and less plausible, or to abandon completely any attempt to interpret the antagonism between the sexes in marriage by means of the intensity of desire. One might consider, for example, that for women marriage is an excessive constraint because it comes on top of other constraints linked to her subordinate status.

Focussing on the impossibility of interiorizing a norm as the fundamental trait of fatalism results in another difficulty, and a no less serious one. This interpretation places the emphasis on what anomie and fatalism have in common, not on what differentiates and opposes them. The reasons for the lack of interiorization of norms – their weakening in the case of anomie, their illegitimacy in the case of fatalism – are no doubt different; but they are not opposites. One might even ask whether fatalism is anything other than a particular kind of anomie: it seems closely akin to what Durkheim calls 'regressive anomie', in which the intolerable character of the norm stems from the fact that it is no longer adapted to conditions. This would be the case for individuals who experience 'increased self-repression' as a result of a loss of status (1897: 280). Or, alternatively, should this form of anomie be subsumed under fatalism?

Answering these questions will require a detailed examination of the features and conditions of anomie, to which we will now proceed. But even at this stage it should be evident that Durkheim's neglect of fatalistic suicide leaves the theory of social regulation incomplete and obscure and, consequently, stands in the way of a precise understanding of the notion of anomie.

ACUTE ANOMIE AND CHRONIC ANOMIE

Anomie is constantly presented in a dichotomous way, subdivided into two modalities. Durkheim analyses two particular forms of anomie, economic anomie and conjugal anomie (though the latter must be distinguished from the domestic anomie arising from the crisis of widowhood, and from sexual anomie, which is the anomie of the unmarried). Durkheim uses two additional contrasts, between acute anomie/chronic anomie and between regressive anomie/progressive anomie. Is there a common principle underlying these various modalities or even some kind of logic making it possible to link them all together?

The distinction between 'acute' anomie and 'chronic' anomie governs the analysis of economic anomie. Durkheim starts off by studying the impact of economic crises and the disruptive effect they have on the suicide rate before contrasting this anomie, which arises 'in fits and starts and in acute crises', to anomie 'in a chronic state', which is a 'regular and constant factor' in suicide (1897: 282–3).[4]

Economic crises, either 'economic catastrophes' or, on the contrary, 'crises of prosperity', in other words 'transformations which are beneficent but too abrupt' (1897: 271, 280), are the first and the principal example Durkheim provides of acute anomie. In both cases the collective order is disrupted temporarily. The anomie which holds sway in 'the sphere of trade and industry' is the same thing 'in a chronic state' (1897: 283). But chronic anomie in this sense is intrinsic to the economic progress characteristic of modern societies, whose ultimate aim is industrial prosperity.

'The liberation of desires' and 'the effervescence' characteristic of trade and industry become extended to include the rest of society. 'The state of crisis and anomie', Durkheim goes on, 'is constant and, so to speak, *normal* here' (1897: 285, emphasis added). Such expressions as chronic anomie or structural anomie are no doubt too weak to describe the case in which anomie is virtually institutionalized in, and lies at the heart of, the system of values of modern society. If it is 'normal' for these societies, it is because their character is pathological.

One cannot stress sufficiently that the concept of anomie entails a vigorous and almost vehement condemnation of the ideology of industrial society. In a typical passage, Durkheim reveals the strength of conviction motivating him through the stylistic flourishes that adorn the sections of *Suicide* devoted to anomie:

These arrangements are so deep-rooted that society has come to accept them and is accustomed to regarding them as normal. It is constantly repeated that it is man's nature to be an eternal malcontent, constantly to advance towards an uncertain goal. The longing for the infinite is daily presented as a mark of moral distinction, whereas it can only occur in unregulated consciences, which raise the lack of rule they suffer from to the status of a rule. The doctrine of progress at any price and as quickly as possible has become an article of faith.

(1897: 286–7; 1951: 254).

This duality between the anomie of crisis and institutionalized anomie is found in connection with the family and marriage as well as in the analysis of economic anomie. The anomie of crisis resulting from an abrupt transition from one state to another (such as widowhood or divorce) is contrasted with conjugal anomie, which is 'inscribed in the law' by the institution of divorce, and which affects married men. This example shows that anomie can be institutionalized, in the strictest sense of the term, since here it has 'become a legal institution' (1897: 307).

But this example also shows us that the two modalities of anomie are not dealt with equally by Durkheim: he grants far more importance to chronic anomie than to acute anomie. After a few lines on the crisis of widowhood and the domestic anomie which results from it, he immediately explains that he will devote more space to a form of anomie (conjugal anomie) 'which is more chronic' (1897: 290). Similarly, he is not interested in the direct consequences of divorce for the individual; he mentions this 'change in the moral and intellectual situation' only in order to pronounce it inadequate as an explanation (1897: 294). There is not a single allusion in *Suicide* to the anomie which might be associated with another change of status: marriage itself. It was no doubt difficult to demonstrate the influence of this transitional state of anomie on suicide on the basis of tables drawn up according to age groups. But using the individual files of suicides, Durkheim could have compared the dates of the suicides to the dates of marriage or used this to explain the relatively frequent suicides among very young husbands. When it suits him, he has no difficulty in employing empirical data to excess. But he does so in contexts where it makes the critical point that interests him: these are the cases of institutionalized conjugal anomie as it affects husbands and the 'sexual anomie' in which the unmarried 'live chronically' (1897: 308).

We are, in the end, given few illustrations of acute or transitional anomie in *Suicide*: abrupt change in economic situation, domestic anomie, and another sudden change, the retirement of officers and non-commissioned officers (1897: 326). Even though Durkheim takes the example of economic crises as his empirical starting point, chronic anomie is in the forefront of his preoccupations, despite the lack of relevant data regarding economic anomie. His motives here are transparent: he wishes to show that 'in our modern societies' anomie is not only a 'specific' but also a 'regular' factor in suicides, 'one of the springs supplying the annual contingent' (1897: 288).

However, it would be going too far to claim that Durkheim treats acute anomie as a negligible phenomenon, or that these two forms of anomie are interchangeable. The two modalities are distinct. But they are not without links since, according to Durkheim himself, chronic anomie encourages the appearance of acute anomie. Economic catastrophes are 'so fertile in suicides' because of 'the moral state' of chronic anomie in which they arise, and, since 'failures increase with risks', their number increases (1897: 285–6). Anomie is no doubt also linked, in both modalities, with change. But in one instance it is the product of an abrupt change in the social world and in the other it results from the fact that the social context of the individual is *characterized* by change and absence of reference.

REGRESSIVE ANOMIE AND PROGRESSIVE ANOMIE

Another duality of anomie is made explicit in *Suicide*: the dichotomy between 'regressive' anomie and 'progressive' anomie. These expressions appear only in the chapter on the individual forms of the types of suicide (1897: 322). But the distinction informs the analysis of economic anomie from the outset. The chapter on anomic suicide starts with the statement of the 'known fact' that 'economic crises have an aggravating effect on the inclination to suicide' (1897: 264). According to Durkheim, this aggravation is not explained by additional misery, because 'beneficial crises, whose effect is to abruptly increase a country's prosperity, have the same effect on suicide as economic disasters' (1897: 267) – or so he believes he can legitimately assert, despite the fragility and the disparity of the empirical data he is using. Durkheim first invites us to deduce the anomic factor from this increase in suicides on the basis of what there is in common between these two symmetrical situations – that they are 'crises, that is, disruptions of the collective order' (1897: 271). In both cases, society is temporarily incapable of performing its regulatory action on individual desires (1897: 280); in both cases, needs are liberated 'from suitable moderation' (1897: 322). The symmetry between 'regressive' and 'progressive' anomie is complete, or so commentators have commonly thought, and indeed such an interpretation can be derived from a superficial reading of certain pages of *Suicide*. In my view, this conception of anomie does not stand up to closer scrutiny. By contrasting regressive anomie and progressive anomie, Durkheim has done no more than pencil in a fake, *trompe-l'œil* window for the sake of symmetry.

The passages concerning progressive anomie are developed at far greater length than those devoted to regressive anomie. The word anomie first appears in *Suicide* (1897: 281) in connection with crises arising from increased wealth, and, not surprisingly, the phenomenon serves Durkheim's ongoing criticism of utilitarianism. The symmetry he establishes between crises of depression and crises of prosperity must be understood in the context of a specific proof. The parallel Durkheim introduces between economic crises in the usual sense of the term and crises of prosperity is first and foremost a means of refuting the generally accepted idea that impoverishment is of itself a cause of suicide. Durkheim stresses that 'economic distress', far from having an aggravating effect on suicide, 'has rather the opposite effect' (1897: 269) and in order to prove this empirically, he compares categories of Departments classified by suicide rate and the proportion of people of independent means in each category of Departments.

The parallel between the two forms is developed beyond this proof. But, try as he might, Durkheim has a great deal of difficulty preserving their symmetry. The passage he devotes to the individual forms of anomic suicide, and in which the expressions 'regressive' and 'progressive' occur, is confused. He says that 'Whether progressive or regressive, anomie, by liberating needs from suitable moderation, opens the door to illusions and consequently to disillusionment' (1897: 322). But how could *regressive* anomie be a source of illusions? In the example Durkheim provides, of a 'man who is abruptly cast down below his accustomed status', one can see how there would be 'disillusionment' and 'exasperation', but illusions and consequent disillusionment can only stem from *progressive* anomie and from the liberation from moderation which it implies.

Durkheim passes over regressive anomie very quickly in order to focus on progressive anomie, in which 'on the contrary, but without rule or moderation, the individual is impelled perpetually to surpass himself' (1897: 322). He distinguishes three typical situations of progressive anomie which lead to suicide. In the first case, the individual 'misses the goal he thought he was capable of attaining . . . ; this is the suicide of the misunderstood, which is so common in an age when there is no recognized social classification'. Durkheim provides no further details of this type of progressive anomie, leaving us with some perplexities. The logic behind the link between the absence of a recognized classification and the excess of aspirations in relation to abilities and the fact of 'being misunderstood' is not readily apparent. The second type of individual situation, the individual who has 'for a time succeeded in satisfying all his desires and his love of change, [but] suddenly comes up against an insurmountable obstacle', is described and illustrated in greater detail. Not only are the aspirations of this individual lofty, they have also largely been attained; an obstacle that arises in the course of this ascending curve can lead the individual to suicide. The obstacle need not be very substantial. In addition to the (dubious) example of Werther, who is 'enamored of the infinite, and who kills himself because thwarted in love', Durkheim illustrates the psychological risks of the ascending curve of success with examples of 'artists who, after having been showered

183

with success, commit suicide because they chance to hear a scornful whistle, because of a rather harsh review, or because their popularity *ceases to increase*' (1897: 322–3, emphasis added).

The third 'individual form' discussed by Durkheim is incontestably the most typical form of progressive anomie. It concerns individuals who 'though having no complaints about men or circumstances, come to tire of a pursuit with no possible conclusion and in which their desires become exacerbated rather than appeased' (1897: 323). In this chapter literary characters are Durkheim's preferred examples, even though he also alludes to the observations of cases by Brierre de Boismont. He finds Chateaubriand's René to be the most perfect embodiment of this type of mind. By contrast with Lamartine's Raphael ('the ideal type of egoistic suicide'), a 'creature of meditation' who 'becomes lost in himself', René is 'insatiate', as his grievances as quoted by Durkheim show:

> I am accused of always missing the goal I am capable of attaining. Alas, I seek only an unknown good, the instinct for which pursues me. Is it my fault if everywhere I find limits, if that which is finite has no value for me whatsoever?
>
> (1897: 323–4)

Later, Goethe's Faust provided Durkheim with 'the absolute embodiment of this feeling of the infinite'. Durkheim saw this as characteristic of the present age, which is sad because 'pessimism always goes hand in hand with unlimited aspirations' (1925: 35).[5] This is the very core of Durkheim's treatment of anomie. People are bound to lose themselves in the infinitude of desire, for the uncertainty of the goal to be attained means that the 'final point . . . progressively eludes one's grasp as one advances' (1925: 35). The limitlessness of aspirations necessarily leads to frustration and torment.

In the three typical situations of progressive anomie described by Durkheim, dissatisfaction is born in the context of the type of ascending mobility likely to foster illusions which will subsequently be dashed. But is regressive anomie any different? Sudden economic collapses, or, in the case of individuals, a sudden reversal of fortune are accidents which occur against a background of chronic progressive anomie. In this respect, there is no radical discontinuity between sudden regression and the phenomenon of stages referred to above. In discussing their individual manifestations, therefore, Durkheim fails to distinguish between regressive anomie and progressive anomie.

This dichotomy is totally inoperative in the cases of conjugal anomie or sexual anomie, which lie completely within the province of progressive anomie. Yet is it appropriate to treat conjugal anomie as progressive? Is it not the indeterminacy of the goal, rather than progress towards a goal which constantly eludes one's grasp, which is the central feature here? To feel the exasperation characteristic of anomie, Durkheim notes, it is not necessary 'to have had an infinite number of amorous experiences and lived the life of a Don Juan. The humdrum existence of the ordinary bachelor is enough for that', for it condemns him to 'perpetual mobility' (1897: 305). But it is easy to see that this potential objection is not valid. The indeterminacy of the goal and the limitlessness of the aspirations are intimately linked in Durkheim's eyes. Because marriage 'assigns to the need for love a precisely defined object' it 'closes the horizon' and places a limit upon desire. But when the conjugal tie can be severed, 'one cannot but look beyond one's present situation' (1897: 304–5).

The close proximity of these two notions, indeed their overlap, is, moreover, a leitmotif running through many pages in *L'Education Morale*. To escape the 'disease of the infinite', human activity must always have a specific object 'which *limits* it by *determining* it' (1925: 35). The purpose of discipline is 'to assign *specific* goals which, at the same time, *limit* their horizon' (1925: 41). It is 'by discipline alone that a child can be taught to limit his appetites, to *limit* and in so doing to *define* the objects of its activity' (1925: 38, emphasis added). This clearly suggests that limitlessness of desire cannot be distinguished from the indeterminacy of the object of that desire. Thus sexual or conjugal anomie must be regarded as a form of progressive anomie. And this is an additional reason for treating progressive anomie as the *true* anomie.

TYPOLOGY OF REGULATION

Defining the notion of anomie as the common core of both regressive and progressive anomie is thus not possible. The symmetry Durkheim suggests in certain pages of *Suicide* between the two modalities is in fact illusory. When Durkheim describes the typical individual situations leading to suicide, it is clear what the two cases have in common: we are dealing here with nothing other than the background of progressive anomie. The experience of individual failure is so painful only because the aspirations were so lofty, not to say limitless. Similarly, economic catastrophes are lethal only by virtue of the yearning for the infinite which characterizes modern societies. Because any limit is considered to be 'detestable', a 'narrower limit' seems 'intolerable': 'when one has no other aim but to constantly go beyond the point one has reached' it is 'painful to be thrown back again' (1897: 286).

The absence of symmetry between the two 'modalities' of anomie is revealed in another way. Regressive anomie in Durkheim's discussions is never anything but acute. There can be no such thing as chronic regressive anomie. Consequently a literal interpretation of *Suicide* would not allow one to reconstruct an underlying typology based on a full,

185

four-fold table using the dichotomies 'chronic–acute' and 'progressive–re-gressive'.

There is, however, a way of giving Durkheim's theory of regulation a degree of coherence. To do so, one must stop treating regressive anomie as a form of anomie: it is, rather, to *fatalism* what acute progressive anomie is to chronic progressive anomie. Such an interpretation is warr-anted by what Durkheim writes on the subject of individuals who are victims of a loss of status as a result of an economic disaster or a setback. They are not 'adjusted to the condition which has been forced upon them' and this 'increased self-repression' is an 'intolerable' prospect for them. They are faced with a situation which they see as unjust and illegitimate: 'their moral education has to be started afresh' (1897: 280). Are these not the essential features of fatalism? There is, certainly, the impossibility of interiorizing new norms which are too constraining in relation to their aspirations (as in the case of husbands who are too young) and are regarded as unacceptable. One can even liken the loss of status to slavery, at least if one considers the situation of those who have just been reduced to the state of slavery. In both cases, highly interiorized aspirations which result from protracted socialization come into conflict with new norms which can only be considered as illegitimate. Another characteristic of fatalism is found in what Durkheim terms regressive anomie: the feeling of having no control over one's fate ('the rule over which one is powerless' [1897: 311]). The man who is abruptly cast out of his class feels 'a situation slipping from his grasp which he thought he was master of' (1897: 322). In regressive anomie, as in fatalism, the horizon of the possible is closed, the 'future is pitilessly blocked' (1897: 311) and desires 'come up against and are dashed' on 'an intolerable obstacle' (1897: 309).

We are now in a position to answer the question raised earlier. Reduc-ing fatalism to a modality of anomie proved impossible. Instead, our conclusion is that regressive anomie belongs to fatalism. The purer and more precise the notion of anomie becomes, the greater the sphere of application of the notion of fatalism. Durkheim had sought to reduce the place of fatalism to almost nothing. But, almost unbeknownst to Durkheim, it is much more in evidence in his writings than first appear-ances suggest, and, far from being confined to a mere footnote, it under-pins a good many of the passages in the chapter on anomic suicide.[6]

All the problems of Durkheim's theory of social regulation are not solved by this recognition, nor are all its ambiguities ironed out. But this reconstruction at least gives it a degree of coherence without at the same time doing violence to it. Among other things, it makes it possible to draw up a typology which combines two aspects: the aspect of regulation as such, which conveys the openness or the closure of the possibilities (anomie/fatalism), and the dichotomy between chronic or institutional-ized situations and acute crises produced by sudden change. See Figure 7.2.

	Regulation	
	−	+
	Anomie	Fatalism
Chronic form	1	2
Acute transitional form	3	4

Figure 7.2 Regulation related to chronic and acute situations

Fatalism, like anomie, appears here in chronic form (Box 2) and in acute transitional form (Box 4). The latter results from the abrupt closing of the horizon of the possible and the sudden imposition of excessively constraining or unacceptable norms. We have seen that it is not difficult to illustrate 'acute fatalism', even if one limits oneself to the examples provided in *Suicide*: victims of an economic crisis, persons reduced to slavery or peoples reduced to subject status, and newly married men. Box 3 is illustrated by crises of prosperity. Yet Box 1 seems to be the anomie which, in *Suicide*, Durkheim places at the center of his concerns: losing oneself in the infinity of desire, the sensation of vertigo when confronted by the unlimited openness of the horizon of the possible. This anomie, which is inseparable from 'all morality of progress and improvement' (1897: 417), is situated at the heart of the system of values of modern societies and is indeed part and parcel of *their* institutions.

THE UNITY OF ANOMIE

The interpretation of the theory of social regulation in *Suicide* suggested here is characterized by the fact that it purifies the notion of anomie of secondary connotations by reducing the number of its possible modalities. However, the distinction between acute anomie and chronic anomie nevertheless remains, and might in a sense even be expressed by an antithesis. In effect, acute anomie refers to the temporary *absence* of norms, or a lack of norms adapted to a new situation: 'all regulation is absent for a time. One no longer knows what is possible and what is not, what is just and what is unjust,' as Durkheim writes in connection with those crises whose origin is 'an abrupt increase in power and wealth' (1897: 280). Chronic anomie, on the contrary, refers to the *presence*, in modern culture, of the ideology of progress at any cost. We are thus faced here with two determining factors of anomie, which should not be confused. If one removes regressive anomie from the category of acute anomie, however, chronic and acute anomie produce the same result. In acute anomie, as in chronic anomie, 'there is no limit to aspirations' and 'appetites . . . no longer know the limits where they must stop' (1897:

187

281). If, then, anomie stems from two social conditions which have to be analytically distinguished from one another even though their respective effects are interlinked and reciprocal, the term nevertheless denotes the same phenomenon: the limitlessness of desire and the indeterminacy of its object.

This interpretation parts company, and in no uncertain terms, with many Durkheim commentators who have thought they could discern, in *Suicide*, two quite different concepts of anomie. According to LaCapra (1972: 159–62), anomie can denote a state of complete absence of regulation and meaning following a collapse of the normative system and is expressed in a feeling of frustration and anguish, but it can also denote the existence of extreme imbalances in the social system (disharmony between means and needs or aspirations). It is thus somewhat akin to the Marxist notion of 'structural contradictions'. Thus 'from Durkheim's viewpoint, exploitation could be seen as a variant of anomie' (LaCapra 1972: 161). To justify this assertion, LaCapra refers to a passage which we have quoted above, in which Durkheim states that discipline is only useful if it is considered just and if it is not maintained by force alone. If a situation of this kind, which in the interpretation given here lies within the province of fatalism, is described in terms of anomie, one must indeed ascribe to Durkheim's concept of anomie a somewhat broad and vague connotation. So it is perhaps not surprising that LaCapra uses the term alienation (1972: 162) and makes it the equivalent of anomie.

The interpretation Giddens proposes (1971: 224; 1978: 107) is close to LaCapra's, though his Durkheim is closer to Merton than to Marx. In his view, Durkheim uses the term anomie to denote two different phenomena: (1) the absence of coherent norms defining a clear objective for individuals, and (2) the fact that a given objective cannot be attained. Giddens claims, though without proving it, that although this second connotation of the term occurs less frequently than the first in abstract discussions on anomie, it is featured in the empirical analyses made by Durkheim. Such an interpretation is unjustifiable not only because it glosses over the notion of fatalism, but also because, contrary to what Giddens alleges, it is totally inadequate for making sense of Durkheim's empirical analyses. In the case of sexual anomie, for example, it is clear that it is not the inaccessibility of the object of desire which characterizes anomie, but its indeterminacy.

These two readings of *Suicide* bring us up against the same fact. The incompleteness of Durkheim's theory of regulation, manifested in his underestimation of the scope of fatalism, contains the seeds of the metamorphoses which anomie subsequently underwent in sociology. The interpretation presented here, on the other hand, even though it may distort certain passages in *Suicide* somewhat (by eliminating regressive anomie, for instance), gives the concept of anomie a narrower and more precise

188

meaning, free of internal contradictions and in keeping with both the empirical data produced in the work and Durkheim's fundamental intuition.

NOTES

1 One may wonder what Durkheim means when he speaks of legitimate hopes as regards conjugal liberty.
2 Subsequently, during the debate on marriage and divorce already referred to above, Durkheim (1909: 279) placed greater emphasis on this second interpretation: in woman 'the sexual instinct is already contained and moderated, even outside marriage, by morals and opinion which, in this respect, are particularly exacting and severe as regards women'. In these comments Durkheim no longer refers to the natural limitation of woman's desires.
3 Durkheim considers it 'probable that marriage, in itself, does not start to have a prophylactic effect until . . . after the age of thirty' (1897: 310, n. 1).
4 'Acute' here means 'transitional' by contrast with structural or permanent (chronic). It is not an extreme form of anomie as was to be the case in the terminology used by De Grazia (1948).
5 Faust was mentioned in *Suicide* (304, n. 2) to illustrate the disease of the infinite. In the same passage, Durkheim made a fleeting allusion to two examples of sexual anomie borrowed from Musset: Rolla and 'the portrait of Don Juan' in *Namouna*. If Durkheim passes so quickly over these two examples, it is perhaps because they do not fit with his argument precisely. Rolla (who, it is true, commits suicide) and Hassan, the hero of *Namouna*, are each romantic figures living a kind of double life: a life of immediate pleasure and debauchery on the one hand and, on the other hand, the search for an all-embracing and unique love, a yearning for lost purity. To my mind, these characters illustrate the romantic quest for an impossible absolute rather than a yearning for the infinite, as described by Durkheim. Their fundamental characteristic is less the indeterminacy of the object of desire than attachment to an ideal object which is inaccessible because unreal or mythical.
6 Apart from the pages which deal with the childless married woman and the husband who is too young (1897: 306–7, 309–11), and apart from the passages relating to regressive anomie (280, 285–6), there is a passage where Durkheim notes that, to be effective, a regulation must be 'considered to be just' and must therefore stem from a power which is 'obeyed out of respect, not fear' (1897: 279). Perhaps one should also include in fatalism the mixed form of 'anomic–altruistic' suicide, under which Durkheim describes cases of regressive anomie: the 'ruined man', 'mass suicides', in particular the suicide of the Jews during the capture of Jerusalem; 'the victory of the Romans, by making them subjects and tributaries of Rome, threatened to transform the sort of life to which they were accustomed' (1897: 326).

REFERENCES

Besnard, P. (1973) 'Durkheim et les femmes ou *Le Suicide* inacheve', *Revue Française de Sociologie* 14: 27–61.
—— (1987) *L'Anomie: Ses Usages et ses Fonctions dans la Discipline Sociologique depuis Durkheim*, Paris: Presses Universitaires de France.

De Grazia, S. (1948) *The Political Community: A Study of Anomie*. Chicago: University of Chicago Press.

Dohrenwend, B. P. (1959) 'Egoism, altruism, anomie, and fatalism: a conceptual analysis of Durkheim's types', *American Sociological Review* 24, 4: 466–72.

Durkheim, E. (1888) 'Suicide et natalité: étude de statistique morale', *Revue Philosophique* 26: 446–63.

—— (1893) *De la Division du Travail Social*, Paris: Alcan. (The page references in the text refer to the second edition of 1902, identical to the subsequent editions).

—— (1897) *Le Suicide: Etude de Sociologie*, Paris: Alcan.

—— (1906) 'Le divorce par consentement mutuel', *Revue Bleue* 44, 5: 549–54.

—— (1909) Text of contribution to a debate on 'Marriage et divorce', *Libres Entretiens* (Union pour la vérité), 5e serie, 258–93.

—— (1925) *L'Education Morale*, Paris: Alcan. (Page references in the text refer to the new Presses Universitaires de France edition of 1963.)

—— (1951) *Suicide: A Study in Sociology*, trans. J. Spaulding and George Simpson, New York: Free Press.

Giddens, A. (1971) 'The "individual" in the writings of Emile Durkheim', *Archives Européennes de Sociologie* 12: 210–28.

—— (1978) *Durkheim*, Glasgow: Fontana/Collins.

Guyau, J. M. (1885) *Esquisse d'une Morale sans Obligation ni Sanction*, Paris: Alcan.

LaCapra, D. (1972) *Emile Durkheim. Sociologist and Philosopher*, Ithaca, NY: Cornell University Press.

Part III

THE ROLE OF THE SOCIOLOGICAL MORALIST AND THE MORALIST

8

DURKHEIM'S SOCIOLOGY OF MORAL FACTS

François-Andre Isambert

The importance of morality for Durkheim can perhaps be measured by the extent of his writing on the subject. It is no accident that the first article he published concerns moral science in Germany and that the last of Durkheim's texts we have aim to found morality (1887: 267–343; 1920: 313–31). Although Durkheim did not himself publish a volume with morality as its explicit subject, the courses he gave at Bordeaux and then at the Sorbonne were collected together posthumously in the *Leçons de Sociologie* and in *L'Education Morale* (1950; 1925). The first volume was a collection of his lectures from 1890 to 1900 on professional morality, civic morality, and respect for human life and for property. The second one explains moral education and its raison d'être, but its first part is virtually a course on fundamental morality, which posits the principle of a secular morality, then places it on three pillars: the spirit of discipline, the attachment to groups and the autonomy of the will. A paper given shortly after these lectures at a celebrated meeting of the Société Française de Philosophie, 'De la détermination du fait moral', a discussion of morality, was to occupy pride of place in the publication *Sociologie et Philosophie*. Finally, V. Karady was able to assemble enough material to fill an entire volume, out of the three volumes he devoted to the publication of Durkheim *Textes*, with writings of Durkheim's on the subject of morality.

But perhaps the place occupied by morality in those of Durkheim's works which do not specifically deal with it is even more important. *Suicide* is concerned first and foremost with morality. *The Elementary Forms of Religious Life* is concerned with morality, not only in the study, but in the desire, expressed at the end of the work, for the unity of science, morality and religion. The first example to occur to Durkheim in his definition of social facts viewed as 'constraints' is moral obligation: 'when I perform my task of brother, husband or citizen, when I meet the commitments I have made, to perform the duties which are defined outside the confines of myself and my acts' (1910: 6). The principal question raised in the *Division of Labor in Society* is whether that division

193

is *moral*. And this question is reinforced by the comment 'that our research is not worth an hour's effort if it is to have no more than speculative interest' (1893: 3).[1]

Durkheim's 'interest' in morality therefore makes him not only a sociologist of morality but a moralist as well, which may seem surprising. In fact, Durkheim did his utmost to link morality with the sociology of morality with a view to establishing morality on a scientific footing. At one stage he even believed he could treat the two projects as synonymous. But the link between the objectivity of 'moral phenomena' and the normativity of morality was always to cause him problems. If morality is a science – and in Durkheim's eyes, it aims to be one – it must be based on facts. Durkheim quoted Paul Janet with approval: 'the facts which serve as the basis of morality are generally accepted duties, or at least accepted by those with whom one discusses this' (1893: 3). More generally, where the moral domain is concerned, Durkheim from the very outset refuses to separate the objective from the normative, what is from what should be. As we shall see, *throughout* the three stages in the development of Durkheim's thought, the *observation* of social phenomena always served as a guide to morality as it *should be* practiced.

MORALITY AS OBLIGATION

Positive morality

As early as his article of 1887, Durkheim was struck by the existence, in Germany, of moralists – a number of whom were primarily lawyers – who, instead of constructing a deductive morality with one or several simple ideal principles as bases, made morality a *positive* science. Wundt, with whom his affinity is greatest, provided him with the term 'fact' (*Tatsache*) in the full title of his work *Ethik* (*Ethik eine Untersuchung der Tatsachen und Gesetze des sittlichen Lebens* [1886]). This term was little used in French to denote phenomena related to moral life. Wundt also gave Durkheim the idea of describing morality in terms of 'obligation'. According to Wundt, 'the particular characteristic of moral ends is that they are conceived as obligatory'. For Wundt, 'moral facts derive their authority from entirely intelligible psychological sources' (Durkheim 1920: 322). The first of these are constraint, either external constraint – in other words, fear of punishment – or internal constraint, which is the product of the interiorization of public opinion. Second are the 'motives of liberty,' which 'originate in the actual conscience of the agent' (the satisfaction of doing good). Lastly, 'there is one final motive which is loftier than the others, but which is accessible only to elite souls: it is the motive which stems from the attraction exerted by mere contemplation of the moral ideal' (1887: 323).

The first and third of these motives, some years later, were to become the antithetical characteristics of the moral act in Durkheim. But instead of treating these characteristics as opposites, Wundt, as we see, treats them as a kind of progressive series. In Wundt, the norms crown the edifice of morality. They are the point at which the goodness of the ends and the imperativeness of duty converge, and the intellectual and the affective spheres are as one. Wundt's morality is a morality of norms in which the justification of the moral act is at the same time what causally determines its execution. Durkheim admires this system, and feels a close affinity to it. He even seems to feel a covert sympathy for the 'breath of idealism' originating in Kant and Fichte. But Durkheim makes a criticism of Wundt:

> There is one of the essential properties of morality which it is impossible to explain: its obligatory force. If one sees it as an order handed down to us by the divinity, then it is in the name of God. If it consists of a social discipline, then it is in the name of society. But if it is neither of these, it is impossible to see whence it can derive the right to issue orders.
>
> (1887: 327; cf. 1925: 129–30)

In this passage Durkheim shatters the unity of the causal and moral aspects of the norm by casting doubt upon the effectiveness of the motives linking it to its ends. Put differently, he accepts Wundt's account of the motives of constraint in obligation but concludes that the acceptance of the moral ideal is a matter of faith.

This review was no more than prelude and criticism. In the first edition of the Introduction to *The Division of Labor in Society* it became a true theory of morality, founded on the notion of the 'moral fact'.

The sanction as a criterion

If there are such things as 'moral facts', and if they are encountered in everyday life, precisely *what* are they and which of the facts of ordinary experience should have this term applied to them? We have already noted a certain vagueness in Paul Janet's definition. Durkheim's simple answer to this is that moral facts 'consist of rules of conduct' (1893: 23). Some years later, in *Moral Education*, he was to clarify this point. By virtue of their regularity, social habits (customs [*moeurs*] in the broad sense) are like rules, and some of them do actually become rules. But most social habits lack the *imperative* character of rules (1925: 31–3). Moreover, we have known since Kant that there are two kinds of imperative. Durkheim has his own way of distinguishing between them. If there are rules which prescribe the means required to obtain a result (Kant's *hypothetical* imperatives), violation of the rules simply brings the whole enterprise to grief. In the case of moral rules, on the other hand, Durk-heim, like Kant, bases the imperative on something other than the result. Because he wished to provide an *observable* criterion, Durkheim noted that every moral offence provokes an intervention by society 'to prevent this deviation' (1893: 23). Summarizing his explanations in a definition, Durkheim concluded that 'every moral fact consists of a rule of conduct to which sanctions apply' (1893: 24).

For Durkheim, the link connecting the sanction to the act is essential. Unlike the somewhat uncertain consequences of a technical error in selecting means toward ends, 'this social reaction follows the offence with true necessity' (1893: 23). The consequence of moral error can sometimes be predicted down to the smallest detail. But it should be stressed that this necessity is not that of an efficient cause operating in the world of pragmatic consequences of courses of action; the constraint arises because the rule has been infringed.

> The sanction does not therefore stem from the intrinsic nature of the act since it can be withdrawn, the act remaining what it was before. It depends wholly on the relation between this act and a rule which permits or prohibits it.
>
> (1950: 6)

Two aspects of the sanction appear here which may seem contradictory, but in fact are not so, for there can be no question of withdrawal of the sanction unless the rule itself disappears. And this only occurs if one moves from one society to another, or if the society itself changes. In a society which remains the same, the same punishments are applied to the same deviations. Conversely, these relations may change if one changes societies. This characteristic makes it possible to speak of a 'moral fact' in the same way as one would speak of a physical fact: the consequences are necessarily the same, but variation is possible when there is a change in conditions.

Morality and law

Durkheim himself objects to this definition's apparent implication. 'If one adheres to this definition, does this mean that all law is subsumed by morality?' These two domains, he sees, are intimately linked, and even interwoven. 'Often,' he observes, 'law cannot be separated from the morals [*moeurs*] which are its very substratum, nor can morals [*moeurs*] be separated from the law which implements and determines them' (1893: 25). Their mutually determining relations force the sociologist to consider them both together. Durkheim reasons that the administration of the sanction rather than the content of the rule distinguishes them. It would be too simple to say that legal sanctions are material and moral sanctions are mere reprobation. Durkheim easily finds examples of corporal punishment for moral errors, and of course infringements of legal rules do not always carry material sanctions. In fact, of the two sorts of punishment, one (the moral sanction) is administered by each and every one and the other by 'specific established bodies'. He succinctly phrases this by saying that 'one is diffuse, the other is organized' (1893: 26).

To anyone considering a phenomenon as extensive in spatial and temporal terms as is the division of labor, this close connection between morality and law will be extremely useful. Morality and law will develop side by side and, since legal sanctions are easier to observe than moral sanctions, it will be possible to use variations in law to infer the associated changes in morality. This enables Durkheim, on the basis of an observable decline in *repressive law*, to deduce a weakening of the morality guaranteeing uniformity of conduct. The expansion of what he calls 'co-operative law' – stipulating the various different obligations of individuals and groups in situations where there is a division of labor – indicates the strengthening of another morality, whose slogan is *'Ensure that you are able to perform a specific function'* (1893: 40).

This development may be dangerous if it entails a relaxation of the common morality. But that morality will need to be replaced – by the diversified morality characteristic of the *organic solidarity* stemming from the division of labor. The less rigid new morality 'has something more human and thus more rational about it':

> It asks us only to be gentle towards our fellow men and to be just, to perform our tasks efficiently, to work to ensure that everyone is called to the function he is best able to perform and receives a just reward for his labors.
>
> (1893: 458)

Under this moral regime, a greater distance develops between the persuasive pressure of morality and the rigor of the law. Those who seek to shirk the division of labor 'are not punished with a precise sentence established by law, but are censured' (1893: 39). But morality continues to be a matter of compliance with rules. Durkheim thinks that the apparent exceptions to this, the non-obligatory element in what we commonly term 'morality' and in generosity, heroism and optional action generally, is not a matter of morality strictly speaking, but of aesthetics. The aesthetic qualities are closely akin to the moral qualities of which they are an extension. Durkheim's thinking on this point was to broaden and become restructured, but without his original convictions being repudiated.

EMILE DURKHEIM

From the normal to the normative

The diversity of moral facts – or in this case moral rules – is one of Durkheim's major insights, and one which he uses against the moralists at every opportunity. It is a dual diversity, on the one hand of the objects of moral rules and on the other of the moral rules governing a given object. The first kind of diversity could accommodate a conception of moral facts according to which any moral rule proclaimed in a given society is considered both as a fact by the sociologist and as a duty by the moralist. But this does not apply to the second kind. A morality worthy of the name must prescribe the same rules, with the same intensity, not only within a given society, but in other societies of the same kind. Yet variation in moral rules does not always exactly match variation in social types. Durkheim was thus to say that moral regulation is sometimes *normal* and sometimes diverges from normality and moves into the realm of the pathological.

The distinction between normal and pathological is explicitly borrowed from biology. Durkheim thinks that through it he is able to make the transition from the moral fact to morality, from the objective to the normative. The normal type is the average type within a given stage of the development of the organism under consideration – in this case society (1893: 33). Thus infanticide was normal in the societies of antiquity; if one of our modern societies permitted it, in spite of the fact that practically all of them condemn it, the rule in that society would be pathological. It should therefore be possible to move beyond the simple observation of moral facts in order to evaluate them and improve the moralities which are actually in place. But Durkheim is skeptical: 'It is not certain,' he says, 'that, even with this adjustment, the normal type will achieve the ultimate degree of perfection' (1893: 37).

Durkheim seems to hesitate at this point between a morality with the limited aim of simple normality and the search for a 'higher perfection' which nevertheless 'can only be determined on the basis of the normal state' (1893: 37).

THE TWO SIDES OF MORALITY

In this initial formulation there is clearly a conflict between a definition based on constraint and an aspiration towards greater freedom. Sanction, conceived as the sole criterion of the moral fact, is never in Durkheim's eyes the *source* of obligation. But in *The Division of Labor in Society*, this fact is stated only in passing (1893: 25). Everything seems to indicate that Durkheim feels constricted by his own rigor in his appeal to this criterion. Years later, he was to stress the contrast between the *source* of the obligation and the criterion of sanction.

198

Here, for the act to be what it must be, for the rule to be obeyed as it must be obeyed, we must defer to it, not to avoid some unpleasant result, or some material or moral punishment, or to obtain some kind of reward; we must defer to it quite simply because we must do so, quite apart from the consequences our conduct may have for us. One must obey a moral principle out of respect for it and for this reason alone.

(1925: 35)

This is precisely the Kantian idea of the act performed *out of duty*. It also proves that Durkheim is less concerned with external criteria and more with the motivation of the act. The very notion of the 'moral fact' broadens to encompass the acts and thoughts which refer to it. From this position Durkheim was to deduce a second aspect of moral facts.

Obligation and desirability

In 'De la détermination du fait moral' the concept of 'morality' is broadened to include a second dimension. Durkheim initially draws attention to the imperative aspect of moral rules. 'We will reassert,' he writes, 'the notion of duty, of which we will give a definition very close to Kant's, but will do so through purely empirical analysis'. But another aspect of the moral act appears. The passage needs to be quoted in full:

contrary to what Kant has said, the notion of duty does not exhaust the notion of the moral. It is impossible for us to perform an act solely because we are ordered to do so, leaving aside what it is. In order to ensure that we are the agents of it, it must to some extent relate to our sensibility, must one way or another appear *desirable* to us. Obligation or duty therefore expresses only one of the aspects, one abstract aspect of the moral. A certain amount of desirability is another characteristic, no less essential than the first.

(1924: 50)

With this, Durkheim takes the antithesis between the characteristics of the moral fact to the point of paradox. What could be more antithetical, at first sight, than *duty* and *desire*? In order to convey a heterogeneity bordering on ambivalence, he compares this to an analogous paradox in the notion of the *sacred*: 'The sacred being is, in a sense, the forbidden being, which one dare not violate; it is also good, loved and sought after' (1924: 51). Durkheim justifies his comparison as follows: the relation between moral life and religious life is rooted in history:

For centuries, moral life and religious life have been intimately linked and even absolutely synonymous. . . . It is clear therefore that moral life has not yet succeeded and never will succeed in

199

ridding itself of all the characteristics it had in common with religious life.

(1924: 69)

Moral Education presents a similar kind of duality, though less sharply and with more emphasis on complementarity than contrast. Although respect for obligation, referred to in a *pedagogical* context as 'the spirit of discipline', is regarded as the first moral sentiment, one must immediately add to it 'attachment to groups'. Each reinforces the other. But the former is obedience to *authority*, whereas the idea of attachment to groups presupposes the idea that society possesses an 'attractive power', in which the idea of desirability is present (1925: 33).

Points of convergence and interpenetration

Durkheim does not hesitate to speak of 'partly contradictory aspects' (1924: 51). But nothing would be further from the truth than to speak in this connection of 'two moralities', one being a morality of obligation and the other of desire, or, as he put it on a number of occasions, one of *duty* and the other of *good*. To begin with, these two aspects of morality are contained in the same acts. 'The notion of good enters into the notion of duty, just as the notion of duty and obligation enters into the notion of good' (1924: 64). That it is impossible for people to act out of pure obligation means that moral goodness must be desirable.

But this is desirability of a very special kind. Whereas one might have thought there was an irreconcilable antagonism between duty and desire, Durkheim considers that there is a kind of permeation of duty into moral desire:

> Something of the nature of duty is found in this desirability of the moral aspect. Although it is true that the content of the act attracts us, its nature is such that it cannot be performed without effort and self-constraint. The élan, even the enthusiasm with which we can act morally takes us out of ourselves, lifts us above our nature, a process which is not achieved without struggle. It is this *sui generis* desirability which is commonly called good.

(1924: 51)

Durkheim comes close to identifying the notion of duty with a particular kind of desirability. But his thought retains a certain vagueness, exemplified by his use of such expressions as 'something of the nature of duty'. The convergence between duty and this 'something' to which it is akin was to be clarified in a subsequent text, 'Jugements de valeur et jugements de réalité' (1924: 117–41).

200

The constraining objectivity of the value judgment

Durkheim never uses the word 'value' in the article on the determination of the moral fact. It is hard to know why this should be. The difference between duty and desirability continues to be marked, whereas that between duty and value would seem to have become less so. When he embarks upon the question of the social status of value judgments, Durkheim would seem to be propelling us towards another sphere of thought, namely one in which judgments of reality and value judgments are logically linked. By the second page, however, one is again confronted by the notion of desirability, and by judgments such as 'I like hunting, I prefer beer to wine, an active life to one of relaxation', etc. False value judgments, Durkheim tells us:

> are just as much facts as the weight of bodies or the elasticity of gases. The purpose of such judgments is therefore not to ascribe a value to things, but merely to affirm specific states of the subject.

Contrast this with the following:

> It is quite a different matter when I say: 'This man *has* a high moral value; this picture *has* great aesthetic value, this jewel is *worth* such and such an amount'. In all these instances, I ascribe to the beings or the things in question an objective character, quite independent of my feelings when I make this judgment.
>
> (1924: 118)

For Durkheim, as we have already suggested, the objectivity of these – strictly speaking – value judgments consist in their identical nature within one and the same society. What is interesting is the way in which such judgments are formed. Try as one might to distinguish value judgments from simple statements of individual preference, desirability remains one of the components of the judgment:

> On the one hand, all value supposes an appraisal by a subject, in a set relation to a specific sensibility. That which has value is good in some way; that which has value is desirable, and all desire is an inner state.
>
> (1924: 119)

How is this subjectivity compatible with the objectivity which is ascribed to value? For Durkheim, the key lies entirely in the fact that, even in our spontaneous appraisals, society exerts its influence upon us: 'We know full well that we are not the masters of our appraisals, that we are bound and constrained. It is the public conscience that binds us'. There is a 'kind of necessity' which we experience and are aware of when we make value judgments (1924: 123). The objectivity of value judgments is thus concealed from us: when we assess the quality of an object or the moral value of an act or a person, we experience it as a necessity felt deep within ourselves. In the case of every moral fact we are faced with the duality of constraint and sanction on the one hand, and with the duality of value and desirability on the other. Yet the social constraint which weighs upon all of them seems to unite them in one single movement of thought.

Maintaining duality

The link between sanction and collective desire would therefore seem to be clear: the two types of the normative would appear to be at least linked, if not actually intermingled. And what better term than 'norm', which Durkheim found in Wundt, could be used to combine two aspects which characterize law, art, morality, those at once real and ideal domains of social life? In contrast with the simple term 'rule', the term 'norm' would only be used for a rule when it contained a value.

Durkheim does not make this link directly. He never abandons the original idea of social constraint as a fact in its own right, nor does he merge it completely with the aspiration engendered by an ideal. He maintains a tension between the two poles.

His refusal to merge the two registers is evident in 'La détermination du fait moral'. Durkheim raises the question of the possibility of making the transition from one register to the other by deduction. But he does not trouble to answer it. It seemed to him self-evident that rules cannot engender desires. But the derivation of rules from the good, the desirable, seems like a more promising strategy. Durkheim is uncompromising in his rejection of this.

> I have received a letter which puts this question and suggests this hypothesis to me. I am extremely reluctant to accept it. I will not go into all the reasons against it; since in all ages, as far back as one can go, we always find these two characteristics side by side, there is no objective reason for allowing even a logical priority as between the one and the other. But even from the theoretical and dialectical standpoint, is it not clear that, if we only have duties because duty is desirable, the very notion of duty disappears? Never can obligation be derived from the desirable, since the specific character of obligation is, in some measure, to do violence to desire. It is just as impossible to derive duty from good (or conversely) as it is to deduce altruism from egoism.
>
> (1924: 69)

Durkheim's spirited reply reflects the fact that utilitarianism was always public enemy number one for him, and permitting this reasoning would be tantamount to accepting utilitarianism. But his discursive characterizations of the orders of duty and of rules are out of step with the order of the agreeable: Durkheim repeats time and time again in his work, beginning with *The Division of Labor in Society*, that the order of duty is not determined by what may be useful and good for society itself. Thus no morality can be deduced from the interests of that society. The register of the imperative and of the evaluative – or, as we might well put it, of the deontological and the axiological – remain without any necessary link. This does not mean that good and duty do not often coincide. But the 'coercive' character and the character of the good remain 'opposites'. Their overlap is no more than coincidental.[2] 'While institutions may impose themselves upon us, we cling to them; they face us with obligations and we are fond of them; they constrain us and we benefit from this function and this very constraint' (1910: XX).

Durkheim's work ends by characterizing the 'superiority' of society, which derives from the fact that its value is much greater than that of the individual. Like God, the supreme value, it is the mainspring of all ideals, of all values. There are thus two characteristics of society that correspond to two antithetical characteristics of moral facts: authority and the ideal. These two characteristics indeed appear to play distinct causal roles in generating the order of the rules and the order of the values.

MORALITY, MORAL FACTS AND MORAL THEORY

Society, foundation of the unity of morality

What is the substratum upon which moral facts are based? Although Durkheim makes the spirit of discipline and the attachment to groups the *two bases* (or at least the first two bases) of morality, he leaves the question of their foundation open. Is the disciplinary aspect of morality an ultimate basis? Durkheim does refer to an *authority*, the authority of moral rules. But what does this authority consist of? 'Yet again,' he says, 'this is a problem which we will have to set aside for the moment but will return to in due course' (1925: 47). Durkheim goes into great detail over the question of the purpose of the moral act, concluding that acts with individuals as their goal cannot be called moral. 'Apart from individuals, there is nothing but the groups formed by them, in other words, societies' (1925: 68). This suggests that attachment to groups is basic. But Durkheim is never explicit about this.

One might conclude that this is a question that Durkheim ought not to try to answer at all. But it is not easily avoided. The term 'authority' is an abstraction. As a sociologist, Durkheim needs a substratum which is a concrete reality. Groups and societies are an obvious candidate for this reality, and Durkheim from his very first writings appeals to them. But does society by itself have the power to ensure that rules are implemented? Is it the source of the rules? Showing that the morality on which we are agreed takes society as its object, as Durkheim attempts to do, is not the same as showing that that society is the source of this morality.

Durkheim's response to this muddle is extremely clear:

> These, then, are the first two elements of morality. In order to distinguish and define them, we have had to study them separately. As a result, they have seemed up to now to be distinct and independent. Discipline seems to be one thing, and the collective ideal to which we are attached something quite different. Yet in fact there are close links between them. They are merely two aspects of one single reality.
>
> (1925: 96)

Begin with the 'spirit of discipline' and its respect for the rule and the authority of the rule. Individuals may exercise self-discipline, but it is the interiorization of the force which makes them obey. This process of interiorization is the chief aim of education. The acquisition of religious conviction is the paradigm of this process, and Durkheim refers on many occasions, and especially in the early pages of *Moral Education*, to the authority of religion. But his point is that the object of religion is the mythologized figure of society. Despite the demise of the moral hold of religion, Durkheim considers that a moral consensus, even if only an approximate one, has been maintained. *Secular* morality enables members of a society such as ours to remain in agreement. It can have no other source than this being, namely *society*, which possesses all the characteristics of the individual, but which dominates the individual: 'Only society in its totality has sufficient awareness of itself to have successfully established this discipline whose object is to express society' (1925: 98). We might add that if morality varies in the way societies do, this is indeed because it is a product of them. Taking his cue from universal history, Durkheim insists that 'if there is one fact that history has placed beyond all doubt, it is that the morality of every people is directly related to the structure of the people which practices it' (1925: 98–9).

One is thus forced to conclude that 'although society is the goal of morality, it also creates it' (1925: 98). To some extent, it makes its own morality. But it does not do so in the mechanical fashion of utilitarian teleology, which Durkheim had rejected ever since *The Division of Labor in Society*. There can be no doubt about this. Durkheim time and again refers to the *ideals* which are the goal of societies, not their simple well-being. Even so-called individual morality is no exception to this:

It [society] obliges us to develop within us an ideal type and it does so because it has a vital interest in so doing. For it can only exist if there are sufficient similarities between all its members, in other words, if they all reflect, to varying degrees, the essential traits of one ideal, which is the collective ideal.

(1925: 99)

If society is indeed the 'reality' which links together the first two components of morality, is it true to say that 'attachment to groups' is based directly on society? In fact Durkheim is so adamant that the attachment to groups must be *inculcated* that one sometimes wonders if this attachment is not the work of the pedagogue rather than of society as a whole. But the characteristics of society are such that it is not *merely* the object of a duty of attachment: it has something about it which *inspires* this attachment in us, and, to put it in the terms of the 'Détermination du fait social', this certainly places it in the category of the 'desirable'. If, by its authority, society is the repository of *duty*, it is also the repository of *good*, 'inasmuch as it is a reality richer than our own and to which we cannot attach ourselves without our whole being becoming enriched thereby' (1925: 110).

But where does this leave us with the duality of the two elements of morality? Does this mean that the duality has been transferred to society itself? Does the same society impose itself on us *and* attract us? What to Durkheim's mind unifies these two apparently conflicting characteristics is the fact that it is 'something superior to individuals' (1925: 105). One wonders whether the question 'Is this the same type of superiority?' should not be posed. Does Durkheim's conclusion rest on an equivocation with respect to the term 'superiority'?

Be this as it may, some things are clear. Moral facts are not merely observable; they can also be explained because they result from a more general, more fundamental reality, yet one which is also a causal fact. In short, whether one enumerates the individual moral facts or traces them back to their origins, one is still dealing with *facts:* society itself is a 'moral fact', one which encompasses all the others. Hence the outlines begin to emerge, in sociology, of a *science* of morality, in the fullest sense, making it possible not only to describe morality, but to understand what it is based on as well.

Scientific knowledge and the autonomy of the will

Durkheim refused to regard sanctions as motives for genuinely 'moral' action, and, echoing Kant, explained that an act which is dictated by duty should also be performed out of duty. But he takes a further step with Kant in positing that the genuinely moral act must be performed

205

through the *autonomy of the will*. According to *Moral Education* this is the third base of morality:

> Only an act we have performed in total freedom, without any kind of coercion, do we regard as wholly moral. But we are not free if the law by which we regulate our behavior is imposed upon us, if we have not freely desired it.
>
> (1925: 128)

This is Kant's conception of the moral act as an act which is free. But Kant conceives a 'pure autonomy of the will', which makes the will into a faculty alien to the rest of our natures. This metaphysical concept Durkheim cannot accept.

If we consider the example of the relationship with the world we have through the medium of the natural sciences, we can see that the sciences make us 'free' in the material universe. Although human reason is not the legislator of the physical universe, we become free within this universe when we understand its laws – in other words, know not only what they are, but why they are what they are. As Durkheim puts it,

> In other words, although it is not we ourselves who, to use a somewhat archaic expression, made the plan of nature, we rediscover it through science, we re-think it and understand why it is thus. Hence, provided we are sure it is everything it should be, in other words, as implied in the nature of things, we can submit to it . . . because we deem it to be good and because we have no alternative.
>
> (1925: 132)

Perhaps it is not just the expression which is archaic. Notice the way in which Durkheim allows a causal necessity to become a final necessity. It is patently the science of morality which is the beneficiary of this shift in meaning. For he takes it that if it is possible to explain why moral facts are what they are, this of itself shows that they must be what they are, and respects this necessity of being.

> We can investigate the nature of the rules of morality which we initially submit to passively and which the child receives from without, through education, and which are imposed on him by virtue of their authority. We can seek to establish the direct or indirect conditions for them, their raison d'être. In a word, we can make a Science of them. Our heteronomy is ended. We are masters of the moral world.
>
> (1925: 133)

Durkheim is closer to Spinoza than to Kant on this point, by virtue of his definition of 'freely desiring' as 'desiring that which is in keeping with the nature of things' (provided that one is able to *understand* what this nature of things is) (1925: 132). Thus morality comes to have two levels, for it is not only the child who receives his morality 'from without'. Most adults, in particular those who receive a religious morality (as Durkheim conceives of it), do so as well. Durkheim's moral education is liberating, in contrast to religious inculcation, but because it is scientific and leads to a higher level of morality, and not because it is not inculcated.

From moral science to moral art

Moral facts are the necessary point of departure for scientists – in this case sociologists – who wish to know what the moral life of a group or of a society is. But by placing themselves on the scientific level, they liberate themselves – as well as all those with whom they share their knowledge – from the local morality which is the starting point of all moral education. Yet it cannot be assumed that autonomy, liberation, has now been achieved; the Science of Morality is still in the process of development. Indeed, there are many passages where Durkheim describes it as being in its initial stages. Sometimes he speaks of individual moral rules, though more often of moral facts in their entirety and of their general relations with society (for example, in *The Division of Labor in Society, Suicide* and particularly in *Leçons de Sociologie*); he scarcely mentions the 'social' explanations of the individual facts.

A Durkheimian 'Treatise of morality' remained unwritten. Durkheim took up this task in the dusk of his life. The last thing he wrote was the beginning of this work. The reader is faced with generalities of the sort one would expect from an introduction. But Durkheim, who had reflected upon this subject constantly, and had acquired a certain distance from his past works, was able to formulate the issues with particular clarity. He also showed that he was conscious of a number of questions beyond those he had already raised. In this introduction Durkheim expressed with great clarity the duality of levels we saw emerging in *Moral Education*. The word 'moral' can have two meanings. First, it can mean the way acts are judged in everyday life, from the standpoint of the moral value to which one is attached. Such judgments are spontaneous: 'We praise or blame by a sort of instinct' (in Karady 1975: 315). 'But "morality" has a second sense: it is also used to mean all systematic, methodical speculation on moral data' (1975: 315).

Durkheim often inveighed against moralists. But he explains that this was only because of their method and not because of their ambition to develop a systematic moral philosophy, an ambition which, moreover, he shares. Durkheim says that the moralists (no doubt with the exception of the German moralists whom he examined in his article of 1887) 'postulate that the complete system of moral rules is subsumed within one cardinal notion, of which it is merely the development' (1975: 318). For Durkheim, morality must be treated as an 'unknown quantity' in observing which it is the 'outermost signs' one begins with (1975: 321). This does not mean that he proposes a psychological approach. 'Man,' he says, 'is a product of history' (1975: 323). Morality, people's own conception of the world and of themselves, has varied throughout history.

It is in historical diversity that we should look for 'moral facts'. But these diverse external facts provide only the starting point for analysis. The 'outward tangible signs are replaced by others' as the analysis proceeds:

> Only when one has moved beyond the level of tangible appearances does it become possible to discover the innermost characteristics of the thing itself, which pertain to its very essence, insofar as this word can be used in scientific language.
>
> (1975: 325)

In Durkheim's view, a theoretical investigation that made it possible to discover such principles would not be merely of speculative interest. 'Moral truths,' he says, are ordinarily 'so deeply rooted in the consciences of all normal people that they are beyond doubt' (1975: 326). The question is rather whether our conformity to them can be reconciled, by means of rational knowledge, with autonomy or freedom. There are of course moments when history hesitates and when moral certainties are shaken. As early as *The Division of Labor in Society*, and in *Moral Education*, Durkheim was preoccupied with the uncertainties of the morality of his own age, uncertainties which stemmed from the changes morality was then undergoing. Hence, one of the keys to the gulf between systematic morality and morality as observed in the acts it inspires is time. In an age when traditional and novel moralities intermingled, systematic scientific morality would be capable of identifying novel developments. The scientific approach also enables us to consider the 'morality of a particular age', the morality actually embodied in moral practice.

Bur Durkheim sought to go beyond the study of actual moral practice, what he considered to be morals 'in a degraded form and reduced to the level of human mediocrity'.

> The science we are outlining, on the other hand, aims to discover moral precepts in all their purity and impersonality. Its subject-matter is morality itself, ideal morality, situated in a region far above the realm of human acts. It is not concerned with the deformations that its embodiment in everyday practice imposes upon it and which can only express it imperfectly.
>
> (1975: 330)

This normative approach, which clearly separates ideal morality from the 'physics of morals', leads Durkheim to introduce a term which until then had been the prerogative of Lucien Levy-Bruhl (1903), the term 'the art of morality'. Durkheim had refrained from using this term, doubtless in order to avoid creating too much of a gulf between knowledge and practice. The purpose of the moral art is to improve morals and perhaps even more to anticipate the morality of the future. But this art, as Durkheim reiterates, can 'have no other basis than this science of moral facts acquired and realized'.

A comment on the family indicates Durkheim's final understanding of the role of this science. The moralist, he says:

> cannot discuss domestic morality for instance unless he first deter-mines the many precepts comprising this part of morality, and also their causes, and the ends to which they correspond. Only later does it become possible to investigate how these precepts can be modified, rectified and implemented. If one is to say how family morality is likely to evolve, one must also know how the family is constituted, how it has come to assume its present form, and what its function is in society as a whole.
>
> (1920: 329)

NOTES

1 The introduction to the first edition contains a detailed discussion of morality and an attempt at a definition. This section was eliminated from the subsequent editions, as Durkheim no doubt considered his first theoretical effort too narrow.
2 A proof *a contrario* of the authenticity of this reading of Durkheim lies in the fact that the two characteristics of society and moral life alike are sometimes confused with one another, though at exceptional moments. Here too one can but quote:

> It is in fact at such moments of effervescence that the great ideals upon which civilizations are based have emerged. Creative or innovative periods are precisely those when, for various reasons, men grow closer together, when meetings and assemblies are most frequent, relations more developed, the exchange of ideas more active. Such times are the great crisis of Christianity, the collective enthusiasm which, in the twelfth and thirteenth centuries, attracted the scholars of Europe to Paris and gave birth to scolasti-cism, the Reformation and the Renaissance, the age of revolutions, the major social upheavals of the nineteenth century. At such times, it is true, this higher form of life is lived with such intensity and exclusiveness that it almost completely dominates the consciences, almost completely driving out egoism and the commonplace. At such times, the ideal tends to become one with the real; which is why men have the impression that the time is fast approaching when the ideal will become reality and the kingdom of God will be established on Earth. But the illusion never lasts because this exal-tation itself cannot last: it is too exhausting. Once the critical moment has

passed, the social fabric slackens once more, intellectual and emotional intercourse slows down, individuals return to their ordinary level.

(1924:143)

At this 'ordinary' level, the rules which had disappeared in the general fusion of the various aspects of society, in which all constraint is forgotten, reappear and with them their coercion.

REFERENCES

Durkheim, E. (1887) 'La science positive de la morale en Allemangne', *Revue Philosophique* 24, 2. (Reproduced in V. Karady (ed.) (1975) *Textes*, Vol. 1, Paris: Minuit.)

—— (1893) *Division du Travail*, Paris: Alcan.

—— (1897) *Le Suicide*, Paris: Alcan.

—— (1910) *Règles de la Méthode sociologique*, 2nd edn, Paris: Alcan.

—— (1911) 'Lecture to the International Philosophy Congress in Bologna', *Revue de Metaphysique et de Morale* 24, 33–58, 113–42, 275–84. (Reprinted in Durkheim (1924) *Sociologie et philosophie*, Paris: Alcan.)

—— (1912) *Les Formes Élémentaires de la Vie Religieuse*, Paris: Alcan.

—— (1920) 'Introduction a la morale', posthumous publication, *Revue Philosophique* 89, 79–97. (Reproduced in V. Karady (ed.) (1975) *Textes*, Vol. 2, Paris: Minuit.)

—— (1924) *Sociologie et philosophie*, Paris: Alcan.

—— (1925) *L'Education Morale*, Courses de Sorbonne, 1902–3, Paris: Alcan.

—— (1950) *Leçons de Sociologie: Physique des Moeurs et du Droit*, Paris: Presses Universitaires de France.

Levy-Bruhl, L. (1903) *La Morale et la Science des Moeurs*, Paris: Alcan.

9

INEQUALITIES AND SOCIAL STRATIFICATION IN DURKHEIM'S SOCIOLOGY

J.-C. Filloux

In the Preface to the first edition of the *De la Division du Travail Social* ([1893] 1960), the reader is informed that 'the fact that we propose above all to study reality does not mean that we should abandon the attempt to improve it; indeed, we would consider that our research was not worth a single hour's effort if it had no more than speculative interest' ([1893] 1960: 3). Durkheim's initial intention was to make 'social science' or sociology (which he considered it was his task to *create*) an instrument of social change. The (political as well as pedagogical) reforming mission Durkheim embraces is closely linked to the theoretical model he constructs: the model enables him to justify the ultimately practical function of a science of society, to justify approaching a society in terms of both what it *is* and what it *should be* given what he calls its 'conditions of existence'. This ambiguous, but characteristic, Durkheimian usage transcends the simple Comtean distinction between social statics and social dynamics, since it serves to diagnose, or even to guide by reference to, the 'normal' becoming of a specific society. The sociologist will reveal *incoherences* characteristic of a social system and *survivals* of archaic traits or structures. It will also be the sociologist's task to assess the *new* aspirations which appear in the system that are the very motor of development. Thus socialism, according to the definition Durkheim was to give of it, could appear to him to be 'implied in the very nature of higher societies' (1970: 235).[1]

PARAMETERS OF A READING

One should approach a reading of Durkheim's texts on the phenomena of social stratification, of the treatment of the questions of equality and inequality in the industrial societies of his age, from this general perspective. If indeed it is true that it is the vocation of the sociologist, like all other members of an 'intellectual elite', by vocation, to be at least the ruler's counsellor if he or she cannot rule, the sociologist's research is not free from practical implications.[2] If these texts are interpreted on the basis of the parameters set by the founding project of Durkheimianism, the structural and functionalist basis of his sociology, the hypothesis of the consolidation of the collective conscience by stages, the humanist thesis – inherited from the philosophy of the Enlightenment and from Renouvier – of the necessary primacy of the cult of Man in the society of the future, their practical implications become clear.

(1) The decision taken by Durkheim during the period he spent at the Ecole Normale Supérieure between 1881 and 1883, to take part in the establishment of sociology as a science, is embodied in the framework of the projected thesis entitled 'Rapports entre l'individualisme et le socialisme', which was to become the 'Rapports de la personnalité individuelle et de la solidarité sociale' at the time that the definitive thesis, *The Division of Labor in Society*, went to press. The basic project of a practical social science is thus embodied in an initial question, which continued to underlie Durkheim's thinking, namely, are individualism and socialism irreconcilable? If not, *what kind of* individualism and *what kind of* socialism are compatible? In what kind of political structure is this reconciliation possible? Although a body of scientific knowledge has to be created in order to answer these 'questions', the final objective is certainly to find practical solutions to them.

(2) Durkheim constructs a 'structural–functional model', with an emphasis on the problem of *consensus*, a notion which he borrows from Comte. We will not dwell here on the fact that this model is part of a very profound imagined vision of *communion* which marks Durkheim as a man. The fact remains that the imagined vision of a unified, consensual society, united by common values, haunts him.[3] The central theoretical themes of his social analyses are *integration* (organic linking of the elements of social structure, solidarity between individuals) and regulation (rules and norms which govern the functioning of this structure and the relations between individuals). One might add that the Durkheimian model leads one to approach the whole integrated and regulated apparatus itself by reference to two notions: the notion of *social needs* (which can be inferred from the way they are expressed, or from an analysis of the 'conditions of existence' of a society); and the notion of *collective representations* (the ideas, opinions, values shared by the members of society).

(3) Consequently, if sociological investigation is to seek to ascertain both the state of a social system and its processes of development, it must take account of relations that develop within time between the collective representations, the institutions, and what Durkheim calls the morphological substratum of the social. In the final analysis, the social can be identified with the 'collective conscience' and its works, as the

collective conscience becomes 'consolidated' and 'materialized' in stages by means of mutual interaction. The framework Durkheim uses to describe the dynamic state of a society may be reconstructed as follows (Filloux 1977: 107–36):

— *substratum:* geographical basis, population, material objects;
— *formalized institutions:* conventions of language, formal precepts of morality and law, professional or family roles, financial systems, rituals;
— *formal representations:* societal values, governing ideologies, myths, symbols, philosophical and religious doctrines, public opinion;
— *free representations:* effervescences, irruptive aspirations, emerging ideals and values, currents of opinion, collective emotions.

Durkheim regards free aspirations as being possibly translated into formal representations, into institutions, as developing a substratum; and conversely, as possibly performing the role of a substratum, that is of the institutions with respect to the collective representations. As one might imagine, this model, which makes it possible to determine both the state of a society and the forces instrumental to its development, in certain respects converges with Marx's base/superstructure model. For Durkheim's, however, the ultimate determining factor is not economics or the material substratum of society, but the collective conscience itself, in the form of the collective representations.[4]

(4) Modern industrial societies are said no longer to be able to 'subsist' save by the common acknowledgement, in the collective conscience, of the Humanity in Man. Durkheim constructs a kind of sociological proof of the necessity for what he calls the Cult of Man, the religion of Man in developing society, which is at once one of the most original and also most audacious aspects of Durkheim's conception of modern societies. In the societies, there are no collective values that unite all its members, apart from the active recognition not merely of human rights but also of the fact that Man possesses a sacred character, that he becomes a God for man, *Homo homini deus.* This enables Durkheim to give sociological content to the concept of 'individualism', which he interprets not as egoism or utilitarianism, in the way these terms are used by economists, but as the *religion of the human individual.* This redefinition (not to say rehabilitation) or individualism, in which one detects the influence of the 'personalism' of Renouvier, enabled Durkheim to write his very fine article of 1898 on the Dreyfuss Affair, entitled 'L'individualisme et les intellectuels'.[5] It also enabled him to consider the possible convergence of individualism and socialism, the latter conceived not as State despotism but as a democratic model centered on respect for the Cult of Man. Sociology reveals the future 'necessity' of a type of society which might be termed individualist, socialist, democratic.

213

Perhaps one should add *meritocratic*, for Durkheim's comments on the inequalities within societies, and on the conditions governing the justification of one form or another of social stratification, seem to lead to a view of society in which social actors within the context of the solidarity of functions are rewarded by reference to social merit. In these pages, one encounters not only that intentional ambiguity between the statement of things as they are and of the things as they should be which is characteristic of Durkheim's political writings. One also finds references to the necessary Cult of Man, to the aspirations and prejudices, in opinion and the collective representations, which therefore constitute their backdrop. Collective assessments or prejudices about merit cannot simply be errors, for they are social products as well. In the period following *The Division of Labor in Society*, the problems posed by the specific social and economic inequalities in industrial societies are examined through the functional necessity of moral individualism in these societies. The social system is approached in terms of what we today refer to as social stratification, of a hierarchy of rewards linked to the distribution of roles, and also in terms of the values of labor and goods, property and social strata or classes. But Durkheim's approach also varies the questions of the ways and extent to which the cult of the individual is expressed and implemented in the beliefs, norms and institutions relating to the allocation and production of resources, and the practical question of how sociological knowledge can help to facilitate the process by which this *individualistic* society will be achieved.

Durkheim is struck by the power of egalitarian aspirations or ideals, which exert pressure for the institutionalization of norms and types of organization aimed at bringing about greater 'justice' in social relations. He is also struck by the contradictory representation of a necessary hierarchy of remuneration linked to a hierarchy of social status. His problem is therefore to find out what types of social stratification are in keeping not so much with egalitarian ideals as such as with the elements in these ideals which can be shown to correspond to shared personal values. For Durkheim, the question is 'What *are* egalitarian ideals in an individualistic and industrial society and what *should they be?*' and 'What should the components of the identity concept itself be, to ensure that it is an instrument for criticizing society's conditions of existence and bringing about ordered change in them?'

The key to Durkheim's response to these questions in his introduction of the concept of *merit*, borrowed from Comte and Saint-Simon. In Durkheim's view, this concept should make it possible both to clarify the question of what elements in the idea of equality are consistent with the demands of individualism, and also to arrive at a preliminary approximation of the type of society which, as a sociologist, he can see emerging from public conscience and institutions. The term *meritocracy* seems appropriate to describe a society which would be founded on the consecration of 'merits' and would satisfy the egalitarian aspirations of modern industrial society. Durkheim the sociologist must therefore help to characterize and justify the form of this society that is 'normal' under modern conditions. This is already tantamount, in a way, to justifying the existence of stratification and inequalities, even if the nature of 'just' stratification is left to be resolved 'sociologically'.

LEGITIMATING A STRATIFIED AND INEGALITARIAN SOCIAL STRUCTURE

Showing that social stratification meets the requirements of 'individualistic' society legitimates such stratification. In all societies where there is extensive division of labor, the highest social rank demands high levels of skills, and hierarchically structured rewards are necessary. In effect, individuals are in competition with one another in performing duties useful to the group. If the cult of the individual implies that people should be declared equal as human beings, it also implies at the same time that the differences which emerge between them in this competition should be recognized. From this standpoint, the whole problem consists in determining the criteria for a stratification which, for the sociologist, could be said to comply, or not to comply, with ultimate societal values. A link may or may not be established between four sets of givens: the *social actors;* the network of *roles* (or functions); the scale of *values* attached to the services (the roles performed); and the hierarchy of *rewards* (or remuneration).

The cult of the individual requires that two demands be met.

The first relates to the congruence between the roles available or on offer and the skills or abilities of the social actors. Actors can be defined in terms of 'talents', which equip them to varying degrees for the task of inscribing their behavior within roles, of becoming *social* actors, bringing into play what Durkheim calls a 'social force'. Yet an individualistic society demands that, in performing the specialized activities of a role, one should be able both to distinguish oneself from other individuals and also to improve onself. If the personal vocation which each person carries within the self (which is precisely what constitutes his or her social force) is stifled, the result is a state of frustration, described at length in *The Division of Labor in Society*. Since one is obliged to perform tasks which are repellent to one's nature, one experiences a feeling of intolerable violation. The demands of personal equilibrium and social cohesion meet; the division of labor is unable to generate either cooperation or solidarity unless natural talents coincide with the tasks to which they are set. Proper harmony between the distribution of tasks and the distribution

215

of skills by means of a range of tasks which is sufficiently open is thus one of the conditions for the emergence of such a society.

The second concerns remuneration, which must enable the actor who successfully performs the activities constituting a role to be *socially recognized*. It should be 'just' and 'equitable', as Durkheim says, meaning in conformity with the *social value* of the services. In the event that an actor is obliged to accept less remuneration than the social value of the service he or she provides, there will be a sense of violation.

The underlying argument may be reconstructed as follows. It is not enough for the remuneration linked to the performance of a role to be intrinsically 'just'; the individual concerned must also have been able to find in the role an outlet for his or her abilities. When social functions are inaccessible to those who possess the requisite aptitudes for performing them and are in effect reserved for privileged individuals who do not always possess these aptitudes, the injustice is a twofold one: not only do certain social actors perform roles below the level of their abilities, but owing to the system of privileges they also receive lower remuneration of their work than it is worth. And this is indeed what happens in the society analyzed by Durkheim and which, to some extent, is his social laboratory. Although personalist values are proclaimed, the fact nevertheless remains that there are distortions in the natural conditions of exchange and competition. It is only when it is possible to compete for the functions, when, for example freedom of contract is guaranteed between worker and employer, that a state of equilibrium is likely to develop in which the division of labor produces the anticipated results.

Every obstacle to the achievement of equality in the conditions governing competition manifests itself in either the suppression of vocations or the maldistribution of rewards. Thus Durkheim comes to argue that individualistic values do not imply either equality between individuals or equality of remuneration, but rather the equality in the *external conditions of competition*, which is necessary 'to link each individual to his function' and also 'to link the functions one with another' ([1893] 1960: 374).

The paradox of an egalitarian, individualistic society is that it is defined by a dual inequality of functions (social inequalities) and individual aptitudes (natural inequalities). If there is equality in the conditions governing competition, the *natural aptitudes* of individuals (the 'social force' they carry within them) will come to be precisely matched to appropriate roles and remunerated in accordance with the 'social value' of the tasks they make it possible to perform. Then, says Durkheim, *social inequalities exactly express natural inequalities*. Then, he adds, introducing Saint-Simon's notion of 'merit', *merits are exactly recognized*.[6] Among the difficulties which this position – and in particular the very existence of so-called 'natural' aptitudes – necessarily entailed for Durkheim, the one which is clearly of most importance to us today is the nature of the so-called 'social value' of functions and the criteria for assessing it.[7]

'SOCIAL VALUE' AND FUNCTIONS

The theory constructed here by Durkheim must be understood in the light of the important role played by the 'collective representations' and their relations with the institutions in the structural–functionalist model he developed, and which we have described in detail above. Durkheim refuses to reduce the problem of the social value of tasks to the problem of economic value as this is traditionally posed. On the contrary, he seeks to develop an argument which takes account of the collective representations, opinion and lastly of the idea of merit in stating what (in a personalist society) the criteria of 'social values' *are* and *must* be.

In *The Division of Labor in Society*, Durkheim admittedly starts from a definition of value which would appear to be the one which goes back to Adam Smith and Ricardo and, in a way, is taken up by Marx: 'In a given society, each object of exchange, at each moment, has a specific value which might be called its social value. It represents the amount of useful work instrinsic to it' ([1893] 1960: 376). But Durkheim is not content merely to establish the conditions for an equitable exchange of objects (exchanged values 'counterbalancing' one another) in the market, but seeks to determine the conditions for such an exchange among social *services*.

The problem of a 'just contract' between employers and workers, in particular, is presented as that of the 'exact reciprocity of the *services exchanged*' ([1893] 1960:376). There is thus a deliberate identification here between the value of an object and the value of a service. It might therefore be thought that, from a standpoint analogous to that of Marx, Durkheim wishes to determine the labor-value of labor considered as a service. Hence he notes that the position of an employer is such that he can 'abuse his position to obtain the labor of the worker on terms which are excessively disadvantageous to him, in other words which are too low an estimate of his true value' (1969: 236).

However, instead of seeking to establish the value of labor in terms of the labor-force, as Marx does, he finds the basis for an evaluation of 'services' and 'functions' in the collective representations as they are expressed in 'opinion'. In *Le Suicide* one finds the clearest expression of the thesis that the hierarchy of social 'services' is founded in collective representations. In the moral conscience of societies, he writes, there is 'an obscure feeling of the respective value of the different social services, of the relative remuneration due to each of them. . . . It is as though the different functions are hierarchically arranged in opinion' ([1897] 1960: 275–6). The result of this is that the degree of well-being, the way

217

of living corresponding to each function, forms a recognized order, whose benefit for the actors is that they know what is their due, accept the lot meted out to them, and do not seek more than they can obtain.[8]

But what 'opinions' are we speaking of – institutionalized, formal opinion, or emergent opinion within the 'free' collective representations? And what are the elements it uses as the basis for the actual assessment of the services? Is it founded on usefulness, on effort expended? Durkheim says merely that the amount of work and its useful effects are *assessed* in relation to prejudices and traditions and also in relation to emergent ideologies, 'effervescent' representations. He also says that the hierarchy of functions is established 'somewhat obscurely'. In the *Leçons de sociologie*, he adds the finely phrased observation that 'an idea of genius, born without effort and created in joy, has greater *value* and *merit* than years of manual labor' (emphasis added) (1969: 239).

So we are again faced with the notion of 'merit', but in a new form, since what is at issue here is the way the public conscience makes the link between the amount of work and its usefulness. The idea of genius is situated high on the scale of merit, because uncommon aptitudes are required to foster its development, but above all because its social usefulness is so pronounced. By referring to merit in terms of a response to social needs, Durkheim is able to come to terms with the fact that social value can be a matter of both quantity of work and opinion, since judgment based on 'merit' is related 'somewhat obscurely' to perceived usefulness. One might even go so far as to say that the amount of useful (though not necessary) work is for Durkheim tantamount to the *degree of merit*.

SOCIAL CLASSES AND EXPLOITATION

In a just society, merit is precisely recognized, because this is what social value is based on. But are we not merely going round in circles? Durkheim, at least, thought that the new form of the notion of merit provided him with a tool enabling him to tackle the crucial question of the exchange of values, which is supposed to serve as a 'counterweight' in the relation between the social functions of employer and worker, as he puts it. According to his observation of *his own* society, there is in fact a conflict between the scale of social values (or merits) and the scale of rewards (or remuneration), a conflict which is more or less part and parcel of the contract between capital and labor. Like those of his contemporaries who were disciples of Saint-Simon, Durkheim sees in the conditions of this contract the possibility that it might be 'a simple means of exploiting one of the contracting parties' (1969: 234). In analyzing the rules or the institutions which in industrial society make it possible to use such a 'one-sided' contract, Durkheim necessarily adopts a position on the nature of profit and on the usefulness of appealing to the concept of social classes.

Naturally enough, Durkheim's point of departure is the identification of *signs* of inequitability in the exchange between capital and labor; the conflicts which result from the conditions of the contract show that, even if it conforms to the rules governing contractual law, the consent of one of the parties is not free, the result being the 'despoilment' of one of the contracting parties. How can this despoilment and the 'abuse' of the victim be explained? Durkheim appeals to the special position of the owner of capital, linking it both with the institution of inheritance, which makes hereditary ownership of the means of production possible, and with the prejudice of respect for wealth. He also stresses the fact that the conditions under which the employer and the worker engage in the struggle to live are antithetical, the constraint upon the latter basically being linked to the fear of death. If, *in order to live*, one social class is obliged to make its services acceptable at any price, while another can do without them thanks to the resources at its disposal, this means that the latter can 'unjustly lay down the law to the former'. This is the origin of 'surplus value created by someone other than him, who has been unjustly deprived of it' – a surplus which is not commensurate with the social merit of the owner (1969: 238).[9]

The similarity to Marx is obvious. But where Marx depicts the worker's as selling the force of their labor and the use of this force as creating a product of greater value, and therefore a surplus, Durkheim describes the worker's as selling the product of their labor through the medium of the individual who places instruments of production at their disposal, yet receiving for this product an amount less than the 'merit' which is ascribed to it on the basis of the assessment of this merit by opinion. Capitalist profit ultimately results from the fact that, owing to the right to inherit capital, the capitalist rewards the merit of the workers with insufficient remuneration, whereas his or her own merit is rewarded with excessive remuneration: exploitation is linked not to the fact that there is profit – in the sense of a difference in remuneration – but to the fact that, in the industrial society Durkheim is observing, this profit is linked to an unjust, one-sided exchange not commensurate with the respective social merits, which is imposed on the weaker contracting party. Durkheim's 'surplus' is thus neither Proudhon's 'windfall' nor Marx's 'surplus value'; it is merely the *excess* of remuneration granted to the capitalist relative to the scale of social values or merits.

Durkheim probably found it difficult to pursue his analysis further than the point where he notes that the value of the labor is ultimately no more than a matter of the collective representations. He is therefore obliged to question the collective representations themselves, to call them obscure and imbued with 'survivals' which help to justify the surplus merit attributed to the social actors from the 'upper classes', for it seems true to say that the public conscience exhibits respect for wealth which helps to guarantee 'despoilment'.

> Under the influence of all kinds of prejudices inherited from the past, we still tend not to consider men of different classes in the same light; we are more sensitive to the undeserved sufferings and hardships that a man from the upper classes may undergo when performing noble functions than to those experienced by men destined to perform humbler tasks and labors.
>
> (1969: 236)

What Durkheim understands by this concept of 'class' is something more akin to Saint-Simon than to Marx. In various texts, he refers to the 'class war', but this is not in order to deduce from it, for instance, that the classes are defined on the basis of their actual struggle itself. On several occasions, he stresses the analogy between 'classes' and 'castes', suggesting that the 'upper classes' form a closed group by virtue of the privilege of inherited wealth. At the same time, he suggests, the trend is not toward the disappearance of classes, but toward a weakening of the caste character of the owning classes.[10]

The problem of classes, for Durkheim, is an aspect of the more basic problem of the basis of the *legitimacy* of property. In an individualistic society, all property acquired by means of a premium exacted on the labor of others, acquired by a one-sided contract and inequality between the values exchanged, is illegitimate. Since this 'premium' can only continue to be levied through the survival of opinion, Durkheim reasons that the development of an opinion which transcended its own prejudices, which institutionalized the emergence of individualistic aspirations on a more just basis, and made a legitimate scale of merits synonymous with the recognition of workers' rights to 'just' remuneration, would be a factor for change: change toward a society which would thus be more in harmony with itself.

What the sociologist can do is precisely to help society to develop in a manner more in keeping with its own conditions of existence. In short, one of the motors of social change is the collective representations, and one of their components is the sociological debate. The sociologist can teach society that, from now on, its integration will be achieved *through* the cult of the individual, and that the egalitarian and socialist aspirations which spring up 'in the depths of society' are moving in the same direction as the development of societies with division of labor, thereby facilitating the transition from a public conscience which is relatively blind to the reality of the conditions of social existence, to an enlightened conscience which can assume responsibility for this reality. The very fact that, within the 'effervescences' producing opinions, a *critical* opinion emerges that is governed by a sense of the unjustifiable nature of the inequalities that arise from the 'exploitation of man by man' shows that the weakening of class conflicts is possible, that the meritocratic system is in a way part and parcel of the future of societies. The opinion which is governed by the archaic prejudices which guarantee the development of the so-called highest class into a caste, in short, may be supplanted by sociologically informed collective opinion in favour of an inevitable meritocracy.

AN INTELLIGENT ORGANIZATION?

The ideal model – that of a society in which every actor finds the place he or she deserves and every social value is assessed according to its just worth – implies a system institutionalized on the basis of these objectives. A society true to itself, and possessing a consensus on respect for the individual (which guarantees freedom of choice and the free exercise of spontaneity and consent in contracts), cannot develop without 'intelligent' organization. In such an organization not only would the rights of inheritance be amended, but consideration would also be given to problems of the relation between present social functions or services and vocations or aptitudes, and of the emergence of new functions and the new individual and social needs that are interlinked in social development.

But what kind of an 'intelligent' organization should this be? Achieving the conditions required for equitable contracts would not be sufficient to ensure that the functions coincided with vocations. Opportunities for pursuing the vocations to be performed would also have to exist, and society's education system would have to provide an opportunity for aptitudes to develop, and to develop into vocations.[11] Thus, when Durkheim seeks to paint a picture of the conditions for the achievement of the meritocratic society which he sees emerging, he comes face to face with the problem of the school and the decisive period in the life-cycle during which opportunities for the development of aptitudes (or inhibitions) arise, and also with the very question of the needs or desires which are born in the actors as their lives are gradually integrated into the roles and functions which confirm their 'merit'.

We will not deal here with the way Durkheim situates the problem of education in the context of a sociology which is critical of the school. We will concentrate solely on the inherent difficulty of the process of change, of becoming, which characterizes all societies which are not immobile.[12]

Durkheim sometimes seems to be describing a society in which social actors, once they have found their place (in keeping with the development of their potential aptitudes) and are remunerated according to the social value of their work, are 'content with their lot' and desire nothing more. Yet Durkheim is also forced to take account of the essential mobility of individual needs, of their formation and development, from the standpoint of their continuous emergence and their legitimation on the basis of existing social needs. He has no doubt that individual desires and needs have to be regulated or anomie will result. Regulation is needed to fix the aims which can legitimately be pursued by the social actors in their search for the social rewards which reflect the usefulness of their work (which is indeed the case, since 'opinion' classifies 'the degree of comfort' which should be the lot of the average worker in each 'profession' and assigns him his 'economic ideal') ([1897] 1960: 275–6). But how are those legitimate 'demands' linked to the egalitarian aspirations towards greater justice, to be incorporated into this model?

However perfectly it may be conceived, a meritocratic system cannot be expected to be stable, not only because the idea of an absolutely equitable projection of vocations into functions is probably utopian, but also because, as soon as the differences which originally separated the classes diminish, it is inevitable that needs should spread from one class to another (Durkheim [1893] 1960: 368). People cannot but compare the rewards they receive with those received by others, cannot but wonder whether it is just that others should be given credit for the needs which they can satisfy. Durkheim sees the process by which needs spread from one social category to another, the comparability between ways of satisfying the needs *which one merits oneself*, and also the needs which *others have met*, in these terms.[13]

In a way, this process ties in with the fact that the system of individualistic values can never totally justify the stratification of the inequalities sanctioned by opinion in a particular meritocracy, because the values call for a constant redistribution of merits and needs. It also means that social change goes through periods in which the criteria of legitimacy is transmitted by channels other than opinion: the new needs emerge not only in relation to external conditions, but also in relation to the individualistic development of individuals.

Durkheim concluded that it was characteristic of individualistic society never to rest content with a given scheme of stratification, with a closed and stable system for defining merit, and that such a society is at all times confronted with the paradox that in the course of development it undermines its notions of merit.

Durkheim goes no further in his examination and discussion of the problems of equalities and inequalities affecting the parameters of observation and speculation about the future of societies than to note the existence of, and the necessity for, equality of opportunity in the struggle between social actors, and the possibility of changes in the scheme of social merits. Durkheim's analysis of these problems reflects the actual

222

objectives Durkheim set himself at the time he was becoming aware of having something akin to a 'mission' as a sociologist.

DURKHEIM'S MISSION

As we have seen, the concept of meritocracy makes it possible to reconcile 'individualism' and 'socialism', a task which always dogged Durkheim, through a 'legitimate' form of social stratification. If one postulates that respect for the individual and the Cult of Man 'in general' is an ultimate value in the society which is developing, it follows that a *humanistic* socialism and a *personalistic* individualism to some extent impose the need for the development of a meritocratic system. But questions about the meritocracy envisioned by Durkheim remain, with respect to how it is to be achieved and also to what might be called its essence.

The model Durkheim proposes is halfway between a static and a 'dynamic' meritocracy or a society which would be able constantly to call into question the stratification of rewards and what it produces. By linking the legitimacy of a given system for the stratification of merits with 'public opinion', or with 'representations' (which are as likely to be progressive as they are to be regressive), he ultimately bases his assessment of equalities and inequalities on a referent whose own 'positiveness' or validity as a goal is difficult for the sociologist to judge.

These are the links between the texts discussed so far and Durkheim's strictly political arguments, his analyses of the role and function of the State and his conception of democracy (Filloux 1971; 1977). The State he conceived as a group of *sui generis* officials whose task it is to assume responsibility for social needs and aspirations, for coordinating and 'socializing' economic activities. Democracy (supposed gradually to become consolidated as time passes) was defined by transparency and by the possibility that the decisions of the State would produce an educated and aware political society. Durkheim's meritocracy, like this briefly glimpsed socialist democracy, has meaning only to the extent that political development actually progresses towards a State which is itself ordered according to the ultimate individualistic values. Yet one may wonder with Michael Young whether, in *essence*, a meritocratic system is not pregnant with risks for the social actors, who are less inclined, as Durkheim puts it, to be 'content with their lot' than to be filled with despair with the realization that they lack the talents which might enable them to rise to higher levels of reward.[14] Viewed in this light, meritocracy might run the risk (if one adopts Durkehim's standpoint) of contradicting the personalist values themselves.

It also appears that, by essentially accusing 'the institution of inheritance' of being the source of the inequalities which stem from 'exploitation' in the contract between workers and owners, Durkheim avoids an analysis according to which inheritance is regarded as appropriating the management of the means of production and which is therefore based on a more solid class theory. If, as Durkheim maintains, inheritance of the means of production plays a role in the permanence of the owners, it cannot alone account for the actual mechanism of 'despoilment'. Abolishing inheritance does not of itself alter the fact that a 'tithe' is levied – that is, if the *social* division of labor as between managers and non-managers of the means of production persists. Durkheim uses the concept of the division of labor in society with a view to the integration of social functions. But his purpose in using the concept of the *social* division of labor within the context of a more radical – in epistemological terms – class theory is not to question the inequality of rewards and responsbilities. The notion of class itself seemed to him, at that time, to be excessively bound up with the idea of the class struggle. The repugnance he felt for the Marxist theme of the struggle of 'class against class' is well known. It stemmed both from his horror of conflict and from his use of class antagonisms in a situation of *anomie* as a metaphor, a metaphor moreover which enabled him to develop the theory of transcending conflicts by means of new and necessary regulations.[15]

These observations tend to emphasize the distance between the objectives Durkheim initially set himself and the difficulties with which he was confronted owing to the dual tendency of the sociology he was developing. On the one hand, it seeks to designate an order which encompasses people in their needs and desires within a normative framework (integration and regulation as the bulwarks against anomie). And on the other hand, it seeks to determine alternatives to the existing order with a view to 'necessary change'.

THE SPIRIT OF DURKHEIM TODAY

These difficulties should not obscure the importance for contemporary sociological thought of the *spirit* of Durkheim's contribution, with respect to the propblem of equality and merit – what one might term Durkheim's latent philosophy. This problem is based, as we have seen, on a host of ambiguities: should sociology focus on integration and/or change? Should social conflicts be taken into account and/or violence minimized? Should one hope that societies will develop democratically and/or feel disillusionment at human nature? One might almost say that these ambiguities are one of the most valuable aspects of Durkheim's contribution to a reading of how society functions today. Consider two Durkheimian themes which are seldom examined: the *theme of warmth* and the *theme of ethics*. The association of the concept of the 'Cult of Man' or of the 'sacred character of the individual' with the concept of the emergence of a 'warm' society over and above the coldness of his society is found throughout his work.

In a lecture early in 1914 to the Union des Libres Penseurs et des Libres Croyants pour la Culture morale, he exclaims:

> We are now in an intermediate period, a period of moral coldness which explains the various events which we are constantly witnessing. . . . But who does not feel that, in the depths of society, an intense life is developing which is seeking outlets and which will eventually succeed in finding them. We aspire to a higher form of justice which in our view none of the existing doctrines expresses satisfactorily. But these obscure aspirations which exercise our minds will some day manage to translate themselves into specific doctrines around which men will rally. . . . All that matters is to feel, beneath the moral coldness which reigns upon the surface of our collective life, the sources of warmth which our societies bear within them.[16]

(1970: 312–13)

This is a 'warm' society because it is a community of fellowship in the new religion, the new sacred being: Man. Texts of this kind can lead one to conclude that Durkheim's sociology is one of the most massive constructs ever assembled in order to justify or demonstrate the humanist affirmation.

Is all this mere illusion, utopia? Durkheim anticipated that democracy would ultimately 'sink without a trace' in the world, and not merely in his society; that State totalism would yield to personalist socialism; that traditional religions would lose ground to the benefit of a new sacred being. All of these predictions have largely been proved wrong. But does this really matter, if Durkheim's deepest wish was to serve a progressive mission? Some of his wishes have already become reality – for example, better-regulated relations between workers and employers, and the fulfillment of more egalitarian aspirations in wage systems in Western societies.

In a sense Durkheim is more relevant than ever, conveying an *ethical message* which is more pertinent than ever before. At a time when revealed religions advocate unacceptable violence, when State totalitarianism tends to crush the individual, Durkheim's appeal for the building of a society or societies incorporating the emblem of human rights into their flags takes on contemporary meaning.[17] His appeal is *also* addressed to sociologists, who now find that they have to give their work an ethical justification, over and above 'practical' or 'speculative' interest. This is the dynamic secret of the Durkheimian doctrine.

NOTES

1 *La Science Sociale et l'Action* (1970) is a compilation of various papers related to social questions. The book includes: 'L'élite intellectuelle et la démocratie' (1904); 'Note sur la définition due socialisme' (1893); 'L'individualisme et les intellectuels' (1898); 'Internationalisme et lutte des classes' (1906); and 'L'avenir de la religion' (1914).

2 'L'élite intellectuelle et la démocratie', *Revue Bleue* (1904), in *La Science Sociale et l'Action* (1970): 'We must, above all, be *advisers, educators*. Our task is to assist our contemporaries to recognize themselves in their ideas and feelings rather than to govern them'.

3 In *L'Education Morale* (1963) he writes that 'It gives one pleasure to say we', in other words 'to blend with something other than oneself'.

4 In a review of the work by Antonio Labriola entitled 'Essais sur la conception materialiste de l'histoire' (1897), in *La Science Sociale et l'Action*, Durkheim writes:

> Far be it from us to maintain that the economic factor is no more than an epiphenomenon: once it exists, it has a special influence of its own; but there is no reason to make it into something particularly fundamental.
>
> (1970: 254)

On the relations between Durkheim and Marx, cf. Jean-Claude Filloux, *Durkheim et le Socialisme* (1977). On Durkheim's position regarding the relations between economics and politics in the context of the moral and social crisis of the period, it is interesting to read Jean Claude Chamboredon's article, 'Emile Durkheim: le social objet de science. Du moral au politique?' (1984).

5 Not only is individualism not anarchy, it is now the only system of beliefs able to achieve the moral unity of our country.' In sentencing Dreyfus when he was innocent to maintain 'morale' in the army, the rights of the individual are flouted and 'everything which makes for the value and dignity of life' is rejected

(1970: 270, 275).

6 'The distribution of things among individuals can only be just if it is in proportion to the social merit of each of them' (1969: 238).

7 The idea that there are 'natural' aptitudes, thoughts unrelated to any environmental condition and which can be quantified, is hard to support. It appears that, by the term 'natural aptitude', Durkheim is thinking of a hereditary factor. Yet even in this form, contemporary writing on intelligence questions the notion of the 'natural'. Intelligence is said to be conditioned both by genetic endowment (two-thirds) and by education and the cultural environment of the first years in a child's life. Whatever the case, it is odd that Durkheim should have wished to put forward the concept of 'natural inequalities' independently of all social factors. If aptitude is developed in and through a combination of hereditary and socio-cultural factors, the hierarchy which is established at a given moment among individuals on the basis of their 'talents' is impregnated with the social and cannot serve as an adequate reference for diagnosing the recognition of merits.

8 Moreover, this scheme can be learned, and one of the functions of education, says Durkheim, is – precisely – to teach children that a specific stratum will one day correspond to the social role they will perform (1922).

9 In addition, Durkheim denounces this situation as *anomic* ([1893] 1960: 235–8).

10 Like Saint-Simon, Durkheim is content merely to observe the latent antagonism between the class of the owners and the class which is defined as 'the
poorest and most numerous'. On the subject of Saint-Simon's 'class theory',
cf. Pierre Ansart (1969).

11 A. Pizzorno has effectively summarized Durkheim's problems in relation to
this point: if aptitudes have to 'marry the tasks', the tasks in which they can
find expression must be available and, conversely, through the socialization
of the child, the vocations must be constructed on the basis of potential
outlets (Pizzorno: 1963).

12 Durkheim's sociology of education argues that the function of school is to be
an instrument through which a society safeguards its own bases by socializing
the rising generations. It thus has a conserving, social reproduction aspect,
and its task is to prepare children for their ultimate function, linked to their
status in the stratification.

But at the same time, the school is (and can or must be) an instrument of
change, for two reasons. First the school system enjoys *relative autonomy*
within the overall socio-political system, and the teachers form a group capable of creating new pedagogical representations. Subsequently, by means of
these pedagogical representations, the school is in a position to accept the
aspirations and needs that arise from various layers of society. Aspirations
and needs are thus translated into new pedagogical doctrines, which tend to
become operationalized and which exert an influence upon the social system
as a whole.

Here too, sociology acts as both observer and critic, able to show that
developments and changes are possible, so that as a result school can be a
motor for the transformation of society into a meritocracy which is more just
and more in keeping with the cult of the individual, who himself or herself
has to be taught (Durkheim 1938; Filloux 1978).

13 As A. Pizzorno has also emphasized (1963). This may be an appropriate
point to refer to the notion of 'mimetic desire', developed by René Girard
(1972).

14 Cf. Michael Young:

It would be betraying our duty as sociologists were we not to stress the
fact that such a general recognition of the arbitration of merit can reduce
to irremediable despair those people, and there are many, who are totally
devoid of talent, especially since the person thus condemned, having too
little intelligence to protest against society, may direct his anger upon
himself

(1958: 99)

15 Durkheim's theory of *anomie* may perhaps be considered in a way as an
alternative to a theory which questions the conflictual relations between the
social classes (Besnard 1987).

16 Durkheim adds: 'One can even go further and say, with some precision, in
what particular area of society these new forces are developing: it is in the
popular classes' (1970: ch 1).

17 In this respect, Durkheim's participation in the foundation of the Ligue des
droits de l'homme et du Citoyen in 1898, at the time of the Dreyfus Affair,
is significant.

REFERENCES

Ansart, P. (1969) *Marx et l'Anarchisme*, Paris: Presses Universitaries de France.

Besnard, P. (1987) *L'Anomie*, Paris: Presses Universitaires de France.

Chamboredon, J.-C. (1984) 'Emile Durkheim: le social objet de science. Du moral au politique?, *Critique*, 445, *Aux Sources de la Sociologie* 460–531.

Durkheim, E. ([1893] 1960), *De la Division du Travail Social*, Paris: Presses Universitaires de France.

—— ([1897] 1960), *Le Suicide*, Paris: Presses Universitaires de France.

—— (1922), *Education et Sociologie*, Paris: Alcan.

—— (1938) *L'Evolution Pedagogique en France*, Paris: Presses Universitaires de France.

—— (1963) *L'Education Morale*, Paris: Presses Universitaires de France.

—— (1969) *Leçons de Sociologie*, Paris: Presses Universitaires de France.

—— (1970) *La Science Sociale et l'Action*, Preface by Jean-Claude Filloux, Paris: Presses Universitaires de France.

Filloux, J.-C. (1971) 'Démocratie et société socialiste chez Durkheim', *Cahiers Vilfredo Pareto* 25 29–48.

—— (1977) *Durkheim et le Socialisme*, Geneve: Droz.

—— (1978) 'Sur la pedagogie de Durkheim', *Revue Française de Pedagogie* 44 83–98.

—— (1990) 'Personne et sacré chez Emile Durkheim', *Archives des Sciences Sociales des Religions* 69 41–53.

Girard, R. (1972) *La Violence et le Sacré* Paris: Editions Grasset.

Pizzorno, A. (1963) 'Una letture attuale di Durkheim', *Quaderni di sociologia* 12(3), 272–309.

Young, M. (1958) *The Rise of Meritocracy*, London: Thames & Hudson.

10

DURKHEIM'S INTELLECTUAL DEVELOPMENT

The problem of the emergence of new
morality and new institutions as a leitmotif in
Durkheim's oeuvre

Hans Joas

The Elementary Forms of the Religious Life, Durkheim's last major work, casts a shadow over the author's earlier writings. While studying this work many readers have become acutely aware of the contrast between the book and his earlier programmatic and substantive studies. The differences are the source of controversial answers to questions of the internal logic of the development of his work and the degree of continuity and discontinuity within it. They suggest a possible rupture in his intellectual biography.

Talcott Parsons's *The Structure of Social Action* (1937) is a famous example of this. He sees Durkheim as moving from positivistic early works to an idealistic later body of thought. The factor which has a decisive influence on this transition, he claims, is the insight into social control via internalized norms which, he continues, is one of Durkheim's essential achievements and revolutionizes his entire frame of reference. He concludes that Durkheim goes too far down the path of normative determinism. This reading, however, depends on omitting much of what Durkheim wrote from consideration. Parsons ignores Durkheim's work prior to the major book on the division of labor and he erroneously attributes his interest in education to one specific stage in Durkheim's development. In fact, the theory of education plays an important role throughout his career. Jeffrey Alexander's more comprehensive interpretation (1982, 1986) represents an attempt to overcome these deficiencies while essentially retaining Parsons's theoretical framework. In Alexander's work, the underlying motif continues to be Durkheim's search for a concept of social order compatible with the free volition of the individual, which results in Durkheim's insight into the sociality of the actor. But, unlike Parsons, Alexander sees Durkheim not as moving from positivism to idealism but rather as progressing from a normativistic early phase through a materialistic intermediate phase to the increasingly normativistic late work.

Alexander's account is distinguished from Parsons's and from the bulk of the remaining literature by Alexander's interpretation of Durkheim's monograph on the division of labor. In his eyes, the interpretation of this book as a critique of utilitarianism rests on the error of considering the first part of the book in isolation. As he sees it, Durkheim does not discover the moral basis of modern society, but rather demonstrates its progressive elimination, and thus finds himself, in the last parts of the book, on the road back to Spencer or Marx. Marx is deemed a utilitarian insofar as he did not advocate any other theory as an interpretation of modern society; in contrast to typical utilitarians, he is seen as merely offering a historico-philosophical relativization of utilitarianism. In order to support this interpretation, Alexander has to impute an extreme measure of internal inconsistency to the *Division of Labor in Society*. Durkheim's subsequent thinking must also be regarded as wildly fluctuating, and Durkheim's next book, *The Rules of Sociological Method*, must be treated as deceptive.

Alexander's need for these ancillary claims could be an indication that an accurate reconstruction can only be achieved by overcoming the exclusivity of the schematization of 'utilitarianism versus normativity', in terms of which both Parsons and Alexander attempt to analyze Durkheim. In this chapter I will suggest that Durkheim's work is best understood as a continuing attempt to answer the question of *how a new morality can emerge*. A great number of interpretations stress that Durkheim situated the subject of morality at the focal point of his theory. However, such readings ignore the fact that Durkheim was less interested in potential ways of preserving a traditional morality than in the conditions that would enable a new morality to develop.

This approach owes nothing to attempts to interpret Durkheim in terms of a supposed longing for community, whether it is regarded as 'conservative', as Nisbet (1974) does, or more correctly as democratic-progressive, as Giddens (1978) does. But the approach has roots elsewhere in the tradition of Durkheim scholarship, namely in René König's work, and more specifically in his *Habilitationsschrift* of 1937 (published in 1975 as *Critique of Historico-existentialist Sociology*) which contained ideas taken up in König's (1976) mature publications on Durkheim. König devoted far more effort than anyone else to interpreting Durkheim as not simply a *moralist* within sociology, nor merely a sociologist for whom the subject was essentially a science of morality, but rather as a thinker in the historical ambience of the *fin de siècle* who was concerned above all with the conditions for the formation of a new morality.

König was able to achieve this not only because he had a better overview of the philosophical and cultural environment in France than many historians of sociology – who paid more attention to the sociologists Durkheim took as his predecessors than to the philosophical contemporaries – but, above all, because he drew on Durkheim in the conviction that the latter provided a way out of German *Lebensphilosophie* and its political and moral consequences. In so doing, however, he did *not* set Durkheim against the philosophy of life as a representative of scientism, but rather as a thinker who pursued the project of reconstructing rationalism. This enabled König to accept valid elements of the critique of rationality embedded in *Lebensphilosophie* and at the same time overcome its consequences. Affinities between Bergson and Durkheim as well as Sorel and Durkheim could be seen from this point of view.

König does not develop the theoretical underpinning of this promising approach adequately and also does not always mark the theories off from one another in the right places. However, his work is a starting point for a view of Durkheim not as a theorist of order and of normativity *per se*, and certainly not of anomie, functionalism, the progressive division of labor, and ongoing differentiation, but rather of the constitution of a new order, or new norms. The theoretical significance of this altered interpretation is that it expands the model of utilitarianism versus normative determinism to include a third position, creativity, concerned with the conditions for the creativity of collective and individual action as well as the linking of creativity and responsibility or normativity.[1]

SOME BIOGRAPHICAL CONSIDERATIONS

Durkheim's interest in sociology derived from a profound sense of crisis on his part. Sociology was part of an endeavour to eliminate this crisis. Most interpreters agree that Durkheim did not want to offset the destructive impact of technical and economic progress on community, bonds and norms by restoring pre-industrial conditions or trusting in the benevolent effects of evolution. His profound insight into the linkages between morality and social structure made him immune to any such idea of restoration: his polemics criticizing utilitarianism were aimed at shattering confidence in evolution. Recent biographical portraits by French scholars have provided solid confirmation of König's description of the hidden passion of Durkheim's apparently compulsive and over-disciplined personality. Durkheim seemed to possess more the traits of a charismatic prophet than of a cold positivist or scholastic rationalist (Lacroix 1981). However, until now too little attention has been devoted to the fact that, for all his sense of crisis, Durkheim by no means saw rationality as a remedy for the problems he saw, but rather from an early date proceeded from the assumption that there was a crisis of rationality as well.

The importance of the young Durkheim's enthusiasm for Schopenhauer has only very recently been considered seriously (Meštrović, 1988a, 1988b), although the fact that Durkheim owed his nickname 'Schopen' to this enthusiasm has long been known (Lalande 1960: 23). Schopenhauer and not Hobbes – the assumption made by Parsons, who had a rather limited background in nineteenth-century continental philosophy – must be seen not only as the source of specific assumptions in, for example, the study on suicide, on the dangers of the anarchy of the individual's instinctual life, but also for the presuppositions of Durkheim's 'rationalism', which from the outset was never a simple rationalism. The frequent description of Durkheim as a Kantian is therefore not very helpful: it would only make sense if we imagined a Kant who would have been able to take up Schopenhauer's challenge. My biographical thesis is thus that Durkheim was not a staunch rationalist who only fought against irrationalism in his writings for reasons connected with his cultural politics, but rather a 'reconstructed' rationalist deeply fascinated, even, by irrationalism, just as he was a lifelong atheist fascinated by religion. Durkheim's personal profile cannot be assimilated to the character of Settembrini as set against Naphta, but is rather characterized by the passionate endeavour to achieve a synthesis of these antipodes, as in the case of Thomas Mann himself or, better still, of Robert Musil.

BEYOND KANTIANISM AND POSITIVISM

Durkheim's early writings, in particular his inaugural lecture in Bordeaux and its program for an empirical science of morality, have been understood in the sense of a radical positivism, one which reduces moral questions to empirical matters. This understanding has been contested by reference to Durkheim's alleged Kantianism. Both views are to my mind wrong – proving the point will form the first step of my proposed interpretation. This part will be the most extensive one because Durkheim's early writings are less well known.

If we interpret Durkheim's early program by drawing on his early reviews, particularly his major piece on 'La Science positive de la Morale en Allegmagne', it quickly becomes clear that Durkheim was concerned with overcoming the contradiction between Kantianism and utilitarianism. Apart from a number of reviews, Durkheim's early writings consist primarily of the two comprehensive reports which respond to his one-year stay in Germany. The reviews dealt mainly with contemporary publications which sought to define the object of study of the new discipline of 'sociology' and to anchor this discipline among the established fields of academic enquiry. Durkheim's commentary on the works of the early German sociologist Albert Schäffle tended to have a political slant. He defended Schäffle not only against the allegation that Schäffle blindly transposed a model of society as an organism onto social issues, but rose to Schäffle's defense in his political differences with the 'socialists of the chair'. Schäffle's antagonists relied on authoritarian means of State intervention to eliminate social inequities, and thus over-estimated the potential of legislative action. Durkheim, by contrast, portrayed Schäffle as searching for a path between the laissez faire of political economy and the faith of the 'socialists of the chair' in the State; Durkheim's sympathies evidently lay with this search.

Durkheim also wrote on religion and participated in the contemporary debate on its future. Durkheim is to be found expressing his conviction that if religion vanished then something else had to take its place as early as his first published works – and not only in his treatment of the theory of religion in the later writings. To be sure, Durkheim in this period – as can be seen in a review of Alfred Fouillée and in contrast to the late works – regarded religion only as a different form of moral rule ('une discipline sociale') *alongside* morality in the stricter sense and law. This narrow understanding of religion was, at the same time, the basis for the criticism Durkheim levelled against Jean-Marie Guyau, the French philosopher who died young. Guyau's concept of an ethics which transcended duty was one of the ideas from which Nietzsche drew his inspiration. For Guyau, modern morality is a form which does justice to the degree to which modern people are individuated; consequently such a morality could no longer be composed of fixed rules, but had to be shaped by each individual. Guyau used the term anomie positively to describe this situation: moral anomie was the morality of this highly developed state and religious anomie characterized an individuated religiosity without ties to institutions of the Church or fixed dogmas. For the Durkheim of this period, who believed morality and religion were characterized by their obligatory character, this concept was a contradiction in terms. Thus he failed to see that Guyau's philosophy of morality and religion was as much as Durkheim's an attempt to overcome the antithesis between Kant and utilitarianism.

All of these early works were, however, limited in scope. They command our attention in retrospect only because we may regard them as preliminary stages en route to Durkheim's later masterpieces. But what made Durkheim well known to his contemporaries were the two reports on Germany. The first, entitled 'La philosophie dans les universités allemandes', served mainly to describe the structures and curricula of German universities and ventured only marginal commentary on German philosophy itself. The study 'La science positive de la morale en Allegmagne' was, by contrast, devoted exclusively to the nature of the humanities and political sciences in Germany. The essay is marked throughout by Durkheim's fascination with the high standards and the breadth of German scholarship. Durkheim has no doubt that these disciplines are more highly developed in Germany than in France; at the same time, however, he hopes that the more developed French public sphere will help these disciplines to obtain a greater practical effect than is possible in Germany.

As Durkheim grew older, the French public put him under increasing pressure on account of this favorable assessment of the state of the sciences in Germany; the tides of nationalism rose in the years leading up to World War I and cast increasing suspicion on the free exchange of ideas between the two countries. This trend climaxed at the outbreak of the war, which prompted each of the warring nations to produce uninhibitedly one-sided interpretations of the intellectual history of its enemies (Joas 1990). Durkheim was thus forced repeatedly to proclaim his strong allegiance to the French tradition in a wide variety of contexts, as well as to convey the fact that he attached the greatest importance not only to German political economists and legal historians, but also to English and American ethnologists and religious historians. He was compelled to claim that the idea of sociology, however, derived from neither the one nor the other, but had rather to be traced back to its French origins in Comte and Saint-Simon. Modern readers of Durkheim should regard these nationalistic statements with caution: it is of far greater importance to identify what substantive achievements of German scholarship were admired by Durkheim and what position he took on these achievements.

The over-riding issue in this essay by Durkheim is whether the contradiction between Kantianism and utilitarianism can potentially be overcome by means of an empirical study of moral phenomena. His first sentence laments the fact that the French debate has had to move exclusively within this spectrum (Durkheim 1975: 267). Later in the essay he explains his attraction to contemporary German moralists:

> The Kantians make morality a specific but transcendent fact, and one which eludes science; the utilitarians, a fact of experience, but one which has nothing specific about it. They reduce it to that notion of utility which is so confused and see nothing more in it than a psychology or an applied sociology. Only the German moralists see in moral phenomena facts which are both empirical and 'sui generis'. Morality is not an applied or derived science, but rather autonomous.
>
> (Durkheim 1975: 335)

The simultaneous opposition to both the Kantians and the utilitarians, in the form in which it is proclaimed here, runs like a bright thread through Durkheim's works. It is visible not only in this early piece, but in the introduction to the first edition in 1893 of the work on the division of labor and in the 1898 commentary on the Dreyfus scandal; even the

234

1906 essay on the definition of a moral fact is marked by the fervid conviction that Durkheim's own theory had achieved the synthesis which he had called for in his early writings. For this reason, and despite the fact that Durkheim makes use of Kantian motifs, I see no point in labeling Durkheim a 'sociological Kantian'. For Durkheim, the similarities of the two feuding schools outweigh the differences, and he sees himself positioned at equal distance from each of them. He accuses both schools of taking not an inductive approach to morality – that is, by exploring moral phenomena – but a deductive one, for they decree moral laws. Both sides:

> begin by reasoning as if the moral law was to be entirely invented, as if they were before a clear table on which they could erect their system to suit their taste; as if it were a question of finding, not a law summarizing and explaining a system of facts actually realized, but the principle of a moral law which would settle everything. From this point of view the schools cannot be distinguished. The argument of the empiricists is no less premature nor summary than that of the rationalists.

> (Durkheim 1933: 420)

This would suggest that the only difference between Kantians and utilitarians lies in the type of principle on which they base their deductions. He believes that the utilitarians take the principle of self-interest as their starting point whereas the Kantians depart from the principle that a moral position is completely detached from any motives of selfishness. The utilitarians work from the experience of the agent, though defining the concept of experience in extremely narrow terms, while the Kantian concept of practical reason has room only for a pure morality, but not for the concrete features of social communities.

In contrast to both the Kantians and the utilitarians, Durkheim and the German scholarly disciplines he admired wished to overcome the deductive method and to provide an exhaustive analysis of concrete moral phenomena. 'One cannot construe all the elements of morality in order then to impose it on things, but must rather study the things in order to derive morality from them inductively' (Durkheim 1933: 278). Durkheim maintained that the works of the German historical political economists constituted an initial step in this direction.

The German school of historical law had gone even further. Durkheim was critical of Ihering's *Der Zweck im Recht*. Durkheim objected to his underlying rationalistic concept of action, which he claimed overemphasized the purposiveness of action. Durkheim's emphasis on how often we act without pursuing a clear objective more closely resembles German *Lebensphilosophie* (for example 1975: 160f in Durkheim's review of Jean Marie Guyau, *L'irréligion de l'avenir*): 'To live is not to think, but to act, and the consequence of our ideas is nothing but a reflection of the stream of events which perpetually unravel in us.'

Durkheim finds a superior approach to the theory of action in the works of Wilhelm Wundt, whose synthetic thrust and comprehensive empirical orientation toward 'folk psychology' ('Völkerpsychologie') Durkheim applauded as the basis for ethics. Durkheim stresses the 'law of the heterogeneity of purposes' formulated by Wundt: all actions produce more consequences than can have been entailed in the motives for action. The consequences of action never coincide with its motive. But as soon as we notice the consequences of our actions, we begin to formulate new objectives. 'The results of our actions always go beyond our motives and, to the extent that they approximate them, they also move away from them at the same time' (1975: 312). Both Wundt and Durkheim regard this action-theoretic conclusion to be a further reason for adopting an empirical-experimental approach in the field of moral theory. It does not suffice to treat motives alone; not through introspection but only in the world of the facts themselves can we determine what consequences actions truly have. We do not know all the consequences of our actions, we do not always act with clear purposes, and the reasons on which we think we act are not necessarily the true reasons (Durkheim 1975: 326). Hence we must rely on more than mere 'raisonnement' in order to achieve progress in moral theory.

Although Durkheim regarded Wundt's work as the crowning glory of German scholarly endeavor in the field of morality, he proposed an even more radically empirical approach than Wundt. In his eyes, Wundt accepted a *unitary* notion of morality or religion and refrained from relativism in the field of moral theory (which is not identical with relativism in morality itself). In contrast, the work of the legal historian Albert Hermann Post applied a historical-comparative method without reservation to the study of moral phenomena. Such a method, Durkheim thought, points to the idea that each type of society has its own corresponding type of morality. Post, however, did not provide such a typology. It was only after Durkheim had concluded his comprehensive survey of the literature that he encountered an attempt to establish precisely such a typology: I am referring to Tönnies's pioneering study *Gemeinschaft und Gesellschaft*, published in the same year as Durkheim's survey. The need to distinguish two primary types of sociality and for a more precise definition of the type of 'community', and the strategy of treating ' "community" as the initial fact from which "society" is then derived as a goal' are all accepted as common ground with Tönnies (1975: 389). Durkheim's suspicion of German state-centeredness however, leads him to read into Tönnies's concept of 'society' traits which Tönnies did not have in mind.[2]

In short, Durkheim resists utilitarian reductionism as well as Kantian

236

transcendentalism; he wants an empirical science which neither misses the specific character of 'ought' as opposed to 'is' nor remains lodged in mere philosophical speculation about that 'ought'. In Germany, of course, this program ends in the relativistic snares of historicism. Let us summarize Durkheim's vision of the empirical study of moral phenomena contributing to the solution of moral questions.

Durkheim supposes that philosophical moral theories contain respectively certain empirical assumptions about moral experience, moral reflection, moral deliberation or moral action. These assumptions, however, can be false or at least falsely generalized, as in the case of Kantian *and* utilitarian conceptions. The initial effect of the study of the historical and cultural variety of morality is to undermine these false ideas of morality. We acquire a more adequate image of what it is actors actually do and experience in situations where morals are concerned. This new image has two contradictory consequences. It expands our own possibilities of action, and it raises our respect for given forms of morality. We become freer, on the one hand, of religious or philosophical ethics; on the other, we reject the illusion of the arbitrary feasibility of moral phenomena. Durkheim stresses both that the science of morality helps us to exercise morality as an art in everyday behavior more effectively and that every superficial modification of morality – for example, by political decree – rules itself out after a study of the internal systematics of morality and especially of the relationship between 'rules' and 'conditions'. One can find further proof for this interpretation in the fact that Durkheim practiced this program in subsequent writings. The penultimate chapter of *Suicide*, 'The relationship between suicide and the other social phenomena', and the 1911 essay on 'Value judgments and reality judgments' are revealing: in neither case are 'ought' questions solved by 'is' judgments. But after reading Durkheim's discussion we also by no means feel that we are as uncertain about the normative issues as we were before reading it. To be better informed on factual matters does not render moral questions resolved, but alters them nevertheless.

Durkheim's approach on this point strongly resembles the pragmatism in ethics championed by John Dewey and G. H. Mead, who also both presuppose a uniform act of reflection in which empirical knowledge becomes an element of moral consideration. This notion is elaborated in pragmatism via the idea of an experiment because they have in mind the actor's situation, which is in principle uncertain and risky and whose future is unclear. Durkheim's plea for historical comparison is also oriented toward an improved means of coping with morally problematic situations by means of reflection on traditions, a reflection which is the prerequisite for developing them further through modification. Science, for Durkheim, does not purport to invent a new morality, nor does it presume to take the place of the members of society in solving moral problems; but by clarifying the conditions which enable a new morality to arise, science promotes the spontaneous formation of a new morality. It is in this sense that a 'science of morality' serves a new morality.

We must keep this model of the relevance of empirical research in the science of morality in mind if we wish to correctly understand Durkheim's *Division of Labor*. This is my second step. This study is without doubt an empirical investigation of the connection between the structures of the division of labor and the structures of morality, and especially of the genesis of a new form of morality. If we think of Durkheim as a positivist, this book contains an empirical theory as to how increasing 'volume' and increasing 'density' compel a division of labor to arise which leads, via interdependence, to organic solidarity. The fact that Durkheim also personally wanted this new morality to assert itself would then be but a secondary, private concern. If, conversely, we think of Durkheim as merely a moral philosopher, then his personal preferences manifest themselves quite clearly. It would appear that the preferences were without any relationship to the observed course of history, or perhaps that he had simply transformed them by means of categorical self-deception, into the automatic result of history, something he had himself previously criticized in the case of the belief in the benevolent moral consequences of modern economy. Both the 'positivist' and the 'moralist' interpretations are far from Durkheim's own understanding of his method and exclude from consideration the moral self-reflection of actors – the sole means by which the comparative method can become morally influential.

The interconnection of the division of labor and morality is conceived in a positivistic way as actions becoming habitualized into rules of action. But if we think of Durkheim as a reflexive moral thinker of the sort I have described, it is plausible to suggest that what Durkheim had in mind in writing this book was the insight into the requirements of cooperation to be gained reflexively by actors. The morality of cooperation he seeks is neither a compulsory morality imposed by rulers nor a voluntary agreement between subjects as to the conditions which appear acceptable to them for dealing with each other, but rather the product of an insight into the functional requirements for egalitarian cooperation.

This conception of Durkheim's purposes fits with further features of the text. Durkheim considered the 'enforced' division of labor to be a 'pathological' form. But if rules were simply habitualized actions, it would be impossible to understand what is pathological about this form. If, however, only just rules fulfill Durkheim's concept of organic solidarity, his concept of the division of labor is intrinsically bound to his notions of justice. Durkheim's argument would not be an argument for the necessity of social order as such, but for the necessity of a just order. Organic solidarity would then be a type of morality which arises in the participants by means of an act of reflection on the universal conditions of their cooperation. The more widespread cooperation is, the more likely the possibility of this reflexive insight would be. The modern division of labor can therefore lead to this new morality, but through the path of reflection rather than unaided habitualization.

Durkheim himself was far from clear as to how this program should be implemented and consequently his efforts were fraught with internal contradictions. For one thing, Durkheim lacked the means in terms of a developmental psychology and a theory of socialization that would have actually enabled him to describe the genesis of a morality of cooperation. This deficiency comes into sharpest relief when compared with the empirical study Jean Piaget published in 1923 on moral judgment in children. Piaget was also the most vociferous critic of this deficiency in Durkheim's work. But this criticism has often concealed the extent to which Piaget based his moral theory on Durkheim and to which Piaget's theory must be seen as a correction of deficiencies inherent in Durkheim's attempt to implement his own program. Piaget expressly bases his argument on Durkheim's distinction between two types of 'solidarity' and also accepts their ties to two forms of moral conciousness. Piaget holds Durkheim's typology to distinguish between a heteronomous and an autonomous morality. In his theory of education, however, Durkheim's attention was riveted on the relationship between the child and the educating authority and did not account for the relationship of children among one another. Durkheim continued to see each type of morality as imposed on the child, even under the conditions of organic solidarity. 'As a consequence,' Piaget writes,

> where we would look upon the 'active school', self-government and autonomy of the child as the only educational methods which lead to a morality based on reason, Durkheim, by contrast, defends a pedagogy which is a paragon of traditionalistic education and, despite all the restrictions, assumes methods that are at heart authoritarian in order to arrive at the inner freedom of consciousness.
>
> (Piaget 1932: 392f)

As a consequence, Durkheim is unable to reconstruct the stages in the development of a child's ability to cooperate. It is therefore by no means a contradiction that Durkheim also construes the division of labor in a profoundly ambiguous manner. He does not distinguish between the antagonistic division of labor by the marketplace and the non-antagonistic division of labor by organized cooperation. Yet the notion of the morality of cooperation refers exclusively to the non-antagonistic division of labor. Modern society based on capitalist industrialization, which Durkheim wants to analyze, is characterized not simply by the extension of cooperative relationships, but rather by the generation of market-like processes and, as Marx would have stated, the contradictory unity which these processes form with the expanded hierarchical cooperation within the factory. Durkheim's thought therefore necessarily itself becomes contradictory. He expects a new morality to emerge from this modern society. But his observations confirm the dominance of anomie. His attempt to interpret the anomic character of the actual division of labor as a transitional phenomenon is clearly an excuse. As Hans-Peter Müller (1993), among others, has shown, Durkheim responds to this discrepancy between prognosis and facts by shifting the weight of unresolved problems onto the level of politics. Organic solidarity is to be produced by an interplay of professional groups, democratic state and individualistic ideal. The study on suicide demonstrates anew the dramatic proportions of the crisis of the day and the sole possibility of resolving it – by means of a new morality.[3]

DURKHEIM'S FINAL WORKS

My third step is to attempt to explain the emergence of Durkheim's mature theory of religion in terms of the problem of the emergence of new morality. My thesis here is that the theory of religion is intended to conceptualize the possibility of the stabilization and institutionalization of a morality of cooperation. Since Durkheim does not recognize the internal conceptual weaknesses of the *Division of Labor in Society*, he hunts for ways of additionally promoting and supporting the desired collective insight into the need for a morality of cooperation. The theory of education always served this end; and the theory of religion now increasingly comes to. These two areas are linked by the question as to how an equivalent for the religious reinforcement of morality is to be found in education.

Ernest Wallwork (1972; 1985) has pointed out in his excellent works on the subject that Durkheim's famous shift to a theory of religion, which Durkheim attributed to his reading of Robertson Smith in 1895, should not simply be viewed as a shift to a discussion of religion, since Durkheim's early works already stress the role of religion as a social phenomenon. Moreover, this accords with the theory promulgated by his teacher, Fustel de Coulanges. In Durkheim's early works, the strength of common convictions is already linked to an experience of transcendentality and this is in turn derived from social phenomena. The early critique of utilitarianism refers to moral and legal obligations legitimated by religion. In other words, the precise nature of this shift still needs to be pin-pointed. It cannot consist simply of Durkheim's adoption of the theory of ritual, as Steven Lukes has assumed (1987), since the latter theory did not appear in his works until many years later. Nor can it consist in the idea of collective effervescence. Although one repeatedly finds references by Durkheim to emotionalized collective states, it is not until later that they start to play a systematic part in his theory. This may be shown by comparing the study on primitive classification systems with the major work on the elementary forms of religious life.

Wallwork maintains that the change is different in character. It consists in Durkheim's recognizing that religion is more than morality, value ideals more than obligation, and sociality more than normativity. As early as the chapter on altruism in *Suicide* it is clear that solidarity cannot consist solely in subjecting oneself to common obligations, but also requires one to be tied to common values. This distinction is also at the root of the interpretation of the intrinsic logic of Durkheim's typology of suicide which enjoys the greatest acceptance among scholars today. The case of educational theory is quite clear. He does not want to retain 'only an impoverished and paled morality under the name of a rational morality' by secularizing moral education, but instead 'to find the rational representatives of these religious concepts, which for so long have served as agents mediating the most important moral ideas' (Durkheim 1963: 7–8). Thus Durkheim accepted, with all the radical consequences this has, the problematic situation expressed in Nietzsche's dictum that 'God is dead' or in Dostoyevsky's fear that all morality would collapse once the transcendental pillars of morality had crumbled away. But he believed that he could show that there could be an intra-mundane substitute for this transcendental pillar. By this he does not mean the artificial stabilization of an outdated and decrepit religiosity or a bureaucratically prescribed substitute for religion.

The whole purpose of Durkheim's theory of religion is to provide an empirically founded theory of religious experience and religious action in order to be able to preserve precisely these modes of experience and action under non-religious conditions. The science of morality is thus transformed into a science of religion, which, however, has the same status: neither science is dogmatic in moral or religious terms, or indifferent toward morals or religion. In the theory of religion, however, Durkheim elucidates not the ways in which the actors relate moral obligations to situations, but rather the manner in which actors are attracted by ideals and are lifted beyond themselves, and how these ideals in turn have resulted from action. Here the question as to the genesis of a new morality becomes the question as to the emergence of new institutions – not only obligatory rules, but rather principles constitutive for one's world. The theory of religion is intended in its most developed form to demonstrate how such structures emerge from the collective, expressive and extraordinary action to categorize the world, create social structures and forge interpersonal ties. It thus represents a step towards a theory of the creative character of sociality, a theory of society as the originating foundation of its own ideals. Morals and institutions are no longer viewed only as fixed forms, but rather are related to the process of their formation.

Just as many interpretations of Durkheim's development have left the earliest writings aside, so too the late works which appeared after his magnum opus on the theory of religion are often ignored. Of these, the lectures on 'Pragmatism and sociology' are worthy of mention. Regardless of precisely what motivated Durkheim to choose this theme – whether, as Robert Bellah thought (1959), he wanted to avoid his work being confused with pragmatism, or whether, as is my contention, he recognized that pragmatism was the only serious competitor in the race to provide a theory of the social constitution of categories – these lectures fit superbly into the outline proposed here. They cannot be grasped in terms of such interpretive concepts as 'idealism' and 'positivism'.

My fourth step is to show that the more Durkheim focussed on the world-constitutive role played by religion, the more important the cognitive processes involved in world-projection that also underlay the moral regulations had to become for him. The debate with pragmatism offered him the chance to clarify his own theory on this point. A careful examination of his argument (Joas 1993) shows that, in a few specifics, his theory of institutionalization diverges from the assumptions of pragmatism. Durkheim believes that institutions emerge only in extraordinary, collective, expressive action. The grounds for these three conditions are not self-evident. The theory focusses exclusively on major dramatic innovations and not on the gradual accumulation of the consequences of action. In contrast to the pragmatists, Durkheim's exclusive emphasis on the creativity of *expressive* action ignores the creativity of *instrumental* action, which is, after all, central to the development of science, technology and the economy. In the theory of religion, the exclusive emphasis on *collective* creativity also becomes problematic: the interplay of innovator and collectivity which is central to Weber's theory of charisma and Mead's conception of science receives short shrift. But this exclusive emphasis appears to reflect Durkheim's subject matter – totemism – as Durkheim is clearly familiar with the innovating individual in other works.

So Durkheim weighs his program down with paradoxes and flaws by concentrating exclusively on extraordinary, expressive, collective experience and attempting to arrive at a social theory of the constitution of moral categories without a conception of everyday social interaction. If, together with Simmel or Mead, and in opposition to the late Durkheim, we continue to regard categories and rules as being constituted in partially anthropological and universal, partially historical and culture-specific structures of social interaction, one might nevertheless agree with Durkheim in maintaining that *comprehensive systems of interpretation* only become viable through collective effervescence. Thus, if we are

242

interested in the *genesis* of a culture's fundamental institutions and its world view, Durkheim's emphasis may be justified.

The arguments Durkheim fields against pragmatism consist for the most part in stressing that action and consciousness are distinct and can be separated from one another. These arguments enable us to show that it is wrong to follow, for example, Stone and Farberman (1967) in viewing Durkheim as being on the road to symbolic interactionism, or to interpret him as a representative of the paradigm shift 'from purposive action to communicative action', as Habermas does (1987). Habermas subsumes Durkheim's theory of action under his own in a manner just as rash as is his use of the idea of the 'linguistification of the sacred' to graft his own theory of evolution onto Durkheim's. Although there can be no doubt that in the field of law, for example, Durkheim presupposes that the sacred core will pass over into political structures of legitimation, this by no means implies, as Habermas assumes, that a 'justified consensus' can serve the socially integrative and expressive functions of ritual praxis. For Durkheim it is much more a question of the interplay of ideals and institutions. Not the ideal of consensus as such but rather the institutional forms that express this ideal can replace ritual praxis. Each particular institutional form is permanently subject to the risk of diverging from and coming into conflict with the ideal which legitimates it. Divergences raise anew the question of new institutions or new versions of the moral ideal. Durkheim is thus not thinking of a linear process of linguistification of the sacred, but rather of the emergence of a new morality and new institutions which express the new, quasi-sacred contents. No ideal can elude this interplay of institution and institutionalizing process.[4]

In the months prior to his death, Durkheim worked on his last, never-completed book on morality. A few sentences from the introduction, the last piece Durkheim was to write, demonstrate clearly how central the question of creativity was to Durkheim's theory of morality and sociology as a whole:

> every morality has its ideal. . . . But beyond this ideal there are always other ideals which are in the process of forming anew. For the moral ideal is not immutable; it lives, develops and changes incessantly, despite the respect surrounding it. The ideal of tomorrow will not be that of today. Ideas, new demands arise which prompt changes and even far-reaching revolutions in existing morality. The task of the moralist is to prepare the way for these necessary changes. Given that he does not allow himself to be delayed by institutionalized morality, given that after all, he avails himself of his right to start with a clean slate if his principles demand this of him, he can create a completely independent work, he can work

EMILE DURKHEIM

to create the new. All the conceivable currents which permeate society and which are hotly debated will, by his agency, become aware of themselves and ultimately manage to express themselves in a reflective way. It is precisely these currents which give rise to moral doctrines; the latter are born to satisfy the former. Only ages characterized by a split on moral questions are creative in the domain of morality. If traditional morality is not thrown into question, if no need is felt to innovate it, moral reflection withers away.

(Durkheim 1975: 316)

NOTES

1 I seek to develop a theory of my own with such a focus in my books *Pragmatismus und Gesellschaftstheorie* and *Die Kreativität des Handelns* (both Frankfurt/Main: Suhrkamp, 1992). A translation of the former has been published by the University of Chicago Press in 1993; a translation of the latter is in preparation.
2 The unpublished papers of Ferdinand Tönnies in the Schleswig-Holstein State Library in Kiel contain a copy of Durkheim's review with Tönnies's marginal notes. These notes indicate that Tönnies felt misunderstood, especially in the case of his alleged state-centeredness.
3 Durkheim's *Rules*, which is certainly more 'positivistic' than any of his other works, also conforms to the interpretation proposed here, as soon as we recognize that in it Durkheim was asserting his own program as well. Furthermore, in devoting a great amount of space to the distinction between the normal and the pathological, he was concerned with the question how the pathological could be cured by means of a new morality. Durkheim's typology of suicide also assumes the turn which I shall seek to elucidate here.
4 Robert Hall (1987) also regards Durkheim's studies of socialism and the history of education as investigations that are studies of the emergence of new ideals.

REFERENCES

Alexander, J. (1982) 'The antinomies of classical thought: Marx and Durkheim', *Theoretical Logic in Sociology*, Vol. II, Berkeley, CA: University of California Press.
—— (1986) 'Rethinking Durkheim's intellectual development', *International Sociology* 1: 91–107 and 189–201.
Bellah, R. (1959) 'Durkheim and history', *American Sociological Review* 24: 447–61.
Chamboredon, J.-C. (1984) 'Emile Durkheim: le social objet de science. Du moral au politique?', *Critique* 445/446: 460–531.
Durkheim, E. (1933) *The Division of Labour in Society*, New York: Macmillan.
—— (1975) 'La science positive de la morale en Allemagne', in V. Karady (ed.), (1963) *L'éducation morale*, Paris: Presses Universitaires de France.
—— (1975) *Textes*, Minuit: Paris.
—— (1975) 'Introduction à la Morale', in V. Karady (ed.), *Textes*, vol. 2, Paris: Minuit.
Giddens, A. (1978) *Durkheim*, New York: Viking.

Gouldner, A. (1959) 'Introduction to Emile Durkheim', *Socialism and Saint-Simon*, London: Routledge.

Habermas, J. (1987) *Theory of Communicative Action*, vol. 2, trans. Thomas McCarthy, Boston: Beacon Press.

Hall, R. T. (1987) *Emile Durkheim. Ethics and the Sociology of Morals*, New York: Greenwood.

Joas, H. (1993) 'Durkheim and Pragmatism', *Pragmatism and Social Theory*, Chicago: University of Chicago Press.

—— (1988) 'The antinomies of neofunctionalism: a critical essay on Jeffrey Alexander', *Inquiry* 31: 471–94 (reprinted in Joas, *Pragmatism and Social Theory*: 188–213).

—— (1990) 'The classics of sociology and the First World War', *Thesis Eleven* 27: 101–24.

König, R. (1975) *Kritik der Historisch-existenzialistischen Soziologie. Ein Beitrag zur Begründung einer Objektiven Soziologie*, Munich: Piper.

—— (1976) 'Emile Durkheim. Der Soziologe als Moralist', in D. Käsler (ed.), *Klassiker des Soziologischen Denkens*, vol. 1, Munich: Beck.

Lacroix, B. (1981) *Durkheim et le Politique*, Paris/Montreal: Presses de l'Université de Montreal.

Lalande, A. (1960) 'Allocution' in *Centenaire de la naissance de Durkheim*, Annales de l'Université de Paris 1, 20–23.

Lukes, S. (1987) *Emile Durkheim. His Life and Work*, New York: Harper & Row.

Meštrović, S. G. (1988a) 'Durkheim, Schopenhauer and the relationship between goals and means: reversing the assumptions in the Parsonian theory of rational action', *Sociological Inquiry* 58: 163–81.

—— (1988b) *Emile Durkheim and the Reformation of Sociology*, Totowa, NJ: Rowman & Littlefield.

Müller, H.-P. (1993) 'Durkheim's political sociology', Chapter 5, this volume, supra.

Nisbet, R. (1974) *The Sociology of Emile Durkheim* New York: Oxford University Press.

Parsons, T. (1937), *The Structure of Social Action*, New York: The Free Press.

Piaget, J. (1932) *Le Jugement Moral chez l'Enfant*, Paris: Alcan.

Schmid, M. (1989) 'Arbeitsteilung und Solidarität. Eine Untersuchung zu Emile Durkheims Theorie der sozialen Arbeitsteilung', *Kölner Zeitschrift für Soziologie und Sozialpsychologie* 41: 619–43.

Stone, G. and Farberman, H. (1967) 'On the edge of rapprochement: was Durkheim moving towards the perspective of symbolic interaction?', *Sociological Quarterly* 8: 149–64.

Wallwork, E. (1972) *Durkheim, Morality and Milieu*, Cambridge, MA: Harvard University Press.

—— (1985) 'Durkheim's early sociology of religion', *Sociological Analysis* 46: 201–18.

NAME INDEX

SUBJECT INDEX

absolutism 79–81, 85, 92, 101
action: moral, sociology of 193–209,
  237; action, social 2–4, 10–11,
  235–6, 242–3; amoral v. moral 141;
  collective 147–51; conformist v.
  non-conformist 144–5, 150, 157–8,
  165; contingency 162; creative 145,
  148–51; ends of 142, 152, 154, 165;
  individual 145–6, 151; theory
  139–41, 144, 149–52, 165
Alsace 27, 40
anachronism 28
ancestor worship 31, 38, 40
ancien régime 27, 29, 105
ancient city 5, 26, 31–2
Ancient Law (Maine) 34–5
Année Sociologique 9, 95, 111–12,
  121–32, 172
anomie 12–14, 95–6, 98–101, 106, 153,
  169–70, 175–6, 179, 222, 224, 231,
  233, 240; acute and chronic 13,
  180–2, 185–7; conjugal 171, 174,
  180–1, 184; progressive 13, 180,
  182–6; regressive 13, 179–80, 182–8;
  sexual 176, 180–1, 184, 188; unity of
  187–9
Anthropogeographie (Ratzel) 123
archon 33
Aryan people 26, 29–30
associative bonds 140, 149, 151, 156,
  161–4
atonement 38
authority 31–3, 141, 148, 150–1, 158–9,
  200, 203–4
autonomy 8, 11, 20, 234, 239;
  consensus 157–60; of the subject
  150, 152–7; of the will 156–7

Bordeaux 5, 34–5, 39, 72, 116–17, 193,
  232
burial 5, 30–1, 37

capitalism 17, 95–6, 99–100, 219, 240
Cartesianism 26, 28
categories 6, 54–6, 62, 67, 242–3;
  abstract 6–7, 53–8, 61–4, 67, 147
causality 6, 11, 53, 55, 63
change, social 3–4, 139, 148, 159, 163,
  211, 214, 220–2, 224; rhythm 144–5
choice of alternatives 151, 161, 165
Christianity 33
Cité Antique, La (Fustel) 5, 25–30,
  33–6
class system 18, 97, 99, 106, 214,
  218–22, 224
classification 6, 53–9, 64, 67, 74, 95,
  121, 125, 130, 241
classificatory concepts 53–5, 58–9
collectivism 6, 8–12, 18–19, 21, 96–7,
  102–5, 107, 113, 117–20, 131, 240–3;
  see also conscience; fusion;
  sentiment
communal meal 33
comparison 5, 28, 30, 34–5, 39, 238
conflict, social 3, 18, 159–60, 224
conscience: collective 4, 10, 16–17, 98,
  100, 115, 140–1, 144, 147–8, 155–6,
  159–60, 165, 170, 212–13, 217, 220;
  moral 194, 208, 243
consensus 212, 221, 243
conservatism 20, 96, 106, 230
contract 72–3, 78, 82, 87–8, 99, 216–17,
  219–21, 223
cooperation 15, 19, 238–40
corporativism 8, 12, 101, 104–7, 156
cosmology 59–64

249